Concepts of
Vice, Narcotics, and
Organized Crime

D1513546

Concepts of
Vice, Narcotics, and
Organized Crime
Third Edition

DENNY F. PACE

Los Angeles Police Department, Ret.
Long Beach City College, Ret.

Prentice Hall
Englewood Cliffs, New Jersey 07632

Library of Congress Cataloging-in-Publication Data

Pace, Denny F.
    Concepts of vice, narcotics, and organized crime / Denny F. Pace. —
3rd ed.
      p. cm.
    Includes bibliographical references and index.
    ISBN 0-13-173691-4
    1. Organized crime—United States. 2. Organized crime—United
States—Prevention. I. Title.
HV6446.P33 1991
364.1' 06' 0973—dc20

                90-48829
                CIP

Acquisitions editor: Nancy Roberts
Editorial/production supervision: Colby Stong
Interior design: Karen Buck
Cover design: Patricia Kelly
Prepress buyer: Mary Ann Gloriande
Manufacturing buyer: Debra Kesar

© 1991, 1981, 1975 by Prentice-Hall, Inc.
A Division of Simon & Schuster
Englewood Cliffs, New Jersey 07632

The previous edition of this book was published
under the title *Organized Crime: Concepts and Control,*
Second Edition.

Printed in the United States of America
10 9 8 7 6 5 4 3 2 1

ISBN 0-13-173691-4

Prentice-Hall International (UK) Limited, *London*
Prentice-Hall of Australia Pty. Limited, *Sydney*
Prentice-Hall Canada Inc., *Toronto*
Prentice-Hall Hispanoamericana, S.A., *Mexico*
Prentice-Hall of India Private Limited, *New Delhi*
Prentice-Hall of Japan, Inc., *Tokyo*
Simon & Schuster Asia Pte. Ltd., *Singapore*
Editora Prentice-Hall do Brasil, Ltda., *Rio de Janeiro*

To Ellie, my girls, my grandchildren, and the friends who have made the struggle worthwhile

Contents

Preface   xv

Part I
The Social Ramifications of Organized Crime   1

1 The Relationship of Organized Crime to the Community   3

The Importance of Public Awareness   *4*
Factors of Social Dynamics   *5*
  Cultural Mores   5
  Social Acceptance and Organized Crime   6
  Entropy in Social Control   6
  The Permissive Society   9
Summary   *10*
Questions for Discussion   *11*

2 Symptoms of Organized Crime   12

The Need for Exposés   *12*
Organized Crime: Myth or Reality   *13*
The Evolution of the Criminal Confederations   *17*
  Nonconfrontation Policies of Organized Criminal Groups   17
  Elements and Purpose of the Confederation   21
  Purpose of the Organization   21
Summary   *24*
Questions for Discussion   *24*

3 Political Influences in Organized Crime Enforcement   26

Politics and the Complex Factors in Organized Crime
  Control   *27*
The Evolution of the Political Leader   *30*
  Political Action Committees   31
  Organized Crime Funds Eliminate Competition   33
  Political Influence by the Party in Power   34
Summary   *35*
Questions for Discussion   *35*

4 Role of the Legal System in Organized Crime Control   37

The Defense Lawyer and the Criminal Client   *38*
  The Syndicate Attorney   38
  Internal Discipline for the Legal System   39
Providing Adequate Laws for Enforcement   *40*
  Consistency in the Law   41
  State vs. Local Laws   42
Legal Agents and the Government Crime Commission   *43*
Summary   *44*
Questions for Discussion   *45*

Part II
Vice Crimes of an Organized Nature   47

5 Gambling   49

The Moral Issues of Gambling   *50*
History of Gambling   *51*
  National History   52
  The State and Gambling   52
  The Function of the Federal Government   54
The Betting Syndicate   *54*
  The Handbook   55
  The Wire Service   56
Bookmaking, Sporting Events, Gambling Devices   *56*
  The Bookmaking System   56
  Sporting Events   62
  Gambling Devices   63
Lotteries: The Numbers or Policy Games   *68*

Skimming and Bribery   *71*
   Skimming   71
   Bribery   72
Summary   *72*
Questions for Discussion   *73*

6 Prostitution   74

History of Prostitution   *75*
Common Methods of Prostitution and Organized Crime
   Affiliation   *77*
   Types of Prostitute   78
   Social Habits and Federal Law   81
Venereal Disease and Prostitution   *83*
   Gonorrhea   83
   Syphilis   83
   The Objective Symptoms of VD   87
   Acquired Immune Deficiency Syndrome   87
Summary   *89*
Questions for Discussion   *90*

7 Organized Crime and Drug Traffic   91

Drug Traffic: History and Organized Crime
   Involvement   *92*
United States Intervention in Drug Control   *94*
   Sealing the Borders of the United States   94
   Curbing Growth and Production in Foreign Countries   95
   Organized Crime Patterns for Drug Distribution   97
Major Drug Types   *99*
   Opium and Derivatives   99
   Morphine   99
   Heroine   101
   Cocaine and Derivatives   101
   Marijuana   102
   Controlled Substances   102
Federal, State, and Local Government Units
   and Confederation Drug Trafficking   *103*
   National Drug Control Efforts   105
   Federal, State, and Local Cooperation   107
   *State and Local Roles in the Future of Drug Traffic
      Enforcement   108*
Summary   *109*
Questions for Discussion   *110*

8 Obscenity and Pornography   112

A Legal and Moral Viewpoint   *114*
   The Legal Viewpoint   114
   The Moral Viewpoint   116
History   *117*
Law Enforcement: Censors Without Laws   *119*
   The Sociological Reasoning Behind Obscenity Enforcement   120
   The Police Position   122
Methods of Enforcement   *123*
   Action Against Material   124
   Injunction   124
   Prosecution   124
Summary   *125*
Questions for Discussion   *126*

Part III
**Other Crimes Related to Organized
Methods   129**

9 Organized White Collar and Related Crimes   131

The Impact of White Collar Crimes on the Social
   Structure   *132*
   Social Impact   132
   Economic Impact   134
   *How Business Enterprises Are Penetrated by Organized
      Crime   136*
Typology of White Collar Crimes and Techniques   *139*
   Racketeering   139
   The Loan Shark Business   142
   Black Markets   144
Techniques and Rationale for Investigating White Collar
   Crime   *146*
Summary   *147*
Questions for Discussion   *148*

10 Organized Crime: Frauds and Thefts   149

Business Acquisitions by Racketeering   *149*
   The Coercive Contract With Public Agencies   150
   Strong-Arm Tactics   150

Manipulation and Embezzlement of Stocks, Bonds, and
Credit Cards   *151*
   Securities Manipulation and Theft   152
   The Futures Market   153
   Credit Card Frauds   154
Special Frauds, Swindles, and Thefts   *154*
   Fraud of the Elderly   154
   Welfare and Medical Swindles   155
   Political Contributions   156
   The Regulatory Commissions   157
   Savings and Loan Frauds   158
   Burglary   158
Computer Crimes   *159*
   Laws That Control Computer Abuses   161
   Computers and Organized Crime   162
   The Potential for Future Crime   163
Summary   *165*
Questions for Discussion   *166*

11 Militant Groups: A Force in Organized Crime   167

Typologies of Criminal Groups   *168*
International Conspiracies   *169*
   Other International Groups   171
   Communist Party in the United States   171
National Conspiracies   *172*
Splinter Groups   *173*
Common Militant Group Strategies   *174*
Summary   *176*
Questions for Discussion   *176*

Part IV
Internal Agency Operation   179

12 Organization and Management Problems for Organized
Crime Control   180

Planning for Organizational Efficiency   *181*
   Structuring the Organization   183
   The Federal System   183
   Regional Systems   185

State Plans: A New Role   185
Regional Metropolitan and Intelligence Groups   185
Policy Development   188
Determining Community Needs   190
Use of Personnel   190
Policies for Expense Accounting   191
Special Administrative Problems   193
The Structure of Administrative Subunits   194
Supervisory Responsibility in Planning Operations   194
Informal Groups Within the Formal Organization   195
Goals for the Officer   197
Violator and Officer Relationship   197
Developing a Philosophy for Organized Crime
Control   198
Summary   199
Questions for Discussion   200

13 Intelligence Gathering and Dissemination   201

Ethical Considerations   202
General Guidelines of the SEARCH Committee   202
Security and Privacy Recommendations   204
Publicity and Release of Information   208
Intelligence Records Organization   209
The Rationale for Intelligence Collection   210
Identifying Functional Aspects of a Record System   212
Common Data Collection Methods   214
Analysis of Collected Data   217
Summary   218
Questions for Discussion   219

14 Methods for Organized Crime Control   220

Education   220
Model Programs   222
Civic Action Groups and Crime Commissions   223
Civic Action Groups   223
Citizen Groups Established Under the Framework
of Government   226
Punitive Enforcement   227
Identifying Organized Crime: How the Patrol Officer
Functions   228

The Common Physical Crimes   *228*
Traditional Confederation Crime   *231*
Summary   *232*
Questions for Discussion   *232*

Part V
Education and Training   235

15 Education and Training for Organized Crime Control   236

Education in Academic Institutions   *237*
   Projected College Outline for the Study of Organized
     Crime   *238*
Specialized Training for the Law Enforcement Officer   *239*
   Organized Crime Training Outline   *240*
Conceptualizing Training and Education Programs   *242*
Summary   *242*
Questions for Discussion   *245*

16 In Retrospect   246

Public Awareness and Progress Against Organized
   Crime   *248*
Prostitution and Gambling   *249*
Drugs   *250*
Pornography   *252*
Business Fraud   *253*
Militant Groups   *253*
Organization and Management of Enforcement   *254*
Summary   *254*

Appendix A   256

Appendix B   260

Appendix C   263

Appendix D   273

Appendix E   278

Bibliography   281

Index   287

Preface

How organized crime is structured and how it can be controlled can be viewed from at least three perspectives. These perspectives are derived from public opinion, academic research, and the criminal justice system itself.

The public's perception of organized crime is based on what it has heard about the Mafia, generally to the exclusion of all other organized crime confederations. Because the public is not informed about the intricacies of organized crime, it is not deterred from engaging in gambling, prostitution, drugs, or pornography. It is not aware that the corner bookie or the pornography distributor is an integral part of a crime cartel; their activities are carefully controlled and orchestrated. The public does not know and does not much care that a prostitute supports a pimp, a drug dealer, and sophisticated burglary and robbery rings. Generally, the public is not much concerned about events it cannot see or understand.

A second view of organized crime comes from college researchers who question activities they find pervasive in society. Because of time and money restrictions, their research is based on reports of government hearings and journal articles written by colleagues. The questions they ask, however, stimulate thinking, which tends to satisfy their goals. In a 1987 report entitled "Major Issues in Organized Crime Control," the researchers themselves stated that documentation for objective research was difficult to obtain because of sensitivity and politicization of the questions involved. This is not to fault the researchers but to criticize the system, which is closed to objective investigations.

The third perspective is found in a small segment of the justice system involved in the enforcement of laws relating to organized criminal activity. This perspective is gleaned from a small number of persons who are investigators, prosecutors, or defense counsel for accused clients.

Most law enforcement personnel do not deal with organized crime activities directly, though they are involved with it tangentially through street drug peddlers and street gang terrorism. Rarely do law enforcement agents concern themselves with covert gambling activities, prostitution, or other organized groups, such as white collar criminals. A part of the mystique of organized crime is that people who know about organized crime rarely talk about it, except among themselves, and then only to seek information, never to give information.

The question "How can organized crime be controlled?" has long been asked by law enforcement agencies. To bring some semblance of control to organized crime, the system itself must improve, and increased public help must be sought. Individuals must take an active role by abstaining from involvement in obvious organized crime–supporting activities, and they must avoid involvement in covert enterprises as well.

Organized crime control is the responsibility of the individual citizen, all law enforcement officers, and all levels of organized government. If a democratic form of government is to prevail and operate under "people control," the individual citizen must actively support the criminal justice system in its attempts to control organized crime. For the past decade, the role of the people in controlling organized crime has been stressed. It is the intent of this text to further that goal.

Several key concepts should be reviewed so that both citizens and enforcement agents will acquire sufficient knowledge to contribute toward controlling organized crime. These concepts are: (1) the interrelation of organized crime to the social structure; (2) symptoms of organized crime in the community; (3) political influence in organized criminal activities; (4) the role of the legal system in organized crime control; (5) specific vice violations; (6) business operations infiltrated and controlled by criminal interests; (7) administrative structures and procedures in agencies for crime control; and (8) the citizen-officer role for organized crime control.

Organized crime is defined in a number of ways. It is viewed by the author as a prohibited criminal activity between two or more persons, which may consist of a conglomerate arrangement or a monolithic system. The term as used in this text implies a more diversified organization than that which describes the activities of the Mafia or La Cosa Nostra. This more expanded definition is based on the descriptions that originated from the Oyster Bay Conference of 1965, in which it was indicated that organized crime is the product of a self-perpetuating criminal conspiracy to wring exorbitant profits from our society by any means. The full operational definition is cited in Chapter 2, but this definition in itself freed the author from thinking of organized crime as a few select crimes committed by a group of henchmen with a common boss. Whether a violation of a penal statute may be construed as organized crime will depend on the scheme or plan used to commit the crime. Thus, no particular crime is excluded from the definition of organized crime.

The importance of organized crime control in the United States is cited in the Organized Crime Control Acts of 1970, 1984, and 1986. The following is a capsulized view of the problem of organized crime:

Organized crime in the United States is a highly sophisticated, diversified, and widespread activity that annually drains billions of dollars from America's economy by unlawful conduct and illegal use of force, fraud, and corruption; organized crime derives a major portion of its power through money obtained from such illegal endeavors as syndicated gambling, loan sharking, the theft and fencing of property, the importation and distribution of narcotics and other dangerous drugs, and other forms of social exploitation; this money and power are increasingly used to infiltrate and corrupt our democratic processes; organized crime activities in the United States weaken the stability of the nation's economic system, harm innocent investors and competing organizations, interfere with free competition, seriously burden interstate and foreign commerce, threaten the domestic security and undermine the general welfare of the nation and its citizens.

Because of the diversification and variety of criminal activities engaged in by organized groups, there can be no true ranking of priority for the criminal activity. Until there are clearer guidelines to identify what organized crime is and the extent of the confederations' involvement in the social order, the true nature of their relationships cannot be shown. There has been an attempt to limit references to the terms Mafia and La Cosa Nostra. These terms reflect an ethnic heritage of some criminal confederations and tend to distort the true ethnic variety of many different organized criminal groups.

This text addresses organized crime so that law enforcement officers and lay citizens can see data brought together to support allegations of the existence of organized criminal groups. By studying how organized criminals ply their trade, the reader will be able to understand the complexity of administering agency enforcement policies.

In the 1980s, several significant changes took place in enforcement agencies' attitudes toward organized crime. Primarily, law enforcement agencies and the public expanded the definition of organized crime to include drug dealers, terrorists who operate with associates, and public corruption when there is a common scheme and design. They now recognize that there is an industry of white collar criminals, such as lawyers, accountants, and financial officers, who fail to comply with the law. The public is awakening to the fact that organized crime has infiltrated legitimate industries such as construction, waste removal, real estate, and dozens of other enterprises that serve the people.

It would appear that pressure tactics of traditional organized crime groups are now less pervasive. Instead, the traditional groups of the past have now eased their way into legitimate operations. The return, in the last decade, to free enterprise values as a national goal has made a culture of fast-buck artists with little conscience for social consequences. Stock frauds, medical rip-offs, telephone boiler room operations, planned bankruptcy, and shoddy manufacturing practices are all examples of the taint that has extended into the business ethics of the community.

There have been some positive movements in the fight against organized crime. These movements include the training of officers for organized crime units, the training of intelligence officers for the collection and analysis of intelligence data, a firming-up of task forces including prosecutors in some key cities, and the increased use of the 1970, 1978, 1984, and 1987 amendments to the Racketeer Influenced and Corruption Organizations (RICO) statutes. But the few positive movements have been overshadowed by the strengthened growth of organized crime activities in most cities and states throughout the United States.

Denny F. Pace

Part I

The Social Ramifications of Organized Crime

America's history is replete with stories of organized criminals. The stories present a variety of ideologies about how criminal groups organize and operate. The criminals are a product of our social system and are often held in professional esteem. They are intricately woven into our economic system because they thrive in our free market economy. And they perform in a conspiratorial fashion, which draws a variety of responses from law enforcement.

The stories reflect patterns of ethnic criminal activities, of corruption in the public workplace, and of mob-influenced corporate structures controlling legal and political systems. The stories tell us how they operate and who their victims are. But seldom are the criminals identified with any kind of specific activity.

Many experts think that street type crime has been given too much attention and social concern. They believe society is overlooking white collar crimes, which, while relatively obscure, are more costly and more dangerous to society than street crimes. For example, few people are aware of the cost of illegal and fraudulent practices used in the cover-up of the danger of carcinogens such as asbestos. Other white collar frauds, such as election frauds, false advertising, and other allied crimes, need to be re-emphasized as a true danger to society.

No crime has as much social impact as drug abuse. Studies have shown that about three fourths of the criminals arrested in major metropolitan areas are drug users. In the 1980s, drug abuse played a crucial role in the growth of street and white collar crimes, public corruption, and the loss of faith in the ability of the criminal justice system to find a solution to crime in society.

With the appointment of William J. Bennett as drug czar, antidrug policymakers hope that new ideas and institutional changes in the nations's inner cities may solve the drug abuse problem plaguing our nation. There is hope that foreign supply problems may be diplomatically negotiated. Drugs, like other organized crime problems, are now part of our social fabric; unless

1

society changes, it is unlikely that drug abuse and concomitant crime problems will be resolved.

This part of the text (Chapters 1 through 4) looks at the issue of organized crime and attempts to examine its influences, gauge its subtle behaviors, and finally assess how this systematic criminality creates a dynamic influence that has a direct impact on the moral and economic fiber of a community.

1

The Relationship of Organized Crime to the Community

LEARNING OUTCOMES

1. Develop an operating definition of organized crime.
2. Be able to identify some of the social and political influences that allow organized crime to exist.
3. Determine the sources of power in a community that can affect organized crime.
4. Know the different cultural patterns of a community and see how these patterns influence the control of organized crime.
5. Be able to discuss the pitfalls and the merits of legalizing or decriminalizing certain prohibited activities that support organized crime.

Within our social structure, many forces establish standards for social conduct. These forces are powerful influences on how society organizes to protect itself against the natural and man-made trends of disorganization that prevail in modern urban cultures. Very brief and perhaps oversimplified concepts about how society adjusts to these disorganizing concepts are presented here so citizens and law enforcement officers may realize their proper role in the control of organized crime.

The amount of organized crime a nation or community has depends on a large number of social, political, and administrative variables. The interchange of these variables dictates how organized criminal violations will be identified and enforced. The basic causes of organized crime allegedly stem primarily from social and individual weaknesses. Thus, the most effective suppression of organized criminal activities will arise from the cultural pressures exerted by citizens, individually and collectively, in a community. It is when these community pressures fail to satisfactorily subdue violations that it will be necessary for governmental enforcement units to intervene.

Formal groups such as legislative bodies, the judicial system, and law enforcement agencies are the administrative units basically responsible for implementing legal controls. Often these controls do not function adequately to protect society. Should this occur, the necessary controls evolve from informal pressure groups such as political parties, churches, social organizations, civic organizations, vested interest groups, or other informal organizations. The interaction among these different organizations in providing just laws, reasonable enforcement, and consistent court processes often determines how organized crime can or will be controlled.

Organized crime control is not solely a law enforcement problem. The solution to the problem of control, if there is one, lies in the application of many control factors. The factors or elements for organized crime control may be conceptualized as being composed of both organizational and individual dynamics that control human behavior within our social structure.

By examining the processes involved in community and agency interaction, the law enforcement officers and citizens involved in social control will be better able to understand community desires, to develop patterns of enforcement, and finally to determine the degree of control necessary to guarantee society reasonable and equitable management of prohibited criminal behavior.

The most acceptable restraints for organized crime control are no longer vested in a policing agency. The roots of effective control are centered in many social entities and are influenced by many forces, one of which is public awareness. Another is the social dynamics of the community. Let us take a closer look at both.

THE IMPORTANCE OF PUBLIC AWARENESS

The ultimate solution to organized crime will not be achieved through enforcement alone. All efforts must be directed toward reducing society's desire to indulge in and sanction these types of criminal activity. Because this is not likely to occur soon, approaches emphasizing control will remain until new behavioral patterns are established. An ideal approach would be the changing of human weaknesses in our social structure, recognizing the fallacy of social acceptability of activities that create organized crime, and developing the ability to establish a consistent public attitude toward the suppression of these crimes. By revealing some of the weaknesses in present control systems, perhaps a more acceptable plan for control may be presented to both the police and the public.

One premise for the suppression of organized criminal activities is to recognize that lack of awareness and concern by the public is organized crime's greatest ally. The efforts of any branch of society directed toward controlling organized crime activities will be largely unsuccessful unless the public is made aware of criminal methodology and the magnitude of organized crime. Publicity and honest exposure of illegal activities is one of the surest ways to dry up sources of revenue for an organization engaged in criminal activities.

The U.S. Chamber of Commerce identified the problem of controlling crime in this statement:

> A formidable problem faced by the nation's Criminal Justice System is insufficient citizen involvement. Indeed, why not leave the crime problem to the professionals who are paid to cope with it? Perhaps the most pragmatic answer is that the professionals themselves are keenly aware and readily admit that without citizen assistance they do not command sufficient manpower or funds to shoulder the monumental burden of combating crime in America.[1]

For example, the President's Commission on Law Enforcement and the Administration of Justice, the National Commission on the Causes and Prevention of Violence, and the National Advisory Committee on Criminal Justice Standards and Goals have all taken the stand that if society is to have a tolerable degree of crime, the citizen must be involved. Active citizen involvement in the control of organized crime is an absolute must.

FACTORS OF SOCIAL DYNAMICS

Basic social factors for understanding and controlling organized criminal activities include cultural mores, social acceptance of criminal behavior, the entropic processes in society, and the permissive attitude present in society.

Cultural Mores

There is a wide divergence in what society purports to believe and what it does. As a result, there are many who, although espousing morality, are inclined to engage in illegal activities and "look away" from a workable enforcement of the law. Cultural mores should serve the purpose in our society that a newel does for a circular stairway.

Before any agency can exert more than a "hit-or-miss" policy of crime control, a new national image of what our society is going to be will have to emerge. If institutions of enormous power that are "quasi" or "in fact"

---

[1]Chamber of Commerce of the United States, *Marshaling Citizen Power Against Crime* (Washington, D.C.: The Chamber of Commerce, 1970), p. 3. Organized crime is a part of society. Also President's Commission on Organized Crime, *Report to the President and the Attorney General, The Edge: Organized Crime, Business, and Labor Unions* (Washington, D.C.: U. S. Government Printing Office, March, 1986. VIII). Also see Eva Pomice, "From Organized Crime to Organized Men," *U.S. News and World Report*, 104, May 16, 1988, p. 44.

illegal can exercise control in our society without being legitimized, we shall have to be satisfied with a gangster-dominated environment. Should society hold to the image that social, political, and economic power may be derived from "any source," the Christian ethic of morality as presently perceived will wither and vanish.

Social Acceptance and Organized Crime

Although nothing is inherently immune from some degree of measurement, organized crime and related activities are about as close as one can come. The reluctance of victims to prosecute and the cloak of secrecy in criminal operations have caused organized crime to thrive. There has never been a wholly objective viewpoint published on organized criminal activities. A number of attempts have been made, but no adequate explanation has been made to the public and/or to law enforcement outlining what must be done to expose organized crime so that legal sanctions may be imposed.

Once established, the effect of a syndicate on the entire legal and political system is profound. Maintenance of order in such an organization requires the use of extralegal procedures because, obviously, the law cannot always be relied on to serve the interests of the crime cabal. The law can harass uncooperative people; it can even be used to send persons to prison on real or faked charges. But to make discipline and obedience certain, it is often necessary to enforce the rules of the syndicate in extralegal ways.[2]

The only logical way to let citizens know about organized crime is for each individual to receive the information that is of public record and that is often buried in police files. This information requires intensive research to assimilate or be put in a format and presented through newspapers, television, and community programs that are understandable to the average citizen. When citizens can understand some of the realities of organized criminal activities, the lack of punitive actions by the police, and the covert political protection given organized crime, they will demand action.

Entropy in Social Control

By applying a liberal social interpretation of Weiner's concept of entropy, we may identify forces that tend to corrupt and disorganize the social norms of society.[3] The disorganizing forces are those that advocate and implement moral misbehavior. In the realm of organized crime control, the

---

[2]George S. Cole, *Criminal Justice: Law and Politics,* 5th ed. (Brooks/ Cole, Belmont, Ca.: 1988), p. 51.

[3]Norbert Weiner, *The Human Use of Human Beings* (Boston: Houghton Mifflin, 1954).

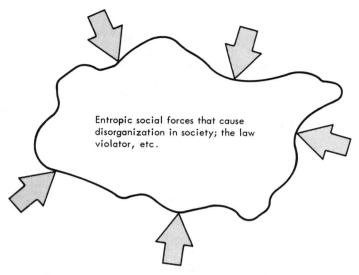

Entropic social forces that cause disorganization in society; the law violator, etc.

Antientropic forces necessary to control the disorganizing element in society, law enforcement, the courts, etc.

FIGURE 1-1   Entropy and social control devices.

disorganizing elements would be people who engage in bookmaking, loan sharking, racketeering, and other assorted violations.

Thus, the anti-entropic forces are those forces operating within society to keep social norms in check. Legislatures, courts, and law enforcement agencies are the primary preventive forces. An illustration of this concept is shown in Figure 1-1.

In the entropic/anti-entropic concept there is no firmly identifiable focal point for intelligent decision making. This lack of decision-making authority makes it nearly impossible for an enforcement organization to achieve a perfect crime control system. Thus, organized crime control cannot be just an effective intelligence squad, an infallible court system, or an enlightened public. It must be a combination of all the desirable elements, such as citizen concern, self-discipline, and a desire for freedom from organized crime dominance, that make up our social system.

This is further illustrated in the conceptualizations made by Stokes in his study of vice in our social order. Stokes cited another closely related social theory in Parson's concept of polity.[4] He uses polity as a conceptual term to discuss the specialized process that handles the input of expectations, reasons, and so on, and the allocation of costs, values, and so on, in our society. These processes are shown in Figure 1-2.

[4]Harold R. Stokes, "Vice Enforcement and Its Dynamic Relationship in Administration of Criminal Justice" (University of Southern California, Los Angeles, 1965), pp. 6–12.

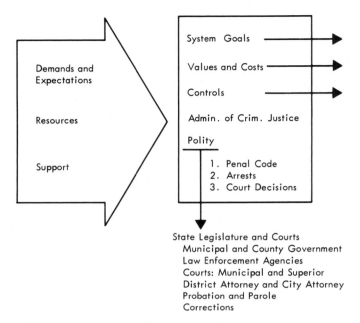

Demands and
Expectations

Resources

Support

System Goals ────────▶

Values and Costs ─────▶

Controls ──────────▶

Admin. of Crim. Justice

Polity

  1. Penal Code
  2. Arrests
  3. Court Decisions

State Legislature and Courts
Municipal and County Government
Law Enforcement Agencies
Courts: Municipal and Superior
District Attorney and City Attorney
Probation and Parole
Corrections

FIGURE 1-2   Inputs and outputs within the polity indicating forces that influence organized crime control.

In organized crime, and especially with those control forces having to do with vice, the powers exercised by pressure groups become an important decision-influencing factor for law enforcement. Stokes illustrated the interaction problems of the administration and the social group pressures when he said:

> The administration of criminal justice becomes a sounding board and a feedback system for groups that try to change the course of events or policies that affect the social system at large, and in particular, their own areas of concern.[5]

This idea is logical in conceptualizing goal attainment for criminal justice and in describing the framework for the control of organized crime.

As Stokes points out, the criminal justice system must transform the inputs into effective decisions or actions on the output side.[6] Identifying how these processes take place requires subjective research techniques. The structural-functional technique of gathering research data has no single dependent variable. Thus, observations made in identifying the problems of organized crime are not comprehensive or empirically validated. There has been no attempt to quantify data in this text.

[5]Stokes, "Vice Enforcement," p. 5.
[6]Stokes, "Vice Enforcement," p. 6, cited in William C. Mitchell, *The American Polity* (New York: Free Press, 1962).

The Permissive Society

There has been a trend in the United States and throughout the world to reduce violations now classified as crimes to harmless deviations that carry little or no punitive action. For example, the manipulation of securities becomes an acceptable business practice, labor union racketeering is looked upon as a nuisance business must live with, and political corruption is swept under the rug by the party in power. Volumes are devoted to the issues of public morals, habits, and how much latitude there should be in human behavior. There is also a reverse process by which harmless deviations become crimes.

Most police thinking today coincides with the following pattern of reasoning. Attempting to dictate the sociological and psychological arguments for or against the legalization of certain crimes is not a legitimate role for law enforcement officers. If the legislature determines a particular act to be illegal, then the statute prohibiting it should be rigidly enforced. If it is decreed to be legal, the police abide by the will of the people and abstain from enforcement activity. The enforcement officer and lower court judges cannot be moralists, but they are commanded to enforce the legal statutes of the nation, state, county, and city. If statutes prohibit and provide punishment when certain acts are committed, the court should see that the crimes are prosecuted within the framework of the law.

The issue of individual morality permeates the whole of our society. It is interesting to note that the same people who speak out vehemently against certain crimes are frequently the ones who ask the local enforcement group for exceptions to the law. For example, lotteries are favorite fund-raising techniques for church bazaars, school carnivals, and so forth.

Many people rationalize that gambling, for example, is all right as long as "gangsters" are not running the show. They contend that gambling is all right if it is conducted in a private home or among friends. If this is the intent of those who create the law, then it should be so stated.

Whatever society determines is prohibited should be set forth in explicit statute form so that those enforcing the law are not burdened with the decision of illegal or unethical enforcement. In spite of allegations that law is a hocus-pocus science, laws can be written that convey the intent of society.

The whole issue of social permissiveness should be of utmost importance to state legislatures. While the federal government is busy enacting statutes to prohibit the interstate transportation of lottery tickets, racing information, and gambling paraphernalia, some states are creating loopholes by legalizing certain types of lotteries[7] and creating lax securities laws and other laws that create a lack of uniformity of enforcement.

---

[7]Two states have casinos, 19 states have lotteries, 32 states have horse racing, and 14 states have dog racing. Exemptions exist in federal laws for state-sponsored gaming activities.

Should a state have the right to pass laws that create national problems? With few exceptions, state-supported gambling has not been as lucrative as anticipated. Some 1300 gambling schemes have gone down the road to corruption and bankruptcy in the history of the United States. A close look at most schemes shows they were ill-conceived by private groups, poorly supervised by the states, and ultimately run by the syndicates.

Americans are not known for strict adherence to the rule of law, nor are they known for their strict morality. The mixed cultures of free-thinking individuals have been famous for initiating rigid rules of self-conduct, then winking and looking the other way as rules and regulations are violated. Prohibition was a grand example of this indulgence. As a result, in recent U.S. history, there have been double operating standards for law enforcement personnel. Each state has adequate laws for the effective control of organized crime. Yet, nearly every major city in the United States has all the organized crime conditions that are common to the other cities. Whereas there are few valid statistics of a local nature to support such criminal activity, the attorney general's First Annual Report and the unpublished and covert meetings held by various intelligence officers throughout the United States support the commonality of organized crime conditions as they exist in the major cities. The attorney general's report merely alludes to the problem and goes on to list isolated activities, such as six gambling rings in New Jersey and adjoining states resulting in the arrest of 65 persons. The Postal Service has expanded its efforts in investigating organized crime involvement in postal-related offenses—there are, without question, data to support the existence of these operations. Yet, the public are not privy to such data because enforcement and political administrators do not view the disclosure of such information as important to crime control.

SUMMARY

Control of organized crime is not such a simple task that enforcement agencies can just go out and accomplish it. Through the influence of formal and informal pressure groups, the criminal organizations will persist in spite of the enforcement effort. By identifying a few of the basic social and cultural influences, the complexity of the control dynamics for organized crime has been shown. Public awareness can strip powerful protection from criminal confederations. There has been an attempt to point out that public action groups, both formal and informal, can influence the degree of pressure exerted against organized criminals. The issue of permissiveness is raised as an important concept in determining if punitive enforcement is a viable method for the control of many types of organized crimes.

QUESTIONS FOR DISCUSSION

1. Why is it not feasible at the present time to establish a taxonomy for organized crime?

2. Identify and discuss the different objectives of the *formal* and *informal* pressure groups.

3. In addition to those listed, identify major processes that influence the control of organized crime.

4. Identify ways in which the public is made aware of organized criminal activities. How are they concealed?

5. Identify specific ways in which different cultural patterns influence organized crime in your community.

6. How does the entropic/anti-entropic theory illustrate the complex factors that comprise social control?

7. Does the interaction described by Stokes indicate that informal and formal group action can change the course of social control in our society?

8. Poll the class on the question of legalized vice. Should certain types of vice be legalized? What is the police role in these crimes?

9. What is the prevailing police attitude toward identifying acts that are illegal?

10. Should the police be active in lobbying activities?

2

Symptoms of Organized Crime

LEARNING OUTCOMES

1. Gain insight into the workings of organized criminals in a community.
2. Understand the need to keep the activities of organized criminals before the public.
3. Recognize the businesses and other activities in the community that are related to organized crime.
4. Determine what is "myth" and what is "fact" about organized crime.
5. Gain knowledge about how organized crime groups have become entrenched in society.

Citizens tolerate so much organized crime because they are not actually aware of its form or magnitude, and when they are aware of its existence, they are not concerned because they do not know how it affects them. The direct link of criminal activity to organized crime is difficult to show and almost impossible to prove.[1] To show the symptoms of organized crime, it is necessary to (1) identify the need for exposure, (2) determine if organized crime is a myth or a reality, and (3) show how the evolution of the criminal syndicates has caused them to be entrenched in our society.

THE NEED FOR EXPOSÉS

A major factor in the growth of the crimes controlled by the confederation[2] is the lack of knowledge on the part of the citizen and the local police officer that criminal activity exists in their community. Activities of the confederations are so covert it is impossible to detect them in casual inquiry or in a normal police investigation. In many cases, this information becomes known only years after an investigation has ended, and in such devious ways

[1]Denny F. Pace, *Handbook on Vice Control* (Englewood Cliffs, N.J.: Prentice-Hall, 1971), p. 27.

[2]"Confederation" is a more accurate term to describe the organization of criminals. This term will be used throughout this book to replace the term "syndicate," which is normally used.

that it would be impossible to prosecute the criminal. Some of the most effective ways for a citizen to know about specific criminal activity is through the exposés of crusading newspapers, television, or other methods such as Senate investigation subcommittee publicity, federal grand jury investigations, and open public inquiries such as the Valachi hearings. Frequently, these are carried out only to the extent that they do not expose clients, friends of clients, and so-called responsible members of the community. Obviously there is need for an informed public, and some effort should be made to see that crime commissions, crime prevention committees, and other citizen groups organize and operate effectively to make the crime picture known. The crime commission and other citizen groups will probably not bring about a concerted effort against organized crime, so the most effective device may be newspaper and television exposés.

There is danger in the exposé because a city in which the exposé is made is cited as the bad example. Citizens of other cities fail to realize the same situation exists within the confines of their metropolitan area. Some law enforcement agencies are satisfied in letting the public believe that an individual under investigation is the only culprit. Most city officials think it is better for a community if the exposé is made in a far removed city.

Even though exposés emanate from local informers, local grand jury hearings, or from investigations developed from within the police department, it is safe to say that organized crime of any nature is not a local matter. An exposé in New York, Chicago, or Miami would find its equal in Los Angeles, Seattle, or Las Vegas. The only differences would be the degree of infiltration, the political temperament at the moment, the vested interests of those making the exposés, and geographic location.

It is amazing how many citizens, judges, police chiefs, and other public officials are surprised when an exposé is made in their community. It is even more ironic when the criminal justice administration of a major city states that its city does not have an organized crime problem.[3] Prostitutes do not have to be walking the streets, nor does each back room of the local taverns need a "bookmaker's layout" for a city to have organized crime. The degree of coordination between courts and enforcement agencies and the corruptive influences of the local political parties are ways in which organized crime may exist.

ORGANIZED CRIME: MYTH OR REALITY

Some law enforcement officials still maintain that organized criminal activity per se is a myth. Findings of the 1967, 1983, and 1986 Crime Commis-

---

[3]See Theodore R. Lyman, Thomas W. Fletcher, and John A. Gardiner, *Prevention, Detection, and Correction of Corruption in Local Government: A Presentation of Potential Models* (Washington, D.C.: U.S. Government Printing Office, November 1978).

sion Reports, however, show a common pattern that must be termed "organized." The structure of the organization is not a formal hierarchy as we normally picture a giant corporation, but it is an offshoot of about 24 main families in the United States, plus other groups. Some of these better known families are shown in Figure 2–1.

During the 1980s, other organized criminal groups gained power. These groups consist of lucrative drug cartels, ethnic gangs, and political splinter groups. For example, in California, Mexican gangs alone accounted for 800 murders during the 1980s. Chinese, Japanese, Vietnamese, and Korean organized groups have taken up extortion and blackmail activities similar to those of the Italians and Irish of the early 1900s. Even the Dixie Mafia continues to operate with success.[4] In black neighborhoods, black criminals control the rackets through affiliation with confederation-controlled services. In 1987, the federal prosecutor for Manhattan was criticized when he booked Wall Street figures for fraud. The "Miami Vice" tactics of rushing in and handcuffing respected members of the financial community shook the stock market.

Organized crime extends far beyond the boundaries of traditional criminal activities, so the cases cited here may be considered only a sample of the overall activities of confederated criminal groups. In organized crime, a dramatic transition is taking place because crime leaders are attempting to move the organizations from activities in illegal enterprises such as narcotic smuggling to lucrative areas of the legitimate business sector.

Data from several sources indicate that stronger federal efforts are needed in the fight against organized crime. The President's Commission on Organized Crime estimated that the criminal confederations reap an annual unreported income of more than $100 billion. This results in federal tax losses of $6.5 billion. The commission estimated that over 400,000 legitimate jobs are lost from the national job market.[5] The very nature of the confederations makes most known methods of control difficult to implement. Most of the criminals who are in control of organized crime activities in the large cities take great care to conceal evidence of their connections. Public officials and businessmen are frequently involved with confederation activities without any knowledge of their affiliation.

---

[4]The "Dixie Mafia" is a loose-knit group dealing in stolen merchandise, fencing, and other types of organized crime. This group operates throughout the southern states. It apparently has few ties with national confederations.

[5]Kathryn Kahler, "The Mob is Winning," in *Criminal Justice, 1987/88,* John J. Sullivan and Joseph Victor, Eds. (Guilford, Conn.: Dushkin Publishing Group, Sluice Dock, 1987). These facts are consistent with the President's Commission on Organized Crime, *Report to the President and the Attorney General, The Edge: Organized Crime, Business, and Labor Unions* (Washington, D.C.: U.S. Government Printing Office, March 1986. VIII).

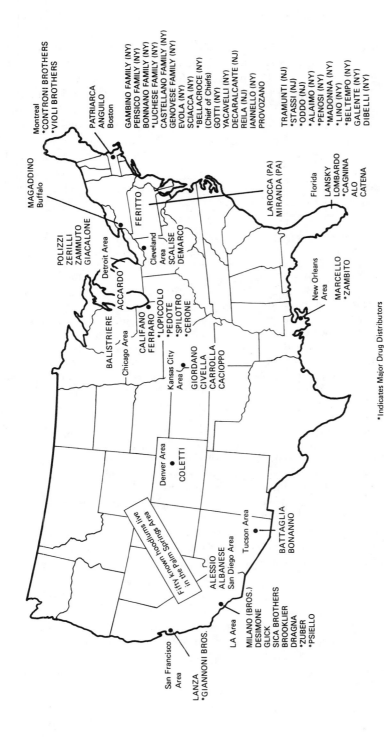

FIGURE 2-1 Identified Mafia leaders and associates in the United States. (List is from contemporary sources such as magazines and newspapers; because of deaths, this list may be inaccurate. It is offered for information only.)

*Indicates Major Drug Distributors

Montreal
*CONTRONI BROTHERS
*VIOLI BROTHERS

PATRIARCA
ANGUILO
Boston

GAMBINO FAMILY (NY)
PERSICO FAMILY (NY)
BONNANO FAMILY (NY)
*LUCHESE FAMILY (NY)
CASTELLANO FAMILY (NY)
GENOVESE FAMILY (NY)
EVOLA (NY)
SCIACCA (NY)
*BELLACROCE (NY)
(Chief of Chiefs)
GOTTI (NY)
YACAVELLI (NY)
DECARALCANTE (NJ)
REILA (NJ)
IANNELLO (NY)
PROVOZANO

TRAMUNTI (NJ)
*STASSI (NJ)
*ODDO (NJ)
*ALAIMO (NY)
*PENOSI (NY)
*MADONNA (NY)
*LINO (NY)
*BELTEMPO (NY)
GALENTE (NY)
DIBELLI (NY)

MAGADDINO
Buffalo

POLIZZI
ZERILLI
ZAMMUTO
GIACALONE
Detroit Area
ACCARDO

FERITTO

Cleveland
Area
SCALISE
DEMARCO

LAROCCA (PA)
MIRANDA (PA)

Florida
LANSKY
LOMBARDO
*CAGNINA
ALO
CATENA

BALISTRIERE
Chicago Area
CALIFANO
FERRARO
*LOPICCOLO
*PEDOTE
*SPILOTRO
*CERONE

Kansas City
Area
GIORDANO
CIVELLA
CARROLLA
CACIOPPO

New Orleans
Area
MARCELLO
*ZAMBITO

Denver Area
COLETTI

Fifty Known hoodlums live
in the Palm Springs Area

ALESSIO
ALBANESE
San Diego Area

Tucson Area

BATTAGLIA
BONANNO

San Francisco
Area

LANZA
*GIANNONI BROS.

LA Area
MILANO (BROS.)
DESIMONE
GLICK
SICA BROTHERS
BROOKLIER
DRAGNA
*ZUBER
*PSIELLO

If organized crime is going to be effectively suppressed, efforts must be directed toward the upper echelons of the organization. The very nature of the structure makes it almost impossible for the local officer to be successful in gathering evidence for more than petty prosecutions. For example, the "handbook" is the only one who has to worry in a bookmaking ring. The "pimp" or "madam" of a house, if they do not become too overt in their operation, need have little fear of prosecution from local sources. Labor racketeering or government corruption have little to fear from local prosecution.

There are a number of reasons why local control is likely to be ineffective in the control of organized crime.

The procedures for investigation are unlike those for a regular crime. The police operator is frequently the only effective technique through which a crime can be solved. This is dangerous and too expensive for local units of government.

The investigations into organized crime activities are frequently conducted over longer periods of time than other investigations. Local cities cannot afford to sustain these investigations.

Undercover operators need funds for extensive investigations. At the local level, these funds are not usually adequate.

Leaders of the syndicates tend to split operations between cities and states, so a complete picture of the operation is unknown to the local officer.

Participating criminals will frequently transfer personnel, thus causing local officers to lose contact with both the violator and the informer.

There is a great overlapping into legitimate businesses, and local laws are not adequate to cover borderline cases.

The crime leaders are so closely affiliated with local politicians that the local officer, if he becomes overly ambitious, finds himself transferred to assignments where he does not come in contact with organized crime.

The lack of wide jurisdiction for local police agencies brings about limitations. Investigation cannot in many cases extend beyond the city limits.

The failure to impose available sanctions through licensing and permits at state and local levels results in less crime control.

Failure of the legislature to make adequate laws limits enforcement action.

Failure of the courts to enforce existing laws rigidly encourages crime.

The dismal lack of public concern toward such crimes is one of the most significant reasons.

To better understand the clandestine operation of organized crime groups, a few brief statements about the history of the Mafia indicate how one of the most powerful criminal groups in America today has sprung from groups organized to protect themselves against encroachment of other ethnic and business groups that extorted and blackmailed the new immigrants to this country.

THE EVOLUTION OF THE CRIMINAL CONFEDERATIONS

In the past, law enforcement agencies were able to recognize participants in the so-called rackets. Because those participants identified with socially unacceptable behavior, by choice, they were alienated from the mainstream of American society. Gradually, the social acceptability of such activities as bootlegging, bookmaking, and legalized gambling has brought about a new attitude toward the racketeers and has made them a part of community life.

Social acceptability of quasi-legal activities and the desire to expand the economic base of the organization have brought the confederations into legitimate enterprises. The dispersion of the criminal element into legitimate enterprises has created covert confederations so powerful that no law enforcement agency can cope with them.

Nonconfrontation Policies of Organized Criminal Groups

Organized crime is unlike any other criminal activity. There is no question of impulse or insanity, nor of ignorance of law or negligence. In organized enterprises, each activity is planned and carefully prepared to avoid direct confrontation with law enforcement. Because of this nonconfrontation policy, the public is not reminded of the millions of dollars that change hands as a part of illegal activities. Confederations would like the public to believe that activities such as prostitution or bookmaking are nothing more than the isolated deviate behavior of an individual. Thus, the conditions emanating from organized criminal activity do not bring pressure to bear on either the police or the public.

No one actually knows the extent of crime that results from these illegal activities. There is no barometer to measure the corruption, legal inconsistencies, and political deceptions that result from the covert activities of organized criminal action.

The history of organized crime in the United States is of importance only to show the interrelationships and the evolution of the families. It is more important to show contemporary problems of society.[6] Law enforcement officers cannot "just go out and put the hoodlums in jail." The complexity of the organizations dictates a more comprehensive view.

At the mention of organized crime, people immediately say "the Mafia" or "La Cosa Nostra." This is, of course, the most notorious and probably

---

[6]For example, see Clair Sterling, *Octopus: The Long Reach of The International Sicilian Mafia* (New York: W. W. Norton & Co., 1990) and William G. Bailey, Ed., *The Encyclopedia of Police Science* (New York: Garland Publishing, 1989).

the most powerful syndicate in America. There are, however, thousands of smaller independently organized groups. Until they become a threat to the "big group," they are permitted to exist and continue to grow. Jimmy Fratianno's testimony when he served as an informer for the Federal Bureau of Investigation is an example. About three decades before turning informer, Fratianno had been a gang member with Johnny Roselli on the East Coast. Roselli, who had been sent to the West Coast in the 1940s by Al Capone, was supposed to obtain some gambling action in southern California. For many years the Roselli group tried unsuccessfully to muscle in on the established West Coast groups. The Roselli group, including Fratianno, was known as the strong arm for anyone who would hire them. With the murder of Roselli and Fratianno's rise to power in one of the local Mafia groups, a murder contract was made on Fratianno. Neither of the gangsters was ever a power figure in the Mafia. Today there appears to be a workable coexistence with a live-and-let-live attitude as all factions quietly rebuild and expand.

Across America "bigness" has become a virtue. Giant cities enlarged from villages of three decades ago dot the landscape. Small businesses have mushroomed into giants or have been absorbed in corporate mergers with complex ownership structures. Into these industries has seeped the money from illegal drug transactions, prostitution, and gambling.

With the investments have come ownership, partnerships, or controlling shareholders who dictate policy for the giant companies. To the companies have come friends, relatives, and gangster partners who seek profitable respectability. They do this without having to relinquish control of lucrative illegal enterprises. Trusted old friends from bygone days become fixtures in the new legitimate environment. By careful planning, company representatives then move into politics, labor unions, or other community service organizations. Thus, the net is woven. Lines of communication from every community endeavor are established. The organization and infiltration process has been completed. New and advanced techniques of modern management make it function.

As with any commercial organization, groups involved in criminal activities must find a product of profit. The organization, which in the past was engaged solely in illegal enterprises, now finds that much money can be made in legitimate businesses. However, there can be no inference that an organized group, which has moved into a legal enterprise, will forsake the riches of the illegal rackets. It is merely expanding its spheres of operation to include legitimate business enterprises.

Fred J. Cook, in his book entitled *Mafia,* presents the history and origin of organized crime.[7] His study supports the findings of several special Senate

---

[7]In Fred J. Cook, *Mafia* (New York: Fawcett, 1973), the documented research on the Mafia has been brought together in one source reference.

subcommittee investigations regarding the existence of a Mafia. These hearings concluded that there is an organized criminal syndicate known as the Mafia (Cosa Nostra) operating throughout the United States and foreign countries. This group has its roots in the Sicilian Mafia. Its revenue is from gambling, prostitution, and almost all other forms of legal and illegal enterprises. The power of the organization emanates from the ruthless enforcement of its edicts, violent vengeance, and intense loyalty of its criminal soldiers.

The Mafia is a semiformal organization. It is ruled by unwritten codes, but its activities are cloaked in a covert organizational structure. It apparently has no allegiance to any legally constituted government, but places the family as the center of allegiance. The following citation shows how the loyalty to the family grew and how the early operation of the Mafia evolved in the United States. While the legend is historically accurate, it has been questioned.

> The Mafia had its origin in Palermo, Italy, in 1282 as a political and patriotic organization devoted to freeing Sicily from foreign domination, and to accomplish this purpose it decreed that persons of French descent must be killed.
>
> Its motto was "Morte alla Francia Italia anela." (Death to the French is Italy's cry.) The initial letters of the motto, MAFIA, were used as a secret password for purposes of identification, and it's from this password that the organization derived its name.
>
> In the early 15th century the Mafia branched out in criminal activities. Intimidation and murder were adopted as weapons. It was an organization of outlaws dedicated to the complete defiance of the law.
>
> After 1860, the organization expanded enormously in Sicily with smuggling, cattle rustling, and extortion as the principal sources of revenue. Administration of justice was openly defied in ineffective drives, but continued pressures against the Mafia caused many members to migrate to the United States. As early as 1860, large numbers of escaped Italian criminals settled in New Orleans. . . .
>
> There is no reliable data on the extent of the operation of the Mafia and its international ramifications. The leaders are in control of the most lucrative rackets. The leadership in the United States is in a group of board of directors. It has infiltrated political offices and some law enforcement agencies, the extent of such infiltration not being known. Its members are not necessarily of Sicilian descent, but include others of Italian extraction.[8]

Family ties created by specialization are no longer feasible in all important posts of the organization. The placing of specialists from outside the family over long-time blood brothers has made it increasingly difficult to maintain discipline and authority, as evidenced in the ability of enforcement agencies to make inroads into the organization. The organizations as identified by the many researchers probably derive their power from an organization structure similar to the one shown in Figure 2–2.

[8]John Drzazga, *Wheels of Fortune* (Springfield, Ill.: Charles C Thomas, 1963), pp. 16–17. Later information has the board consisting of twelve members.

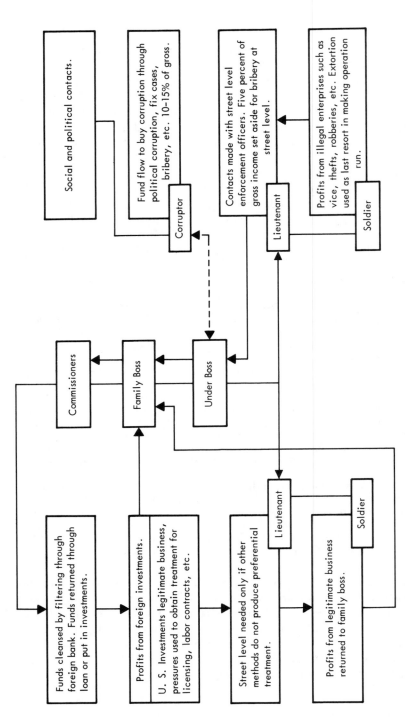

FIGURE 2-2 Source of power for organized crime members. Left-hand column shows the flow of confederation money and involvement of their personnel to stimulate the flow of money and its disposition. Involvement of a lieutenant and soldier is used only as a last resort. The right-hand column shows how contacts are made in the community from an underboss, or capo, through a lieutenant to pay for protection. Payoffs to higher-ups go through a person who has the appearance of legitimacy, often an attorney.

Elements and Purpose of the Confederation

Confederated criminal activities extend into many areas other than vice-type activities.[9] A confederation implies an organization conducting activities under a coordinated plan of action. By setting aside melodramatic adjectives frequently used in the descriptions of "organized crime," we can identify some of the major common elements and activities of the confederations.

There is an unlawful conspiracy between two or more persons.

The agreement may be actual or implied.

There is a semipermanency in its form much like the modern corporation.

The organizational structures are in a continuous fluid transition to compensate for political and criminal misfortunes of its members.

The regional organizations are heteronomous; thus, the fear, corruption, totalitarian influences, and the insulation of leadership have a common pattern throughout the United States and even in many other parts of the world.

The type of organizational control varies with the charismatic personalities of individual leaders. Control can be authoritarian or a loose-knit laissez faire structure. Both may be equally effective.

Activities may frequently be contrary to good public policy, yet they may not constitute a crime. An example is the donation of funds to a political campaign by a criminal confederation.

Failure to understand the basis or organization in the criminal confederation causes many persons to doubt its existence. Cook's documentation of the New York area families in his book entitled *Mafia* establishes a model that could be related to any area in the nation. The patterns of organized crime are difficult to distinguish because few overt individual criminal activities can be traced to an organization; consequently, how the groups can be controlled cannot be precisely or simply stated, nor can the present attempts at control be accurately or objectively evaluated.

Purpose of the Organization

Organized criminal groups are simply business organizations operating under many different management structures and dealing in illegal products. A requisite of the organization has been the establishment of illegal enterprises to produce large profits, which are then converted into channels of influence and legitimate enterprises.

How an organized group generates illegal profits is generally known to the chief of police, but he is unable to maintain a sustained enforcement

[9]Office of the Counsel to the Governor, *Combating Organized Crime* (Albany, N.Y.: 1966), pp. 18–22. The James Fratianno investigations of 1979–88 showed the diverse interests of organized crime.

effort against the confederation. Because of the organization's policy of "insulating" the higher-ups in the organization, it is unlikely a local agency will prosecute more than street agents at the lowest echelon in the criminal hierarchy. The organized groups are structured to accommodate the loss of a large number of street agents because of arrests and intergang violence. Thus, organization is vital to the survival of these confederated groups. The confederations are active in all phases of American life; they have a grip on real estate involving hundreds of millions of dollars; control of numerous banks, loan firms, and financial institutions; control of prostitution, gambling, narcotics, and other vice activities. As early as 1964, for example, *U.S. News and World Report* stated that the Mafia was deeply involved in the garment industry. The U.S. Senate's Permanent Subcommittee on Investigation listed two hundred trades or types of business with which organized crime has become involved.[10] And the degree of involvement is still being expanded at a rapid rate.

Organized crime is somewhat synonymous with principal types of underworld criminal activity. One expert explained organized crime in the way shown in Figure 2–3.[11]

The presence of organized elements in a city may be influenced by geographical location, ethnic group population, historical heritages, and many other physical, cultural, and social traits.

A city such as a seaport, a transportation and convention center, or a boomtown naturally attracts organized elements. Frequently these settings create the "open city" atmosphere with liberal attitudes toward organized crime enforcement. Pressures from business favor laxness in law enforcement. Businesspeople believe that overlooking certain violations will enhance the attractiveness of the city. Conversely, however, the closed city may be a greater attraction to the syndicates. For example, the so-called dry areas, with reference to liquor availability, have always been spawning grounds for organized criminal activity and government corruption.

Whether civic leaders adopt an open or closed city attitude does not deter the influences of the confederations. The highly industrialized, the tourist spas, and the prosperous cities attract commercialized crime, which then infiltrates into local legitimate businesses. Once these inroads are made, illegal business and informal pressure groups exert just enough influence to see that their vested interests are allowed to operate.

Ethnic group composition of a city may promote the growth of organ-

[10]"How Criminals Solve Their Investment Problems," *U.S. News and World Reports,* March 30, 1964, pp. 74–76. In a 1979 article, it was alleged that at least 200 companies are owned or controlled by organized crime in California.

[11]National Conference on Organized Crime, *A National Strategy for the 1980s,* University of Southern California, November 8–9, 1979. For update see The National Institute of Justice, *Major Issues in Organized Crime Control.* Symposium Proceedings. (Washington, D.C.: U.S. Government Printing Office, 1986).

FIGURE 2-3 Defining the scope of organized crime.

ized crime. Some ethnic groups have different values, cultural mores, and ethics, and as such do not readily adapt to white middle-class standards. These ethnic groups, frequently of lower economic status, find hope in promises of a big lottery win or a long-shot win with the street corner bookie. Perhaps, because of intense social frustration, these groups find emotional outlets in gambling and prostitution. Through necessity they patronize the loan shark, and because of ignorance they become victims of organized frauds and swindles.

Historically, gambling has been the financial foundation of organized crime. In the 1970s and 1980s drugs became the major source of revenue. It is estimated that more than one-half million drug addicts in the United States depends on a constant flow of drugs. *Fortune* magazine recently identified Orientals from the golden triangle of Southeast Asia, Mexicans, or South Americans to be some of the major suppliers for this flow of drugs.[12]

[12]Roy Rowan, "The 50 Biggest Mafia Bosses," *Fortune*, November 10, 1986, p. 38. This is expanded in the President's Commission on Organized Crime, *Report to the President and the Attorney General, America's Drug Habit: Drug Abuse, Drug Trafficking and Organized Crime* (Washington, D.C.: U.S. Government Printing Office, March, 1986).

By combining expertise of the federal government and the strike force operating units, there has been a reasonably successful effort against the confederations in many major cities. Such operations have in the past ten years caused substantial changes in the operation of the five New York families. The families, which are estimated to number about 2500, have been forced to tighten security in internal operations, to make business connections more covert, and to contend with rebellion among the young members.

There appears to be little question of the existence of organized crime. How it will be ferreted out and prosecuted remains the prime problem.

SUMMARY

The existence of organized crime does not indicate massive societal dishonesty. A more logical reason for its pervasiveness is because citizens are not actually aware that organized crime as such exists. Because of the covert nature of organized crime, there is a need for exposés as a method of enforcement. The organizational structure of the present families derives from Mafia history. The elements of the national confederation have a loose formal organizational structure. Because the organization's business moves through the informal or family-based structure, organization members are practically impossible to arrest and prosecute successfully. Factors that are present in a community with a high degree of infiltration by organized crime have been shown. These factors are so subtle, however, that most citizens accept and tolerate acts such as lottery, bookmaking, and others under the mistaken belief that they are individual violations.

QUESTIONS FOR DISCUSSION

1. Identify possible sources of organized crime related to government functions. Can they be eliminated?
2. Discuss the "nonconfrontation" policies of major organized criminal confederations.
3. Why is "confederation" a more descriptive term than "syndicate"?
4. In the history of the Mafia, how have family ties been instrumental in the evolution of the organized crime structure?
5. Draw a sociogram on the blackboard and indicate how communications move through the entire class. Note that certain members can be insulated from the feedback by having spokespeople.
6. Identify the so-called business activities indulged in by organized crime.
7. What are the legitimate enterprises that are subject to pressure from organized elements? How are the pressures exerted?
8. With reference to organized crime, does a "closed city" necessarily indicate a "clean city"?

9. Explain how minority neighborhoods affect syndicate operations.
10. Why are local efforts at enforcing organized criminal activities basically ineffective?
11. Identify differences between traditional and organized crime.

	Traditional	Organized
Structure	Operates independently or with ad hoc group	Loose knit confederations, two or more persons, conspire on a continuing basis
Law	Specific statutes	Broad statutes, Omnibus Crime Bill, RICO
Enforcement Policies	Tightly enforced	Selectively enforced
Enforcement Procedures	Publicity, exposure, public indignation	Secrecy, no acknowledgement that organized crime exists
Personality of Criminal	Social isolate, sociopathic	Sociopathic, strong peer identity, money oriented
Other Differences	Occasional criminal based on monetary need. Not guided by group action.	Seeks career indentity, adheres to group's ethical and moral standards. Lives by code of gang, which is administered summarily to keep discipline.

3

Political Influences in Organized Crime Enforcement

LEARNING OUTCOMES

1. Become aware of the risks and benefits of a democratic society with reference to organized crime suppression.
2. Be able to understand the dynamics of political campaign financing, and how favors are paid off by the political candidate.
3. Understand why citizens or police cannot go out and eradicate organized crime because of political influence.
4. Become aware of political pressure groups and how these groups influence the passage of laws.
5. Recognize that the party in power sets the enforcement policy of the enforcement units in government.

Our democratic republic is viewed as the utopia of political organization. The preservation of an organization that provides for individual liberty has been the basis for its strength. What happens to that system when organized criminal elements move in? In recent years, it has been possible in some instances for organized elements to allocate sufficient financial resources and exert enough influence at the local level to dictate who will or will not be elected. At the state level, organized criminals subvert the processes of government sufficiently to kill or enact a legislative bill. At the national level, organized criminal lobbies exert an untold amount of political pressure on our lawmaking bodies.

Political contacts with organized crime flow from the apex of the criminal hierarchy. The political representatives of the crime confederations, however, are not linked to the operating processes of the criminal conspiracy. Those in politics who deal with representatives of criminal combines do so in complete freedom from the stigma of known hoodlum association and may be totally unaware of confederation connections.

A good deal of guesswork is involved in identifying the political links that bind elements of the legitimate society to organized crime; some links exist in almost every phase of social and business interaction. The stronger ties, however, come through the political and legal systems. It is natural for an attorney, who represents a criminal client, to also become that client's advisor. While it is easy to be hypercritical of certain legal practices, it must be remembered that allegations of an attorney's criminal ties come to the investigators in bits and pieces. Thus, conclusions derived from these bits of information lead to certain unsubstantiated assumptions regarding political and criminal ties. Therefore, many criminal-attorney relationships may border on unethical rather than illegal collusion.[1]

Patterns and trends used to identify political corruption are shown in Figure 3–1. The cases cited in this chapter are from intelligence files and other documented events. The problems of political influence are divided into three major categories: (1) politics and the complex factors in organized crime control, (2) the evolution of the political leader, and (3) political influence by the party in power.

POLITICS AND THE COMPLEX FACTORS IN ORGANIZED CRIME CONTROL

The political influence in the growth of organized crime should not be underestimated. New legal ways or means should be developed to minimize the deleterious effects of political corruption both in law enforcement and with political decision makers. Law enforcement is going to be ineffective unless there is the honest cooperation from all political leaders of a community. Corruption of political-legal organizations is critical to the success of the crime cabal. The study of organized crime is thus a misnomer; the study should consider corruption, bureaucracy, and power.

This story of political corruption could be played out in nearly every major city in the country. The report by the Chamber of Commerce of the United States acknowledged that local groups must supply the impetus for crime control.[2] Thus, major cities did not have the wide support necessary to eliminate organized crime.

---

[1]The ties between the legal and political corruptors were clearly established in the 1972–73 Watergate conspiracies. This was also shown in ABSCAM and "Irangate" in the 1980s.

[2]Chamber of Commerce of the United States. *Marshaling Citizen Power Against Crime*, p. 77. Also see California Department of Justice, *Proceedings of Symposium 87: White Collar/Institutional Crime—Its Measure and Analysis*. Sacramento, 1987, p. 52, which gives prosecution rates for official corruption in key areas of the United States.

Participants	How Obligations Are Incurred	How the Debts Are Paid
Elected officials (Federal)	Support in political campaigns Trips, vacations on company expense accounts, cash through foundations, and cash bribes through lobbyists, etc.	Political appointments Contracts Personal favors Paroles, pardons
Appointed staff	Campaign workers Liaison with revenue sources Cash payoffs	Hired as staff worker Retains contact with revenue sources Conducts business for elected official
Elected official	*State* Campaign contributions Trips on private accounts Cash through lobbyists Tips on investments, i.e., public franchises and licenses	Contracts Allocations of franchises Granting licenses such as liquor Contracts for local service— garbage, ambulance, towing, etc.
	Local Campaign contributions Promise to self-interest groups—gamblers, etc. Money to citizens' committees during preelection campaign Cash payoffs through lobbyists	Abstain from enforcing certain type of laws
Judge	*All Levels* Campaign contributions Cash payoffs	Favorable decisions Probation, parole and select court assignment
Lawyer	Client contacts and referrals Campaign workers Liaison with business and criminal clientele Cash payoffs (fees)	Appointments to positions to keep contacts with proper clients Consultants on contracts, crime commissions, etc.
Police	*All Levels* Political patronage Campaign contributions to elected offices Budget manipulation Cash payoffs	Select enforcement methods Preferential treatment in the degree of enforcement Lack of enforcement

FIGURE 3-1   Patterns of political corruption.

Because there are few valid statistics about organized crime, the political leaders of a community can dictate the degree of enforcement merely by the allocation of money and personnel. How corruption infiltrates the social structure of a community was shown as early as 1978.[3]

The contrast between honest administration and corrupt practices is, of course, not exclusively directed to the elected politician. The citizen who overcharges customers, cheats on repair bills, and misrepresents a product is as guilty as the criminals who are being indicted. The citizen, in cases where fraud and collusion are "a way of doing business," may not class him- or herself as a member of the criminal confederation, but he or she is equally effective in subverting good government.

Once the life pattern of "dealing under the table" is established, it is only a very short distance to the total seduction of honest government. Many situations that put political figures in compromising situations are not created with criminal or even malicious intent. The political compromises are a part of the system that must be changed if political honesty is to become a reality. These situations are cited as examples:

Ever since Lincoln Steffens charged in *The Shame of Our Cities* that "the spirit of graft and lawlessness is the American spirit" we have almost tacitly accepted the role of corruption in the politics of the American city.[4]

The "third legislature" (lobbyists) in a state may exert enough power to keep out state regulation of certain transportation, utility, and interest rates. Whether state-regulated rates are desirable is questionable; many states have decided it necessary to protect consumer interests. The very fact that this type of influence may be exerted over a political body is cause for concern. The second example of how poor political policy subverts the processes of justice is the provision that allows a legislator to be retained as an attorney for a criminal client. This means the case will be continued until the expiration of the current legislative session. The abuse of this provision is obvious when a legislator is identified with a case on a retainer basis even though the legislator will not be a part of the defense for the client.

These are only examples of what can happen. However, similar abuses are not unusual. In time of "pressing manpower needs" most cities accept the philosophy that the less heard about the problem of organized crime, the less of a problem it will be. This is exactly what the confederations desire and strive for.

The corruption of American politics is summarized in this statement:

[3]Theodore R. Lyman, Thomas W. Fletcher, and John A. Gardiner, *Prevention, Detection, and Correction of Corruption in Local Government* (Washington, D.C.: U.S. Government Printing Office, November 1978).

[4]Francis A.J. Ianni and Elizabeth Reuss Ianni, "Organized Crime: A Social and Economic Perspective," paper prepared for The Academy of Criminal Justice Sciences, March 1980. See also Lyman, Fletcher, and Gardiner, *Prevention*, p. 1. A survey of 250 newspapers from 1970 to 1976 showed 372 incidents of corruption in 103 cities.

> In the estimation of the [Pennsylvania] Crime Commission, the most harmful effect of the crime syndicates is what they do to government. To ensure the smooth and continuous operation of their rackets, they finance political campaigns or bribe and corrupt political leaders and criminal justice personnel—either the policeman, prosecution, court clerk or judge depending on the type of protection desired and also on who is the weakest link in the criminal justice chain.[5]

The big fixes are replaced by thousands of "little fixes." For example, during 1977, news stories[6] reported the Orange County, California, grand jury's investigation into reported links between a supervisor and a man with county contracts to salvage scrap from county refuse dumps. Before sealed bids were opened, the contractor had contributed $2500 to the supervisor's campaign. Two days after the supervisor was elected, the contractor contributed another $2500 to the campaign fund. In another case, a businessman and political fund raiser was indicted on charges of bilking various companies of $1.5 million through the operation of a bogus pension fund program. Fifty thousand of these dollars were used to finance the campaign of another Orange County supervisor.

Another case cited in the *Los Angeles Times* and national news services in 1988 gave the appearance of impropriety and the abuse of political influence. The Robert Wallach law firm was investigated by independent counsel looking into the background of Attorney General Edwin Meese's ties to outside interests (specifically, money collected as referral fees from Wallach by Meese). In a lawsuit, a fee of 57% of a $1.74 million settlement was assigned the Wallach firm. The fee was eventually reduced to $322,000 after investigation by the state bar. What raised the issue of impropriety was that the judge hearing the case, also a close friend of Attorney Wallach, was appointed to a federal judgeship four months later.

As the complexity of government increases, so do the policy-making processes. As the number of governmental processes increase, the pressures of special interest groups prevail and the merry-go-round of politics opens a way to lay a firm foundation for unethical and illegal activities. The first goal of a crime commission must be to lessen the influence of organized crime on the agencies of criminal justice.[7]

THE EVOLUTION OF THE POLITICAL LEADER

A political leader will rise in power partly because of a charismatic personality and partly because of an ability to raise money. Typically, this latter activity

---

[5]Pennsylvania Crime Commission, *Report on Organized Crime*, Scranton, July 7, 1970, p. 2.
[6]*Los Angeles Times*, February 17, 1988. The second example was also carried in the *Times*.
[7]Pennsylvania Crime Commission, *Report on Organized Crime*, Scranton, July 7, 1970, p. 2.

is done through legitimate contributions. Money from illegal sources, however, has a way of creeping in.

Political manipulation by organized confederations is not new. Some criminal figures were made powerful by support from organized conspiracies, and many were famous for riding the crest of political fortunes. The important point is that money from the confederations seldom backs a loser. In part, this is due to clever planning. Several public relations firms have announced that with a "proper candidate" and an "adequate" amount of campaign money, they can produce a winner, and they have.

Political Action Committees

Political action committees are the latest method used by politicians to hide the sources of donations. For example, one politician's campaign committee complained that a political actions committee charged nearly a quarter of a million dollars raised in 1985 and 1986 to activities other than the candidate. They alleged that less than $1,000 had actually gone into the candidate's campaign. The remaining money was used for other things.

In another case, a California assemblyman received over $20,000 from a land developer to get approval on a large property development. When the assemblyman was caught failing to disclose his financial interest in accordance with state law, he apologized, saying he would immediately file an amended report. This type of abuse has been rampant in the political processes throughout the United States.

In late 1988, a federal sting operation conducted against California state legislators brought to light corrupt procedures in the political arena. During this investigation, some of the criteria used by federal investigators in the conduct of undercover operations involving political figures were made public to show the integrity of the investigation:

> When a law maker is suspected of committing a political crime, often the best way to investigate these violations is through undercover sting operations. The agency does not buy or pay for legislation in a sting operation that would be illegal, no matter the number of arrests that would result.
>
> Once an "undercover bill" is introduced, efforts will be made to get it defeated. If this fails in the normal process, the Governor will be notified so that he/she may veto the legislation. Thus, no illegal legislation is enacted into law.
>
> Infusion of cash into a corrupt candidate's campaign should be minimized so that a corrupt candidate will not be elected with undercover funds.
>
> Undercover investigations should not surface between September and the election in November, but should terminate in early Spring.
>
> Under no circumstances will there be leaks.

These processes have been marginally effective in preventing organized crime influence. Other methods and processes have been shown in studies by Tyler, who shows the workings of the organized gangs:

Organized crime deprives many individuals of their inalienable rights, not by turning the overwhelming power of the state against the citizen, but by exercising the power of private government against the nonconformist. Strikers lose their right to picket; businessmen lose their right to buy, manufacture and sell as they please and are forced to accept unwanted junior or senior partners; citizens lose the right to testify and others are forced to bear false witness. Even the right to honest and free election is repeatedly jeopardized.[8]

Next to having a well-informed public scrutinize the total election operation, it is important to have a branch of the local political clubs analyze "the candidate" and "his or her money." Frequently, well-meaning political groups at the local level are victims of too much syndicate money being funneled through political action groups (PACS) to a candidate that is unknown to the local political party and who would not otherwise be supported by the local political party. The dramatic increase in candidate spending for these offices are shown in Figure 3–1.

Frequently, a "ready made" candidate will come to the party trained in showmanship and possessing personal campaign funds. Through the "campaign money," "friends" are made in local businesses. Many of the "friends" have a vested interest in the candidate. An honest candidate operating through campaign managers may not have recognized the encumbrances to donors. For example, in a recent California election, a major candidate's representative was openly entertained and given financial support by a known West Coast mobster leader. This social connection could have far-reaching consequences with respect to power centers, political appointees, and sources of campaign expenditures.

This type of activity may appear petty and, when viewed as an individual donation to the political party, insignificant. However, when a syndicate leader and hundreds of wealthy friends donate to their "favorite candidate," the sum can be staggering. The intelligence files covering this type of activity are impressive.

The "ward heeler," or, more politely "field office representative," has an increased need for massive amounts of money for campaign funds, thus putting the power structure directly into the hands of the corruptible. To survive, local politicians must follow the person with the money. To have politically appointed department heads, judges, and people in lesser positions who are well connected with money, from whatever source, may become necessary.

---

[8]Gus Tyler, "An Interdisciplinary Attack on Organized Crime," *The Annals*, 347 (May 1963), 109. The reader is referred to this and other publications by Tyler for a comprehensive documentation of political influence. This basic premise is supported in the President's Commission On Organized Crime, *Report to the President and Attorney General*, Vol. VIII, (Washington, D.C.: U.S. Government Printing Office, 1986). The formation of political, ethnic and social coalitions are also illustrated in the National Institute of Justice. *Major Issues in Organized Crime Control.*

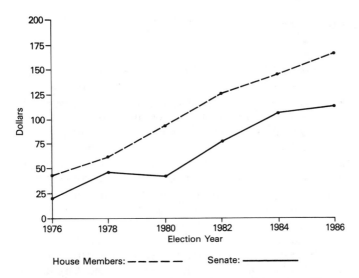

FIGURE 3-2 Amount spent by winning candidates in millions of dollars—Who pays?

Organized Crime Funds Eliminate Competition

Tyler alleges that corruption can almost be assumed.[9] There seems to be no reason to disagree. Strangely enough, not all money spent by the mob is spent to create corruption. Some years ago a vested gambling interest in Nevada was reported to have spent several million dollars in Mexico to dry up "illegal gambling" in Rosarita Beach. It took them two nights to wipe this operation out and close other operations that would keep customers from the tables in Las Vegas.

The same Nevada gambling interest finds it expedient to keep anti-gambling laws rigidly enforced in surrounding states. Whenever there is illegal activity that tends to draw action away from the tables of Nevada, quick work by local police vice squads eliminates the threat. It is no accident that information on gambling games in the adjoining states is funneled into the police departments in an almost hour-by-hour account. The political policy makers cannot be criticized for rigidly enforcing the laws (see Figure 3-2). A select number of "political ambassadors" benefit financially from this type of activity. The fact that this control exists gives the political manipulators an "in" for any other type of pressure they desire to exert.

[9]Tyler, "An Interdisciplinary Attack," *The Annals*, 347 (May 1963).

Political Influence by the Party In Power

The history of political exposés indicates that the party in power feels it is entitled to certain benefits.[10] The political pressures are felt even in the lowest echelons of law enforcement. Whether the selection system of a department is political or whether it is "merit" makes little difference. No selection system devised can eliminate politics from personnel policies.[11]

Political pressures may be illustrated in a different way. In a recent state election where power shifted from one party to another, a political appointee who handles more money than all but two other persons in the state government was retained by the incoming party. This appointment came after a grand jury investigation strongly suggested the appointee had solid connections with organized criminal elements who were doing legitimate business with the state.

How do the organized gangs manage to operate so covertly? The public assumes there must be no criminal activity of an organized nature because they do not hear about it. Nothing could be further from the truth. Organized crime flourishes in peace and calm. With few exceptions, most major cities have been fairly free of open warfare in recent years. There were nearly eight years of peace between the Gallo-Profaci feud and the Colombo shooting of 1971. There have been more than 20 years of gangland peace in Los Angeles. Other cities have had exposés that resulted in the prosecution of members from small theft and burglary gangs of semiprofessionals. Most of the major confederations, however, have learned to live in harmony. Areas of dispute are now settled by arbitration. Merely because a city does not hear of widespread organized criminal activity does not mean crime is not present. The corrupt politician cannot afford to be without these violators. The honest politician who is either uninformed or lacks the courage to challenge them must suffer in silence.

The professional politician should begin to look at organized crime as a real problem in our society. The politician should realize organized elements are creating a subculture that is out of step with the rest of society. For example, in the ghettos of American cities, ineffective vice control is one of law enforcement's most critical problems. In a minority neighborhood, vice-type crimes serve as a catalyst for political unrest. No other crimes cause so much conflict, bitterness, and lack of confidence between police and the minority community as do these violations. The basic problem in the ghetto is not more police but a better system of operation so the police can take impartial and consistent action on law violations. When a "policy runner"

---

[10]This attitude was evidenced in the ABSCAM investigations and in recent national elections where known organized crime figures were actively engaged in overt election activities.

[11]John A. Gardiner and David J. Olson, "Wincanton: The Politics of Corruption," *Task Force Report, Organized Crime* (Washington, D.C.: U.S. Government Printing Office, 1967), pp. 62–64. The same condition still exists in 1990.

or a "bookie" roams the same neighborhood for years without an arrest, the citizens can rightfully assume corruption. When prostitutes and narcotic users stand on the same corner year after year, the honest minority will lose confidence in any type of enforcement activity. There is not much incentive for this social group to be law-abiding.

SUMMARY

Organized crime is not simply the result of lax or corrupt police practices. These practices may contribute to the growth of organized crime, but the unseen manipulations in the political and legal arenas share a major responsibility. Several sociologists have made statements implying organized crime could not exist without the connivance of law enforcement agencies. To be more precise, organized crime cannot exist without the connivance of the participating public, and corrupt politics at all levels of government. No government agency can do more than attempt to control the most obvious forms of crime. The very complexity of the organized criminal organizations indicates they operate in many fairly large cities without the actual operations being known to the police. This may be due to a lack of police expertise, a lack of money and personnel to sustain investigations, or a lack of interest by political officials.

The nature of the democratic process offers a breeding ground for all types of organized crime. The fine line between individual freedom and social chaos is of prime concern in the area of organized crime. For a person to understand why organized crime cannot be easily controlled, the link to political influence must be shown. Through the illustrations of political influence one must be made aware of the tenacious grip that corrupt politics has on the entire community. Through a brief insight into some of the more common techniques of corruption, a person will be more aware of the magnitude of criminal organizations.

Closely related to the political governing element is the legal system. An understanding of the legal system's role in organized crime control is important for the well-informed citizen and enforcement agency representative.

QUESTIONS FOR DISCUSSION

1. Why do the so-called democratic processes encourage the growth of organized criminal influence?
2. How does the "use of cash" assist the confederation's influence in the community?
3. Are people involved in supporting the goals of organized criminals without being aware of it?

4. Can methods be devised to shield local political parties from the criminal-influence peddler?
5. How do the appointive processes in our system of government tend to shield criminal inroads into the system of justice?
6. May the rigid control of vice assume a form of corruption?
7. What are the ramifications of organized crimes in the city ghettos?
8. What do the police statistics indicate in describing the number of organized crimes in a community?
9. Discuss the political ramifications of such issues as statewide utility regulation and local franchises such as those for taxi, bus, and other business enterprises.

4

Role of the Legal System in Organized Crime Control

LEARNING OUTCOMES

1. Understand the importance of the legal (judicial) system in organized crime control.
2. Recognize how the activities of attorneys who defend organized crime figures tend to be insulated.
3. Gain knowledge about the failure to discipline members of the legal system whose activities are illegal or unethical.
4. Recognize how inconsistency in law creates natural loopholes for organized crime.
5. Gain an overview of the functions of crime commissions and other investigative agencies emanating from the legal system.

Without diligent development and maintenance of an honest legal system, no efforts by citizens or enforcement agencies will be effective against most types of organized crime.[1] The legal system personnel (the defense lawyer, the prosecutor, and the judge) are the keystones to the control of organized crime. Important areas over which the legal system exercises almost exclusive domain are: (1) the defense lawyer and the criminal client, (2) providing adequate law for enforcement, and (3) legal agents and the government crime commissions.

---

[1]The National Institute of Justice, *Major Issues in Organized Crime Control*, p. 7. Organized crime depends for its existence on the implicit support of otherwise "respectable" citizens— those who purchase its goods and services, and those who, perhaps inadvertently, create the conditions that insulate it from investigation and prosecution.

THE DEFENSE LAWYER AND THE CRIMINAL CLIENT

The moral and legal question as to where legal advice stops and criminal conspiracy begins is critical to the control of organized crime. Without the collusion, and frequently outright conspiracy, on the part of a lawyer, organized crime would wither away by sheer pressure. The involvement of a defense counsel in an organized crime operation raises the following interesting theoretical social questions:

1. Who are the groups that support organized crime legislation? Does this legislation support vested interest groups, or social norms established by the majority of society?
2. Is so-called white collar crime, so closely allied with organized crime operations, really a crime or merely nonconformity with accepted business practices?
3. Are laws governing organized crime mere social conventions and thus subject to case-by-case interpretation in courts of law before acts can be adjudged crimes?

When the issue of defense counsel involvement rises above the pragmatic level it becomes easier to understand why a lawyer acting beyond his or her "legal charge" might be willing to lend active and constructive support to many organized criminal activities.

For example, in 43 states legislation has been passed that makes the state overseer of the gambling enterprises in that state. Thus, it is not difficult to defend a man against felony bookmaking charges in the states where it is illegal.

It is easy to see how a lawyer becomes involved with an organization dealing in criminal enterprises. Schwartz illustrated this in his study of lawyer involvement in organized crime.[2] He indicated that the lawyer, merely by agreeing in advance to represent or counsel members of a confederation at a criminal trial, would raise questions of proper involvement. Until there is some reconciliation of this question, law enforcement has very little opportunity to exert effective control over organized crime.

The Syndicate Attorney

There are lawyers who are well known for their defense of persons deeply involved in organized crime. They are not, however, exclusive

---

[2]Murray L. Schwartz, "The Lawyer's Professional Responsibility and Interstate Organized Crime," *Notre Dame Lawyer,* 38, 6 (1963), 711–26. National Institute of Justice, *Major Issues in Organized Control,* p. 7. "Corruption is the device that enables syndicates and criminal ventures to achieve a de facto immunity from regulation and investigation, and provides them with the ability to penetrate the legitimate economy." The police, the legal system, and the politicians share an equal responsibility.

representatives of the organized element. They will also represent many local individual violators as a front for their major clients. A close scrutiny of their clientele could show the major portion of their income is derived from the confederations. While those individuals who are clients are entitled to legal counsel, the public should be aware that there are lawyers who serve on retainer for the confederated groups.

A person, merely because he or she is a lawyer, has no legal right to compound a crime. If an attorney becomes an integral part of the planning and development of legal subterfuges for organized criminal activities, then it is time to reappraise the delicate distinction between what is unethical and what is illegal. The ethical relationship of lawyer and client is a matter that should be rigidly enforced by punitive sanctions if necessary. The American Bar Association and the different state associations have the authority to take such action. As a matter of practice, such action is rarely taken, and it is even more unusual to find very many actual sanctions. While there is no attempt to vilify the good job done by most members of the legal profession, when an attorney assumes the role of "middleman and fixer," the problem of ethical standards exists.

Internal Discipline for the Legal System

There is a double standard that our society accepts in apprehending criminals. If the thief is without the protective cloak of professional societies, he or she becomes a subject of prompt police action and prosecution. If the person belongs to certain state and national associations, he or she has a strong cushion of judicial protection. For example, the California state constitution does not permit the Commission on Judicial Qualifications to make public the names of the judges who quit or are dismissed for illegal or unethical conduct. There is no such protection for the criminal, for police officers who are dishonest, and for many others who do not belong to the cloistered organizations. Although it is recognized that the legal system (lawyers and judges) may require some protection from the public, there is certainly no reason for letting their own peers decide what illegal or immoral acts the public should know about. Until such practices are ended, there is little hope for expecting effective cooperation from organizations that are outside the coveted protection of the professional associations. Organized criminal confederations have built-in security for their representatives in the legal system.

A crucial area for maintaining internal discipline within the legal system is the division of function and authority between law enforcement and prosecution. The Cornell Institute on Organized Crime published a comprehensive report on these units and their relationships and came to the conclusion there is no common pattern of operation between these critical units.[3] The legal (judicial) system, it appears, has tended to extend its jurisdiction into the functional areas of organized criminal investigation. The "task forces" have tended to be dominated by the prosecutor's office, the determination of who to investigate and the mode of investigation being more frequently made by this arm of the legal system.

In outlining how each unit was organized, the Cornell Institute identified four functional patterns of operation.

These patterns of operations are:

(1) The functional unity between a rackets unit, (2) interaction with police departments within its jurisdiction, (3) relations with other prospective agencies will be as varied as the personalities and (4) the quality of the interactions and relations will vary with the experience of the unit's director.[4]

The precise organization is not important. The failure to have checks and balances between the executive and the judicial branches of government will result in a long-term, self-defeating effort to control organized crime.

PROVIDING ADEQUATE LAWS FOR ENFORCEMENT

No other segment of society has more responsibility than the legal system for the control of organized crime. No segment, unless it is law enforcement, has been more thwarted in its performance. Members of the legal system initiate and conduct research and make recommendations for the legislative and administrative branches of government. Semiprivate legal organizations, such as the State Bar Associations and American Bar Association should be staffed with personnel of allied disciplines (sociologists, psychologists, and criminologists) to formulate realistic and workable laws. The fact that a law is technically sound from a mechanistic point of view does not mean that it serves the public. Many of the laws that support vice and other organized crime are of this category. Many of these statutes are not realistic in an enlightened society. For example, within the environs of the city of Los Angeles, three different applications of the law prevail for the control of gambling:[5]

[3]G. Robert Blakely, Ronald Goldstock, and Charles H. Rogovin, *Rackets Bureaus: Investigation and Prosecution of Organized Crime* (Washington, D.C.: U.S. Government Printing Office, March 1978). Also Robert M. Morgenthau, "Police and Prosecutors: A Professional Partnership," *FBI Law Enforcement Bulletin,* March 1981, pp. 6–7. A *Los Angeles Times* staff story, dated September 21, 1987, part 1, quotes John Feerick, chairman of the New York State Commission on Government Integrity: "The last several years may be remembered as the most scandal plagued in the history of New York state." The internal discipline apparatus of the various levels of government is not working in New York and in other major cities of the United States.

[4]Morgenthau, Ibid., pp. 4–5.

[5]California Penal Code section 330 and Los Angeles Municipal Code.

1. It is illegal to bet on a horse unless you wager the bet at a state-licensed track.
2. It is illegal to wager on any game of chance (except draw poker, which the legislature of the 1870s decided was a game of skill).
3. Draw poker may be played only if authorized by local ordinance.

In Texas and other states, the local option law for distributing over-the-bar alcohol is equally absurd. A person cannot attach a very strong feeling of wrongness to laws based on abstract whims. These inconsistencies of law create a multi-million-dollar morally acceptable racket in illegal betting activities, in racketeering, and in abuses of liquor laws. Realistic laws in these and other organized crime areas would minimize the opportunity for corruption and profit for the confederations. Under the federal 1970 Organized Crime Control Act (amended in 1978, 1984, 1986, and 1988), realistic statutes have been designed. The states are gradually bringing their own laws into a consistent pattern with this law.[6]

Consistency in the Law

The legal profession, while defending the need for more lawyers, is not expected to recommend statutes that would not be liable to a legal challenge. But in legal practice, changes should be sought for statutes and procedures that follow a doctrine of consistency. A doctrine of consistency is mandatory for any acceptable degree of legal control, but is rarely found. For example, in California and many other states it is a felony by statute to engage in bookmaking. Yet, statistics will bear out that bookmakers seldom go to prison. Even long-time recidivists who are punished with summary probation can, if arrested within the probationary period, have the case transferred to another court. Thus, the terms of the summary probation are nullified. The reason is simple: money and legal talent to see that the case gets to the right court. With this lack of consistency in conforming to the code, a few judges and lawyers have acted as effectively in perpetuating organized crime as has any of the syndicate bet takers.

It is interesting to note that a few attorneys who are mentioned in the 1950 Crime Commission Hearings in California and the Kefauver hearings are still the legal representatives of the same bookmakers who were being arrested from 1945 to 1950. This is no coincidence. The same allegations could be cited for New York or Illinois.

Because of the need for consistency, the application of law should not be a part of a "drive" or a "war on crime" by politically ambitious crusaders.

---

[6]In National Institute of Justice, *Major Issues in Organized Crime Control, Symposium Proceedings,* (Washington, D.C.: U.S. Government Printing Office, 1987), Ronald Goldstock pointed out that there is a radical contrast between federal and New York state law when he discussed inter-jurisdictional and interagency issues.

This type of activity is likely to pose a threat to a normal legal protection of the accused. In crusaders there is a tendency to abuse immunity from prosecution provisions so that quick information is available at exactly the right time for news releases. This technique is regularly overworked when there is an overlapping of state and federal statutes under which the suspect may be tried.

One of the most maligned uses of the legal system by confederation criminals has been the use of the Fifth Amendment protection guarantee. Rufus King, a Washington, D.C., attorney, identified the problem this way:

> The Fifth Amendment privilege of silence combines three disparate elements: (1) the privilege of the accused, formally charged with crime, to remain silent at his own trial; (2) the privilege of a suspect to be free of sanctions applied to make him confess; and (3) the privilege of unsuspected persons to conceal guilt known only to themselves. It is felt that the Fifth Amendment privilege should have been confined narrowly to the protection of persons accused of crime when they appear as defendants in their own trials; it has been intended to protect two other classes: persons merely suspected and under investigation, and unsuspected persons who have, in fact, some guilt to conceal. This extension has worked harmfully to limit the interrogator and to prevent the public's right to everyman's evidence from being carried out. The immunity device is suggested as a valid palliative for this situation, but no new enactment of immunity legislation should confer immunity automatically as some of the immunity provisions of the federal regulatory agencies do. Any law should exclude the offenses of contempt and perjury from the scope of their immunization, and, perhaps, all should require the concurrency of the Attorney General or of a federal judge before their provision could come into play.[7]

State vs. Local Laws

Local communities jealously guard the historical concept of local option. With communication and transportation systems drawing the communities of a state closer and closer together, the need for a "model of adequacy" appears to be more important than laws of doubtful legality in every "incorporated crossroads" of the state.

Technology in police service has made it desirable to have similar laws that extend across city and county lines. The state should give law enforcement an adequate system of laws to regulate those crimes that confront the people of the state. There are no situations, especially in the field of organized crime, that the state cannot adequately legislate for local protection. The legislatures of states with inadequate state laws should preempt areas of vice law and other local ordinances that furnish organized criminals an opportunity to "beat the system."

---

[7]Rufus King, "The Fifth Amendment Privilege and Immunity Legislation," *Notre Dame Lawyer*, 38, 6 (1963), 641–54. Also see G.R. Blakely, *Investigation and Prosecution of Organized Crime and Corrupt Activities* (Washington, D.C.: U.S. Department of Justice, 1977).

LEGAL AGENTS AND THE GOVERNMENT CRIME COMMISSION

It is impossible to determine how extensive the corruption of the public and/or public officials by organized crime has been. We do know that there must be better identifying and reporting of corruption. There must be better ways for the public to communicate information about corruption to appropriate government personnel.[8] One of the ways in which information may come to appropriate authorities is through established crime commissions. The placement of the investigative commissions, although a responsibility of the executive branch of government, is nevertheless subject to control through judicial appointments and acquaintances. Whether a government crime commission functions depends greatly on the cooperation offered by prosecuting agencies, courts, and defense attorneys. The very fact that the judicial branch of government exercises such great power over a legitimate executive function offers perhaps the weakest link in the reporting and prosecution of organized crime violations.

Crime commissions can come in many forms. The most prominent ones in the organized crime field have been the Senate Permanent Subcommittee on Investigations and the Senate Select Committee on Improper Activities in the Labor and Management Field. These two subcommittees, which are serving in place of specified crime commissions, have been responsible for substantial investigations. A great deal of information about organized crime has been revealed. These two committees and dozens of lesser committees are charged with the investigation of hundreds of criminal violations involving organized crime. These committees have many shortcomings. For example, there is little preinvestigation, so certain types of criminal activity may be excluded from the hearings. The autonomy of past crime commissions has also revealed problems of whitewash, favoritism, and conspiracy simply because selected representatives of important interest groups— "sixty-year old smiling public men" or "eager, pink-cheeked, name-seeking friends of the fraternity"— constitute the typical investigative subcommittees. Their participation, it is alleged, is essential to make funds available from other congressional subcommittees. A new selection process for commission members is desirable.

To have effective organization in government commissions or subcommittees, they should be set up according to the President's Crime Commission, which recommended:

---

[8]John A. Gardiner and David J. Olson, "Wincanton: The Politics of Corruption," *Task Force Report, Organized Crime* (Washington, D.C.: U.S. Government Printing Office, 1967), pp. 22–23. Perhaps the most definitive study has been Alan A. Block and Frank R. Scarpitti, *Poisoning for Profit: The Mafia and Toxic Waste in America* (New York: William Marrow and Co., 1985), which claims that the toxic waste industry embraces corruption in nearly every facet of the operation.

...a permanent joint congressional committee on organized crime. States that have organized crime groups in operation should create and finance organized crime investigation commissions with independent permanent status, with an adequate staff of investigators, and with subpoena power. Such commissions should hold hearings and furnish periodic reports to the legislature, governor, and law enforcement officials.[9]

In the past, few local units of government have provided such support simply because there was no coordination between units engaged in the organized crime control effort.

Because many states are, in fact, politically controlled by attorneys and judges, they are the ones who must be made aware of the potential of the crime commissions for the control of organized crime. The legal segment of the criminal justice system can ensure that crime commissions are composed of qualified representatives rather than of cronies who may bargain away favors for appointments.

Government investigative committees exist for the purpose of putting before a lay audience clear and credible information taken from immensely complex and detailed accounts. Intelligence information must not only be gathered, it must also be analyzed by experts who are in the business of crime control. The issues raised and identified by an investigative commission must be documented, thoroughly investigated, and followed by prosecution if necessary. Sufficient time and money must be allocated for ongoing studies and analyses of local crime conditions as revealed by the crime commissions.

By singling out the legal system for criticism there has been no intent to take blame for the existence of organized crime from either the legislative or administrative branches of government. The position of the legal system is so critical that any effort at organized crime control must use this system.

SUMMARY

The importance of a noncorruptible legal system cannot be overstressed. It is not enough that most attorneys and judges be honest. A small minority allowed to omit ethics, and frequently legality, can defeat the efforts of the entire system of criminal justice. The relationship of the lawyer to a criminal client should be subject to research, and more stringent rules of conduct should be imposed. The issue of honesty also includes the enforcement of realistic laws and consistency in the courts. The legal system is the catalyst for crime commissions as a means of investigating organized crime. Appoint-

---

[9]*Task Force Report: Organized Crime*, pp. 22–23. This recommendation was also supported by speakers at the National Conference on Organized Crime, Los Angeles, November 8–9, 1979. The President's Commission on Organized Crime is the result of these recommendations. This type of commission, however, should not relieve Congressional sub-committees from conducting investigations and hearings throughout the United States.

ments to these commissions as presently structured are almost exclusively in the hands of the legal power structure. The system of selection can be self-defeating. It is no longer the local police agency that can dictate whether organized crime will exist. It is the total criminal justice system with the power centered in the legal subunits that dictates how much organized crime will and does exist.

QUESTIONS FOR DISCUSSION

1. Why is the legal system termed the "keystone" to the control of organized crime?
2. Where should legal advice stop in advising a criminal client of methods to subvert the law?
3. Do the operating patterns of "syndicate lawyers" show a consistency over the past two decades?
4. What steps should the legal system impose for better internal ethics?
5. Identify the local and federal laws most commonly used in your community. Are there wide variations in content and enforcement application?
6. Why don't people attach much "wrongness" to organized crime?
7. Do the crime commissions, as presently constituted, offer a solution to the identification of organized criminal enterprises?
8. How can liaison among the various levels of organized crime control agencies be improved?
9. How can the legal system be used to increase the efficiency of organized crime control?
10. Identify provisions in the federal 1970, 1986, 1988 Omnibus Crime Bills for providing crime commissions made up of lay citizens.

Part II

Vice Crimes of an Organized Nature

The financial keystones for organized confederations have been the crimes commonly classified as vice. With vice being defined as a moral failing, evil or wicked conduct, corruption and depravity,[1] there are a great number of crimes that fall into this category. For all practical purposes, vice crimes, as they relate to organized groups, are gambling (Chapter 5), prostitution (Chapter 6), narcotics trafficking (Chapter 7), and obscenity and pornography (Chapter 8).

Generally, vice crimes are viewed by the public as an act of individual moral weakness and the decision to engage in such acts as one that should be left to the decision of the individual. Many allege that legislation against this type of moral behavior is fundamentally wrong. This concept may be right and if such control were to be removed, perhaps vice crimes might be less susceptible to control by organized confederations. But because of the right of society to impose sanctions that it believes are necessary for the regulation of human behavior, the right of self-determination, while being increasingly liberalized, is not apt to soon become general in our culture.

The relationship of vice to organized groups has had much publicity. However, many people refuse to believe that the prostitute in the local bar may work for a national confederation or that the bookie in the local barbershop may have the same boss as the prostitute. The direct link between vice activity and organized criminal groups is frequently difficult to show and almost impossible to prove. Activities of vice confederations are so covert that it is impossible to detect them through normal investigative methods. By their very nature, vice crimes are a catalyst for criminal activity.

The evolution of organized crime has been synonymous with the expansion of these vice crimes. The growth of vice crimes has remained fairly constant in relation to increased population and trends toward urbanization

[1]*Webster's New World Dictionary,* College Edition. Copyright © 1987 by The World Publishing Co., New York & Cleveland.

in spite of campaigns to clear out the bawdy houses and eliminate the red light districts.

A double standard exists for sanctions against vice crimes. The citizens who pressure for the elimination of vice crimes are the same ones who patronize and engage in these illegal activities. This double standard has caused the confederations to gain public support while the criminal coffers grow rich from vice profits.

In 1988, a new problem emerged when the Drug Enforcement Administration (DEA) accused the State Department of turning a "blind eye" toward friendly nations engaged in drug trafficking. For example, the DEA said the golden triangle area included large areas of the People's Republic of China and that after the 1972 opening of relations with China, 24 narcotic refineries disappeared from the map in the redrawing of China boundaries. The DEA alleges the 24 refineries disappeared on paper only.[2] Thus, the double standard in the political handling of the drug problem still exists. To compound the double standard, prior to the 1988 elections, Congress hastily passed drug legislation that many civil libertarians alleged were unconstitutional. It has been most difficult to keep Partisan politics out of the drug enforcement scene.

The trend in vice crimes today is toward bigger and more lucrative crimes. In spite of increased enforcement, the monetary take from gambling, narcotics, and pornography continues to spiral upward. Television sports coverage has contributed to gambling on events that in the past were ignored. In 1978, the federal government passed legislation that enables newspapers, radio, and television to report the results of state-run lotteries without running afoul of federal laws. At that time 13 states ran their own lotteries, while 25 other states authorized lotteries conducted by some other organization. Some states have both forms of organized lotteries.

It is difficult for the citizens to distinguish psychologically between gambling conducted by organized crime and that conducted by government. Because the citizen fails to make this distinction, the illegal activities of organized crime continue to supply the ever-increasing citizen demand.

---

[2]Editorial, *Insight Magazine*, March 28, 1988, p. 7. All states except Hawaii, Indiana, and Utah now permit some form of legalized gambling. Sports betting generally has become a socially accepted pasttime.

5

Gambling

LEARNING OUTCOMES

1. Know the ways in which organized crime perpetuates gambling empires.
2. Understand the structure of confederation gambling operations and realize why local enforcement agencies cannot eliminate organized gambling.
3. Gain knowledge about the ways in which gambling operations are conducted.
4. Recognize that society has a dual standard for enforcing gambling laws.
5. Associate community activities that pertain to gambling with a common scheme or plan designed by syndicate members.

This chapter covers three traditional vice crimes commonly associated with the confederations: (1) gambling; (2) bookmaking, betting on sporting events, and gambling devices, such as cards, dice, and slot machines; and (3) miscellaneous lotteries that are partially or completely dominated by the confederations.

Confederation domination and operation are identified with many major gambling activities. For example, there are no bookies who do not owe allegiance to the confederations. Gambling activities are the direct link to street crimes.

The evolution of gambling may be described in this manner. Gambling begins as entertainment for the family and a small circle of friends. It is perpetuated by fraternal groups and social gatherings, where it is still looked upon as entertainment. There is little danger of antisocial behavior in this type of activity as long as it is a form of social entertainment. The next step, however, is the identifying and bringing together of mutual groups whose only interest is gambling for profit. When this occurs, friendships vanish and what was formerly social entertainment becomes a lucrative commercial enterprise.

Municipal governments, although obligated to enforce the gambling ordinances, frequently find it expedient to encourage or turn their backs on illegal gambling operations to placate vested interest groups.

Newspaper accounts document gambling operations throughout the nation that apparently have public approval and political collusion enabling them to survive. For example, Hot Springs, Arkansas, long renowned for its vacation spas and gambling, closed the doors of its "locally favored" commercial operations. Only after Senator McClelland exposed vice and corruption in major cities throughout the United States did public pressure cause them to close his hometown gambling spa. Other cities of major size have condoned gambling for a time due in part to the indifference of citizens. Active local citizen support is what makes gambling flourish. There seems to be a feeling in America that life itself is a gamble, so risking money in a game of chance is just another acceptable part of our social system. This is exactly what the confederations want the public to think.

THE MORAL ISSUES OF GAMBLING

Sociologists, psychologists, and theologians universally are in favor of and expound on the issue of legalized gambling. Most studies indicate no empirical basis for the adverse influence of gambling in a society where it is legalized.

Fred Cook believed, however, that when gamblers are sheltered by the law, as they are in Nevada, the morals and ethics of the gamblers become a part of the accepted pattern of life.

Virgil Peterson, a leading investigator of gambling influences, states:

> Whenever the light of public attention has been focused on the unsavory gambling racket, when gangland killings arouse some measure of public indignation and when corruption arising out of alliance between hoodlums, politicians, and law enforcement officers is exposed, there recurs agitation for the licensing of gambling. Whether gambling should be licensed or not is a highly controversial question.[1]

An honest difference of opinion exists among many who are strong advocates of licensing and those who are in opposition. The position to be taken is that as long as the activity is prohibited by statute, it should have no positive recognition in our society.

Some of the more common comments for and against gambling illustrate how behavior patterns tend to form around mysticisms. Gambling is a belief in the supernatural. However, the *Encyclopaedia Britannica* states

---

[1]Virgil W. Peterson, *The Problem, Gambling—Should It Be Legalized?* (Springfield, Ill.: Charles C Thomas, 1951), pp. 3–7. The position of this author is updated and supported by Seth Kupferberg in "The State as Bookie," *The Washington Monthly,* July–August, 1979, p. 57. Also, in the *Los Angeles Times* of January 19, 1989, Part IX, officials of two cities where a lottery is legal complained that they had been threatened by a group seeking approval of their application to play Bingo. Even legalization has problems.

no society has the rise of rationalism brought about a decrease in the incidence or volume of gambling."[2]

Gambling is a natural law because life itself is a gamble.   This is accepted by many groups in society. Yet, most religions maintain that there is a spiritual design in every life that may preclude a commitment to the concept of gambling.

Gambling is nonproductive and immoral.   Jewish, Muslim, and most Christian faiths have held gambling to be immoral. Oriental religions and modern Roman Catholics have held that gambling for amusement does not offend a deity.

Gambling should be legalized and taxed to provide revenue for the governing functions.   Several states have chosen this alternative, and most have had only moderate success in terms of raising operating revenues. The late Los Angeles Chief of Police, William Parker, had this to say on the subject of gambling as a source of revenue: "Any society that bases its financial structure on the weakness of its people doesn't deserve to survive."

Gambling is justified for the financial support of churches and private charities.   History indicates that in many societies scholars connected with religion conducted gambling. Priests with divinatory devices and occult activities sustained gambling. In modern society, it is very questionable whether such enterprises contribute to the public welfare. In England, many private clubs have been the benefactors of the 1968 Gambling Act and now serve under license as public betting parlors.

Thus, with this reasoning, the ethic against gambling is established. To see how this ethic has applied to gambling throughout history, a brief review follows.

HISTORY OF GAMBLING

The history of gambling has been fairly well documented through the centuries. From artifacts found by archeologists, there are indications that people, rich and poor, have always been gamblers. There is little question that most people at some time in their lives will gamble. The great social problem to be resolved is this: *How can society regulate gambling so that people may afford the luxury of indulgence?* Whatever the argument, for or against gambling, one can look to documented history and see that gambling in most of its

---

[2]*Encyclopaedia Britannica*, 15th ed., (Chicago: Encyclopaedia Britannica, Inc., 1987), p. 104.

forms has existed since the beginning of recorded history. Because of that long history, organized crime has attached itself to a reliable profit maker.

Many authorities document the evolution of gambling. The ancient Greeks considered gambling on athletic games a quasi-religious observance. Yet most philosophers, including Aristotle, grouped gamblers with nonproductive thieves. Following the Greeks, the Romans imposed strict regulations against gambling except during the December holiday called Saturnalia. The opposition to gambling was in only rare instances repulsive to the religious deities, but the waste of resources was a severe drain on the economy. In the early Middle East cultures, chess was the one game of skill that was not forbidden.

Historians believe card playing started in Europe around the early fourteenth century. English and French laws were enacted at this time for the purpose of keeping the common person away from the card and dice tables and diverting his talents to archery, which would be of benefit to the state. Penalties for gambling were minor.

For at least 300 years there has been government control over licensing of gambling. "The need for tax revenue from indirect—hence not unpopular—sources has persuaded nearly every sovereign entity, including forty-seven states of the United States, to license some form of gambling. . . ."[3]

National History

In the American colonies, there was differing public reaction toward various forms of gambling. It is quite possible that cards came to this country soon after the Pilgrims, or possibly with them. As early as the seventeenth century, the law, influenced by New England Puritans, established a fine of $5 for one or more individuals who brought cards into the colony. About 1645, the Massachusetts General Court prohibited all gambling and gaming and included in the category bowling and shuffleboard. In spite of the sanctions against gambling, there was a steady increase in the activity. Each of the thirteen original colonies conducted public lotteries as a source of revenue. As public sentiment changed, card playing was punished by the stocks in many areas of New England. In other parts of the colonies, it was looked on with some degree of tolerance.

The State and Gambling

To what extent is the guilt of the casual participant distinguished from the gambling house proprietor's or the horse bettor distinguished from the bookmaker? As would be expected, the answer fluctuates from state to state.

[3]Ibid., p. 105.

The laws prohibiting gambling are enforced in various ways throughout the United States, usually quite inadequately. Large segments of our population feel that such laws are proper and necessary, but they reserve for themselves the privilege of deciding whether or not the laws apply in their own particular case. This rationalization complicates the enforcement of laws and creates a haven for organized criminals.

In the 1970s, many states decided that gambling was going to be a "something for nothing" bonanza for financially troubled states. The number of state lotteries increased from 2 to 19. Four states legalized gambling on jai alai, and New Jersey legalized the first casinos outside Nevada. State lotteries have suffered only minor scandals. However, New Jersey's casinos figured heavily in the Justice Department's ABSCAM probe of bribery of congressmen and state and local government leaders in 1981.

The history of legalized gambling in the United States would indicate it is only a matter of time before most of the gambling ventures will be counterproductive because of the drain on law enforcement resources and the corruption that surrounds gambling enterprises. The present trend in this country is mixed and confused; the federal government is attempting to crack down on professional gambling in general, and on bookmaking activities of an interstate nature in particular. Although there are occasional proposals for a nationally sponsored lottery, they have generally met with public disapproval. In many states, the movement is in the other direction. The game of Bingo, which is a form of lottery, is now legal in many states and others are considering legalizing other forms of lottery.

Those states that now allow horse betting (32) are adding extra tracks and expanding racing days. Fourteen states permit dog racing. In addition, there are trotting races and other sporting events to stimulate the bettor. In the encouragement of new race tracks some states take a very realistic view. Laws usually provide that a specific total be taken from the bettor's dollar but permit state officials some latitude as to how much of the total various track operators will be permitted to retain. Live video racing with pari-mutuel betting and Indian lotteries are the latest concessions to organized crime.

Whether corruption is a result of gambling or gambling is a result of corruption is a matter of individual decision. The Pennsylvania Crime Commission identifies the problem this way:

> A U.S. Senate subcommittee, studying organized gambling in depth, concluded that "organized crime in the United States is primarily dependent upon illicit gambling, a multi-billion dollar racket for the necessary funds required to operate other criminal and illegal activities or enterprises." Illegal gambling provides a steady source of lucrative profits which organized crime syndicates then invest in either more profitable or high risk ventures.[4]

[4]Pennsylvania Crime Commission, *Report on Organized Crime,* Scranton, July 7, 1970, p. 25.

Today organized criminal groups are "pyramiding" their wealth. They are able to flaunt this wealth because they service their customers by promoting illegal enterprises alongside the state-run gaming enterprises. It is estimated that 8 to 10 percent of the total gambling take in Nevada is from an unlicensed and illegal source.[5] Other state lotteries are playing second fiddle to the organized crime enterprises. State-run lotteries tend to run for the convenience of the state, while crime-run enterprises are designed for the convenience of the gambler. Until legislators recognize this is a competitive enterprise, no state will be free from the influence of the corruption of gambling billions.

The Function of the Federal Government

The United States has federal laws prohibiting lotteries and wagering across state lines.[6] In the past three decades, many new laws, such as the Omnibus Crime Bill, have been passed to combat the syndicate operation. These laws have, to some extent, discouraged the movement of persons and information in interstate travel for racketeering purposes. For example, it is a felony to transmit bets and wagers between states by any means.[7] This law has caused changes in techniques for transmitting information. The information today, however, moves more rapidly and as freely as it has ever done.

THE BETTING SYNDICATE

Some of the largest segments of the organized crime groups and allegedly the most profitable are those that handle horse and sports betting. The very nature of this operation dictates a highly sophisticated communications network. Through the wire services, instantaneous information is available for the bookmaker's "business office." Figure 5–1 illustrates this system.

The recordkeeping function of the business offices closely parallels the information flow. As each bet, taken by a "handbook," is recorded in the business office, a flow of information on new races and events is transmitted back to the "handbook."

---

[5]Information from a member of the Organized Crime Strike Force Los Angeles and partially confirmed in an article by Frank Fortunato, *Betting with Bookies,* reference unknown.

[6]The U.S. Code has several sections on carrying, knowingly taking or receiving chance, share, interest, etc. In a lottery a gift, enterprise, or similar scheme is in violation. You are referred to the following sections: 18 USC 1301, 1302, 1303, 1304.

[7]U.S. Code 1084.

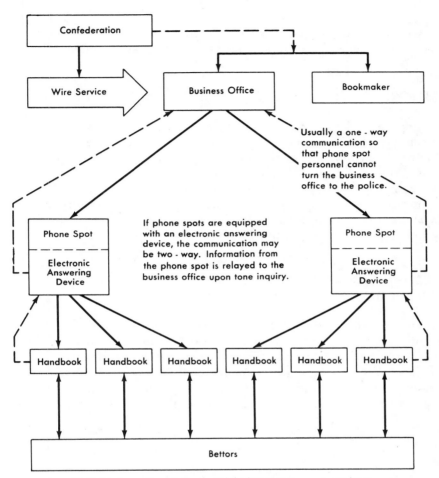

FIGURE 5-1 The bookmaking empire. New techniques use a programmed mini-computer in the business office; this gives on-line access to the wire services.

The Handbook

The handbook, or bookie, is the member of the organization who must contact the bettor and relay bets into the organization's recordkeeping service. The handbook's operation depends solely on the imagination he exhibits. Frequently he will have an established pattern of operation. Thus, the investigator must observe and study the mode of operation until a weakness can be detected in the handbook's system. A number of clever techniques by the bookmaker will create problems for the enforcement officer.

The Wire Service

The wire service providers analyze data such as injuries, weather, team morale, and past performance. They then set a *line* that evenly divides the betting public, with half the money backing one team and half the other team. A perfect point spread can pay off the winners with the loser's money and keep as profit the 10 percent commission known as "vigorish" or "juice." Computerized results of data from local newspapers and sheets such as the *Gold Sheet,* a Los Angeles-based publication, make wire services to the gambling industry a highly sophisticated service.[8]

BOOKMAKING, SPORTING EVENTS, GAMBLING DEVICES

A two-dollar bet, multiplied by thousands, gives organized syndicates throughout the United States a prime source of revenue. Each state regulates its own horse racing and parai-mutuel betting. For the customer who cannot make it to the track, there are many obliging bookies. From the local barbershop to the largest missile manufacturing complexes, the handbook finds a niche to ply his trade. (The handbook is the agent who actually takes the wager from a bettor.)

The Bookmaking System

As part of a large organization, the bookmaker does not actually risk his own money in bookmaking activities. He is merely an instrument of the confederation, which has agents take the bets and make payoffs to the winning bettors when necessary. For a fee, the local bookmaker can "lay off" bets with the syndicate. To "lay off" a bet is similar to the underwriting techniques used by insurance companies as a guard against large losses. This technique enables an individual to share the loss, if there is one, with a larger organization or combination of medium to small organizations. Thus, the losses are spread over a large number of bettors, bookmakers, and race tracks.

---

[8]Las Vegas Sports Consultants, Inc., projects the spread on over 200 teams, thus, furnishing illegal bookmakers with vital information.

The law of probability dictates odds in favor of the larger bookmaking organizations.

Figure 5–1 shows the sequence of betting information. To maintain this information sequence, the bookmaker, with new developments in electronic communications systems, is now able to eliminate the "phone spot" person. Now a small, inexpensive instrument can receive the bets from the handbook and store this information until queried by the business office with a simple "tone inquire" device.[9] This system eliminates a weak link in the bookmaking enterprise. Under present search and seizure laws, there are few legal techniques by which the local vice operator can apprehend anyone higher in the organization than the "handbook."

The memory system. Perhaps the most difficult handbook to apprehend and prosecute is the one who takes bets solely from established clientele, commits these bets to memory, and calls the business office only after every 30 or 40 bets. Many handbooks have phenomenal memories and never write down bets, nor will they accept a bet written on a piece of paper. All business is committed to memory until the handbook is called by the business office, or contacts the phone spot or an electronic answering device.

The employee bookie. Another difficult handbook to apprehend is a messenger, toolman, or representative in large plants who contacts the same people daily on business matters. He will come to know those who are sports minded and through his contacts may operate so covertly the worker on the next bench will not be aware of his activities. The wins and losses are frequently handled at payday. If the handbook keeps records in codes that cannot be interpreted,[10] his longevity is practically guaranteed. Plant owners frequently do not wish to cooperate with police investigators because every employee is a member of some employee group. To have an employee removed from the job can be done only for cause. Usually, one handbook removed is only replaced by another. The plant owner's attitude is usually live and let live rather than incur the wrath of organized employee associations.

The traveling bar bookie. One of the most common operations is to have a bookie cover several bars or cafes in a given area. The bookie will drop in, pick up the bets, and move on to the next establishment. If the patrons of a bar, for example, sit and study a scratch sheet or racing section

---

[9]In 1979, two separate cases were prosecuted in which programmed computer systems were used to record bets. Computerized codes have given "back offices" protection in contemporary bookmaking systems.

[10]The court requires that an expert in bookmaking be able to interpret what is written in code. A coded message on a tool room requisition may appear to be a legitimate tool request yet be a handbook's record.

of the newspaper, chances are good the bookie will be around at intervals preceding every two or three races.

Frequently, a bar patron will study the races, then go in search of the bookie. By following, the police investigator can frequently be led directly to the transaction between bookie and bettor. Once consummated, these betting transactions are then relayed to the bookie's office from phone booths along the route.

An establishment that caters to the traveling bookie or one that has its own bookie usually receives rent from the confederation as part of normal business.

The fixed spot.   From sophisticated "horse rooms" to telephone spots, the bookie must take chances in order to meet the bettors. The spot where a bookie can come and socialize with betting friends is very popular. The front of the spot may be a small grocery, a book and record shop, or any other small business that should have a high incidence of pedestrian traffic.

A popular fixed spot is a newsstand on a busy metropolitan corner. The operator is a natural because of multiple contacts with people, especially employees of department stores or offices who cannot afford the time to visit the race track. It is virtually impossible to detect a betting transaction during the sale of a newspaper. However, an operator who leaves the stand to make frequent telephone calls may be calling out bets.

A good news location that has betting action will frequently sell for $70,000 to $90,000. The news vendor is usually an independent contractor and is not usually an employee of the newspaper publisher. This type of fixed spot is often "wired politically" and can survive only where corruption exists.

Fixed "phone spots."   The technique for placing an off-track bet by phone is quite simple. If a person is well recommended, he or she may contact a bookmaker and place the bet by telephone. (From time to time, the bookmaker will change phone numbers as a precaution.) All betting transactions are handled over the telephone. At predetermined times, the bookie will send a runner to the bettor to collect for the losses or pay the wins. Appointments with the runner are sometimes unscheduled, private, and secretive. Only cash is involved, and there is no exchange of receipts or written memorandums.

Phone spots will frequently have the added protection of a "drop line," "a black box," or "a wire out" so that the bookie sitting on the phone spot will have time to destroy the evidence in case of a police raid. This technique is shown in Figure 5–2.

Numerous types of equipment are used by bookmakers to avoid detection. One type is the "blue box," which enables the user to simulate a touch-

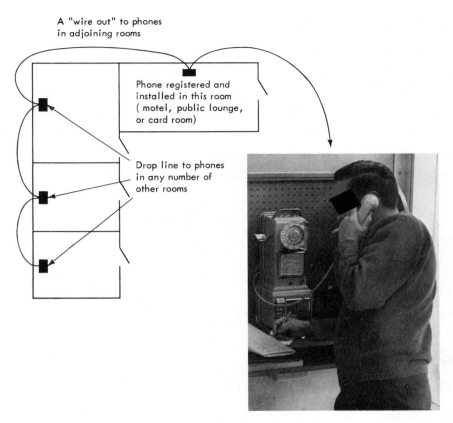

A "wire out" to phones in adjoining rooms

Phone registered and installed in this room (motel, public lounge, or card room)

Drop line to phones in any number of other rooms

FIGURE 5-2   A phone spot with a "wire out" to phones installed in adjoining rooms. (This technique is often called a cheesebox.)

tone signal and use toll-free 800 WATS telephone numbers. Used in this manner, there is no charge for the call and no toll record.

The betting marker.   One of the most desirable pieces of evidence to come into the vice operator's possession is the betting marker. The betting marker may be a piece of paper with the race, the horse's name, and the amount to be wagered (2nd, Rose Red, 2.2.2). It may also be a stick of gum, a piece of ceramic tile, or an intricate group of numbers on an adding machine tape. The variations for recording bets are limitless. The notations made by the bettor on a slip of paper and handed to the bookie along with cash for the bet is still the most common technique in bookmaking. Figures 5–3 and 5–4 illustrate the various types of betting markers.

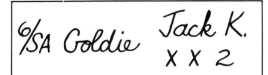

	Interpretation
	The bettor 6th race Santa Anita Race Track The horse $2 to show

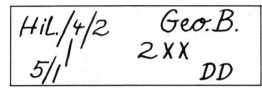

	The bettor 4th race Hialeah Race Track 2nd post position If horse wins bet Parlays to horse in 5th race 1st pole Position $2 to win

Hap				Schizo				
SA 6 JK			2	2				Hap is the agent Schizo is the bettor
Hil 4/2	2			2				
Hp 2/4	2	2	②	6	6.80			Information from above markers to indicate the track, the race, the horse and the amount wagered
GG. 1/7	10			10				
				20	6.80			This record shows a total of $20 bet and a payoff of $6.80 or a loss of $13.20
				+13.20				This may be a daily or weekly record

FIGURE 5-3 Typical betting markers with interpretation and the professional betting marker found at phone spots and offices to record action.

Pimlico

– OFFICIAL JOCKEYS AND POST POSITIONS –
Percentage of winning favorites corresponding meeting
1965, .36; current meeting, .30. Percentage of favorites
in the money, .59. Daily double on first and second races.
United starting gate. Confirmation camera.

★ Indicates beaten favorite last time out.
Horses listed in order as handicapped by EL RIO REY

WEATHER CLEAR—TRACK FAST

Used for racing information by
legitimate racetrack bettors.
If notations are made, the reporter
becomes a betting marker.

FIRST—Purse, $3,300   Probable POST 10:00 A. M.
1 1-8 Miles. 4-Year-Olds and Up. Claiming
Colts and Geldings

Hcp.		Last Finish	P	P Odds	Jockey
1	§Red Erik	13	11	3-1	R.Adams
2	Beech Time	3 116	14	7-2	G.Patterson
3	News Wire	4 116*18		4-1	C.Baltazar
6	Keb	5 122	6	5-1	J.Brocklebank
8	Friendly Cat	9 116	1	8-1	W.J.Passmore
9	Milrutho	3 116	7	8-1	J.Block
10	Even Swap	7 116	10	12-1	C.F.Riston
11	Sterling Prince		12	15-1	R.J.Bright
12	*Mr. Songster	9 107	15	20-1	E.Belville
13	‡Jambar	9 109*	8	30-1	N.Reagan
16	‡Spider Spread	5 109	9	30-1	A.Garcia
17	Billy Giampa	12 116	4	30-1	R.McCurdy
4	Congratulations	1 122	17	——	SCRATCHED
5	Dumelle ★	5 119	16	——	SCRATCHED
7	Fast Answer	3 116	5	——	SCRATCHED
14	Regal Lover	6 116	3	——	SCRATCHED
15	Little Rib	10 116	13	——	SCRATCHED
18	Graf Smil	11 116×	2	——	SCRATCHED

SECOND—Purse, $3,300   Probable POST 10:26 A. M.
6 Furlongs. 3-Year-Olds. Claiming

1	Broken Needle	2 111×	7	2-1	G.Patterson
2	Woodlake Witch	111	5	4-1	P.Kallai
3	Lady Macbeth	11 117	7	5-1	F.Lovato
4	‡Mink Boy	6 109	8	6-1	R.Nolan
5	Craig's Fault	8 116		8-1	B.Phelps
6	Fast Lass	3 111	10	8-1	C.Baltazar
7	Tora Tora	10 116	11	8-1	P.I.Grimm
8	Hawkins	7 116*	3	10-1	T.Lee
13	*Carole A.		6	12-1	N.Reagan
14	Its a Star	9 116	4	15-1	T.Guyton
16	Mr. Cricket	11 116	12	30-1	R.Kimball
17	*Marv's Joy	10 111	2	30-1	J.Taylor
9	‡Blocker	— 109	14	——	SCRATCHED
10	Yokel	— 116	15	——	SCRATCHED
11	Drag Pit	— 116	16	——	SCRATCHED
12	Little Nancy	— 111	18	——	SCRATCHED
15.	Ginnygem	8 111	13	——	SCRATCHED
18	Jovial Lady	12 111	17	——	SCRATCHED

THIRD—Purse, $3,300   Probable POST 10:52 A. M.
6 Furlongs. 3-Year-Olds. Claiming

FIGURE 5-4 The *National Daily Reporter,* a publication, annotated as a betting marker.

Sporting Events

Gambling confederations usually are not content with accepting wagers just on horses. They also give odds on contests, such as football games, basketball games, prize fights, political elections, and so on. Usually the bookmaker does this by "handicapping." For example, if through careful analysis competitor A is thought to have a better chance than competitor B, a handicap given in money odds or a point spread is given to equalize their chances. The customer may choose either competitor on the basis of the handicap. Thus, a weak team may be given points to compensate for a superior rival. Those betting on the stronger team can win if that team wins by a larger margin than the handicap. This system can also work for betting on elections, with the underdog given a handicap of so many votes.

It would be unusual for horsebets to be taken in regular working offices, but sporting pools are widely accepted by some businesses on the grounds that they promote office morale. The office baseball or football pool, although not usually of an organized criminal variety, will find its criminal counterpart in the bars and betting parlors that are confederation-sponsored.

As for the sports bookmaker, there is little gambling involved in the operation. The bookmaker is simply the middleman, charging a commission for sevices rendered. The bookmaker seldom bets against the bettors; they actually bet against themselves. If the books balance, the commission will vary from 4 percent to 8 percent, depending on the price line the bookmaker quotes the bettor.

Like the "morning line" in horse racing, the "opening sports line" is made up of handicappers who sell their services to bookmakers in the United States, Canada, and some of the Caribbean Islands. The opening sports line is believed to originate in four places: Houston, Las Vegas, Chicago, and Seattle. The basic research for this information requires scores of daily newspapers, college publications, and sports releases. From these, vital statistics are obtained on past performances of players and teams. For last-minute and more detailed reporting, they employ scouting systems composed of sportswriters, bookies, assistant coaches, players, students, and professional tipsters. The goal of handicapping is to make the underdog team as attractive as the favored team. To do this, the underdog is given a point or spot handicap. The initial line is based on the relative ability of the teams; the final line is adjusted to the national betting trends. The line is frequently juggled to protect the profit margin of the confederations.

Each succeeding sporting season reaps a richer gambling harvest than the previous one in terms of dollars bet. For example, college and professional football, which is the leading sport for gambling, may have as much as $20 billion bet annually on the outcome of games. The televising of championship games and the New Year's bowl games may cause the betting action to double. In horse racing, the Kentucky Derby brings out the bettors.

The championship series in basketball and the World Series are the bookmakers' delight.

The Crime Commission report indicated the take by organized crime in gambling profits to be approximately $6 to $7 billion per year.[11] Sports betting is the leading contributor in the gambling enterprises.

Gambling Devices

Devices used to gamble are unlimited. New electronic games are great devices for fun and for gambling. It is not the device used that makes the game illegal, it is the purpose for which it is used. Gambling laws vary from city, to state, to federal. Many laws are without logic.

Cards are a popular gambling device well-suited to house-run games. House-run games, however, have no common method of operation. Some professional houses, such as those in England, charge a membership fee to enter the club, and play at the table is free. In Nevada, where all forms of card playing are legal, and in Gardenia, California, where draw poker is legal under local option, the gambler may enter without paying a club fee. The house collects periodically from individual tables, and amounts collected from each player usually depend on the size of the game.

A broad general rule that seems to apply in most states is that any card game based on chance, not skill, is illegal unless specifically permitted by law. Any wager made on the turn of a card in such a game completes the elements of an offense. The amount wagered does not increase the severity of the crime (exception to this rule is made in the 1986 Omnibus Crime Bill). Court decisions have held that the intrinsic value of the thing bet is sufficient for prosecution.[12]

A police investigator who is to testify in court as an expert should be well-versed in rules of the game. It is not necessary to identify a suspected gambling game by name.[13] If a suspected illegal game is being conducted and money or an item of value is being wagered, an arrest will usually be made.

Common card games.   A few of the more common games are cited for illustrative purposes:

Poker. Draw, stud, and low ball games are so common that the average teenager knows how to play. Note: In an illegal professional house game, the house will

[11]*Organized Crime: Task Force Report* (Washington, D.C.: U.S. Government Printing Office, 1967), p. 6. Some sources report $20 to $25 billion per year.

[12]This will vary from one locality to another. You are referred to applicable state laws and local ordinances.

[13]In California, where draw poker only is allowed by local option, it would be necessary to prove the suspected game was not legal under local ordinance.

frequently sell poker chips to the players so that no money is on the table.[14] In an investigation, there should be an initial attempt to locate the bank. Money seized, if it can be related to the game, should be booked as evidence. The Internal Revenue Service will be interested in larger games.

Black Jack or 21. Play is against the dealer, each player is dealt two cards. In this game aces count as 1 or 11, numbered cards are counted as their numerical value, and face cards count 10. The object of the game is to get 21 or closer to 21 than the dealer. The odds in this game favor the dealer because the players must make their hand before the dealer. The bank or the house has approximately a 6 percent advantage.

In England, laws require that games do not have odds favoring the house; thus, to satisfy the law, house dealers offer the deal to a player when he has black jack. In reality, most customers cannot afford to bank against the table and refuse the deck.

Pique. Frequently referred to as the "Chinese game," pique is played with cards or blocks similar in shape and appearance to dominos. Combinations of red and black dots are used to denote winners. As many as eight players may participate. Side bets may be made by any number of players. In the investigation of pique, the investigator may distinguish the game by the sound of fast clicks of the blocks. In Mahjong and dominos, the clicks will be slower.

There are an unlimited number of card games that lend themselves to gambling operations. Games that are well known with *fast action* are the most desirable.

Dice.   Dice in various forms are the oldest gaming implements known. Innumerable game variations are and have been played with them. Dice is probably the most prevalent and fastest way for the gambler to invest money. From the plush layouts of London, Las Vegas, and Atlantic City to the back rooms of many towns and cities, gamblers gather in small and large groups to try their luck at the crap tables.

Archeologists claim the forefather of the modern die was the astragalus bone in the foot. Six-sided cubes resembling our present dice have been found in ruins of the Egyptian tombs of 2000 B.C., the diggings at Pompeii, and Greek burial vaults from the year 1244 B.C. The dice found were made of stone, ivory, porcelain, and bone. There is evidence that many of the dice were crooked. Recent artifacts from Britain and France indicate that "Roman crap shooters" lived there from 55 B.C. to A.D. 410.

In the past two decades, explorations under the London financial district have revealed artifacts proving that dice games are not new. "Shaved dice" and "loaded dice" were fairly common. Many of the dice found under

---

[14]Frequently equipment supply houses will furnish equipment to private clubs. A donation to enter the room is collected and free chips are supplied to the donor. If more chips are desired, a new donation must be made. These types of transactions are legal under the laws of some states.

London were made from the knuckle bones of sheep or goats. Thus, today, dice are frequently referred to as bones.[15]

The evolution of dice indicates that they were probably used primarily for religious purposes. Each society evidently chose a dice form and retained it through several centuries. For example, cubical dice were used by both Egyptians and the Chinese. The American Indians used waferlike dice having only two effective faces.[16] Various other forms of dice have been found in the different societies.

Dice as a modern gambling device is perhaps the most prevalent illegal game operating. It is easy to conduct, any number of persons may play, and the action is fast. In ghetto areas of the cities, dice games are a way of life. It is not uncommon to find games that operate around the clock. These games may operate in a fixed location, or they may "float" from location to location. When a game operates at the same location for a period of time, it is reasonably safe to assume that payoffs are going to local officials.

Games played with dice. Early in the twentieth century, *craps* became the principal gambling game of the United States. This game is popular because any number of people may play and betting is fast. The shooter bets as much as he likes, and the bet may be covered by one bettor or split among a group. Side bets, wagers between bettors, may involve any amount of money and any number of bettors. The game has much fascination for gamblers because money is being exchanged on nearly each roll of the dice. Confederations are active in this type of gambling.

Poker dice. Five standard dice may be used, but there are also special dice with six faces marked as playing cards with ace, king, queen, knave (jack), ten, and nine. The dice are normally thrown from a dice cup. By following the regular rules of poker, the winner may be determined. This game is frequently found in bars where the house will roll the customer for drinks and money. Depending on local and state laws, this technique may not only be a gambling violation but may also be prohibited by liquor laws.

Barbudi or barbooth. This is a two-dice game of Balkan and Levantine origin. It is played in the United States chiefly by persons of Greek, Armenian, and Italian ancestry. Alone among popular dice games, it provides no mathematical advantage for any player or for the gambling house. Two persons play against each other.

Crooked dice operations. Dice are popular for house games and portable outfits that may be set up easily. Floating games are common and lend themselves to loaded dice activities or to electromagnets under the table, or in the wall, that can control the roll of the dice.

It is important for an investigator to recognize the more common forms of crooked dice operators. The presence of crooked dice in a game may supply the elements for a grand theft (bunco) charge against their owner. Figures 5–5 and 5–6 illustrate some of the more common types of crooked gambling devices.

[15]*Encyclopaedia Britannica,* 15th ed., (Chicago: Encyclopaedia Britannica, Inc., 1987), p. 104.
[16]Robert Charles Bell, *Board and Table Games* (New York: Oxford Press, 1960), Chap. 5.

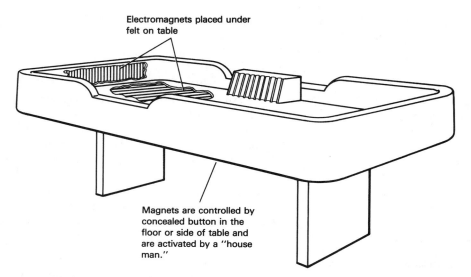

Electromagnets placed under felt on table

Magnets are controlled by concealed button in the floor or side of table and are activated by a "house man."

FIGURE 5-5 Typical dice table with electromagnets.

Slot machines. Four decades ago, nearly every diner along the transcontinental highways had some form of slot machine action either as part of the dining room attraction or to lure customers to the back room. Most states now prohibit slot machine operation, either statewide or via local option. Federal law prohibits their interstate transportation.[17] The law also, in certain instances, prohibits transportation to a place where gambling is being conducted (gambling ships). Many states make it a misdemeanor to possess a slot machine. These statutes are frequently loosely enforced. Some states, such as California, make it a felony to possess a slot machine, and the statute is rigorously enforced.

Slot machines have a unique role in American gambling habits. No other form of gambling appeals so strongly to the woman gambler. A study conducted in Las Vegas, Nevada, indicated that the average woman gambler spent $17 per day on slots. The reasons for their preferences were summarized by Zimmerman.[18]

Receive a lot for their money in terms of action.

Lack knowledge of other games.

Requires small investment.

Feel sexual excitement while gambling.

[17]It shall be unlawful knowingly to transport a gambling device to any place in a state—from any place outside of such state—, 15 USC. 1172.

[18]Gereon Zimmerman, "Gambling," *Look,* March 12, 1963, pp. 21–35. Also, Diane Weathers, et al., "Gamblers Who Can't Quit," *Newsweek,* March 3, 1980, p. 70.

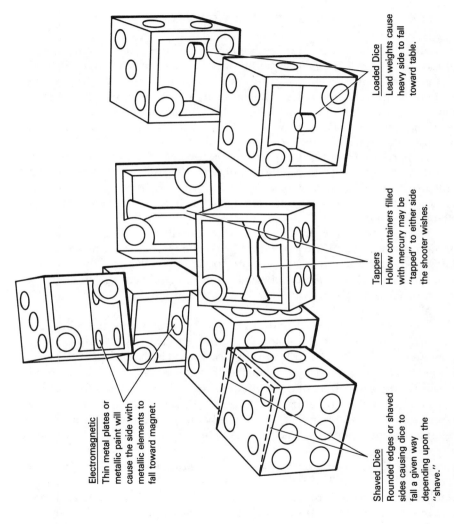

Electromagnetic
Thin metal plates or metallic paint will cause the side with metallic elements to fall toward magnet.

Shaved Dice
Rounded edges or shaved sides causing dice to fall a given way depending upon the "shave."

Tappers
Hollow containers filled with mercury may be "tapped" to either side the shooter wishes.

Loaded Dice
Lead weights cause heavy side to fall toward table.

FIGURE 5-6 Cheater dice.

The average woman would hesitate to play if she knew that large jackpots pay off at about 1 in 2700 times. The house will keep at least 5 percent and frequently up to 50 percent of every dollar played.

LOTTERIES: THE NUMBERS OR POLICY GAMES

Whereas cards, dice, and horse betting may satisfy the professional gambler, millions of people from every echelon of society like to participate in a "little game" of chance. Number games are popular because they are simple and may be played inexpensively. Ten cents to a dollar per chance is the usual price, and all a player must do is draw a number or bet a hunch. For the numbers bettor, there is very little chance to win. For the numbers operator, there is absolutely no risk of loss.

To participate in the numbers game, for example, a bettor will draw a number between a preset number limit (1 to 1000). The operator will have regular drawings. These drawings may be by chance or they may be associated with race results, policy wheels, stock market figures, or other attention-getting gimmicks.

The term "policy" is frequently used to identify the numbers game. This derivation comes from the early days, when poor people set aside nickels, dimes, and quarters to pay on insurance policies. Frequently, they invested the money in numbers for quick profit, only to find that the odds of 1 in 1000 did not pay off very often. In the southern United States, it is called "bolita" or "the bug."

The numbers game is usually an integral part of a poor neighborhood. The chances for quick riches make it attractive to those who cannot afford the luxuries of race tracks and gambling casinos. The "quick profit" or "big winner" atmosphere overshadows the fact that at least 25 percent of all money bet will go into the coffers of the confederations. Figure 5–7 is a hypothetical model of the numbers organization. A numbers ticket is usually nothing more than a simple form in triplicate. Frequently, only a simple plain number is used. Colors, number style, and special codes to avoid forgery will change daily.

In the past, drawing of the numbers was dramatic enough to bring out a crowd. For example, a Chinese numbers game was conducted in Los Angeles each morning. Bright and early, the numbers writers would make their morning rounds, sell their tickets, and inform the bettor of the location of the noon drawing. At noon, at the prearranged place, a truck would pull up to the gathered crowd and park. There would be a rapid drawing of numbers from a washtub and the winners would be announced. The truck would then speed away before police arrived to take violators into custody.

In one Eastern city, more than 1500 "number writers" collected in excess of $90,000 daily. There was a well-established "banking system" where

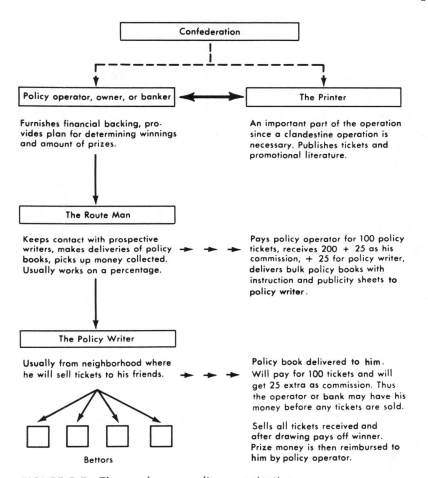

FIGURE 5-7 The numbers or policy organization.

the employees received full fringe benefits. Enforcement against this type of operation is nearly impossible because of public participation and apathy. Lottery or policy is becoming more a part of everyday activities and receives a high degree of public acceptance.

A legal lottery system will not interfere with the illegal lotteries now found in major U.S. cities. The twenty-five cent to one dollar lottery player likes action. He will buy his ticket and expect a payoff within hours. Most gamblers will not be happy with daily, weekly, or monthly payoffs based on just a few drawings per year, as used in the state systems.

Lotteries may be chain letter schemes, raffles, bingo, football pools, baseball pools, and hundreds of similar schemes. One of the most prevalent lottery schemes in use is shown in Figure 5–8. These illegal lotteries are in

FIGURE 5-8 Typical football pool ticket.

violation of federal and state law. They are the object of continuous enforcement action.

Most lotteries are controlled by federal statutes as well as by state and local law. Basically, federal lottery regulations state it is a violation to:[19]

---

[19]U.S. Code 1301–1304 prohibits the carrying, knowingly taking, or receiving of chances, shares, interest, etc., in a gambling scheme. In 18 U.S. Code 1084, there is prohibition against the transportation of wagers across state lines.

Bring into the United States, for the purpose of disposing of the same, or
Knowingly deposit with any express company, or
Carry in interstate or foreign commerce, or
Knowingly take or receive (when so carried) any paper, certificate or instrument:
Purporting to be or to represent a ticket, chance, share or interest in or dependent upon the event of
A lottery, gift enterprise or similar scheme, offering prizes dependent in whole or in part upon lot or chance, or
Any advertisement of or list of prizes drawn or awarded by means of such a lottery, etc. (Title 18 U.S. Code, Sec. 1301).

Federal law also prohibits the use of the U.S. Postal Service to send any offer, ticket, money, money order, etc., for tickets or any newspapers or publication advertising lotteries or containing any list of any part or all of the prizes. In spite of these prohibitions, millions of Irish Sweepstakes tickets are sold in the United States annually.

SKIMMING AND BRIBERY

Gambling is more of a problem for others than those directly involved in losing to the system. The following problems will be present where gambling exists.

Skimming

One of the profitable gimmicks for organized gambling has been the skimming of money from legal casinos. Skimming is defined as the taking of gambling profits from legal machines without the payment of license fees and taxes. From the 1960s through the 1990s, continuing investigations of skimming operations in legalized casinos in Nevada and New Jersey have turned up innovative schemes to beat the tax on profits. In 1983, the Stardust Hotel was cited in a 222 violation count for skimming more than $1.5 million in a so-called fill-slip scheme. While "skimming" has little interest for local enforcement, the investment of this money is bound to show up in the liquor business, the financing of prostitution activity, and other enterprises. Skimming rackets in Las Vegas and the group that is engaged in them read like a chapter from the "blue book" on organized crime.

Some of the money skimmed off the top will leave the country for foreign deposit; some will go to special funds to ensure that nearby states do not have gambling. Much of it may go into legitimate business.

In spite of adverse publicity, federal investigations are still being conducted and offenders are being prosecuted with evidence obtained from "listening devices." These cases in the next years will establish legal guides on how prosecutors must handle future cases of skimming. The Omnibus Crime Bill of 1970 contains provisions for utilization of listening devices, and Justice Department policy has made them operational. Most state laws, however, prohibit the use of listening devices such as phone taps.

Bribery

Some professional gamblers who concentrate on sporting events resort to bribery to make their bet a "sure thing." They bribe or attempt to bribe participants who can shave points to lose the even margin or cut down the winning margin. These are characteristics of the types of third-party criminality that become by-products of certain forms of gambling.

By implication, the relationship between sports and big business investments will probably always border on ethics rather than law.

Major organized sporting groups have kept investigators on their payroll to protect the player from this influence. Only in isolated instances have the major sports been tainted by bribery. However, those who know the business report bribery as a constant and continuing problem.

SUMMARY

Gambling is one of the most lucrative and the most difficult to regulate of all the vice type crimes. Individuals and communities sanction organized gambling operations, in an unconscious manner, merely by participating.

There are many viewpoints regarding the issue of punitive police sanctions imposed on select types of gambling operations. Many well-informed citizens believe gambling will always be with our society; thus, it should be regulated and taxed as a normal business. Others believe it is morally wrong to legalize an activity that preys on the weaknesses of human nature.

Throughout the history of civilization, there is evidence of the human propensity to gamble. There are also indicators that laws regulating gambling have been token gestures of societies that are divided on "how much" gambling can be tolerated.

Statistics, gathered for decades, indicate that society as a whole does not attach great moral or legal wrong to gambling. As a result of the diverse attitudes about gambling, law enforcement officers and administrators are placed in the position of interpreting social attitudes in the application of the legal statutes. These facts lead to the breakdown of legal sanctions and superimpose a criminal confederation on every community.

The criminal confederations are not represented by overt gamblers hustling bets from strangers on the street. The confederation representatives are the neighborhood bookies, the football pool sellers, and club friends who just happen to always have lottery tickets of some variety. The gambling empires are built around the twenty-five cent to two dollar bets. Only with massive public participation can they exist.

Law enforcement cannot presume to make much of an impact on gambling organizations. The organizations are "wired into" every level of government. Only through legal collusion and, frequently, corruption can professional gamblers exist.

This chapter illustrated a few of the more common gambling schemes. These schemes are not unusual; they are known by nearly every teenager and adult in the United States. The popularity of gambling creates vice enforcement problems that make acceptable regulation extremely difficult.

QUESTIONS FOR DISCUSSION

1. Discuss what is meant when the term "malum prohibita" is used in referring to gambling.
2. What proof do we have that there are degrees of disagreement on the issue of legalized gambling? Poll the class and discuss the different viewpoints.
3. Is there a double standard in many church and civic organizations with regard to gambling?
4. There tends to be a cycle in the dynamics of gambling—as amount of gambling increases, prohibitory legislation increases, legislation becomes poorly administered, which prompts repeal of local laws for revenue purposes, causing increased gambling and the cycle to repeat. Explain.
5. The federal and state governments may impose sanctions against gambling, but the problem must ultimately be resolved in the community. Explain.
6. The organizational structure of the betting syndicates makes them nearly immune to legal arrests. Why?
7. There are five specific booking activities cited in this text. Explain why the number could be ten or fifteen.
8. The betting marker is perhaps one of the best bits of evidence for prosecution purposes. Why?
9. Sports bookies are generally said to work on a commission. Why?
10. Why are there differences among the "morning line," the "opening line," and the "initial line"?
11. Why are cards and dice such popular gambling instruments?
12. What are the paradoxes of lotteries that make them so difficult to control?

6

Prostitution

1. Learn why law enforcement is involved in the control of prostitution.
2. Understand how the organized confederations gain control of prostitution activities.
3. Recognize the common modes of operation of the prostitute and the relationship to ancillary crimes.
4. Realize that control of prostitution has always created a social, ethical, and legal problem.

Law enforcement interest in the control of prostitution is based on a number of criteria. First is the crime itself: Society finds it repugnant to have the prostitute barter sex for favors without an emotional attachment between partners. Second, society has become a moral moderator of activities it will approve. Prostitution, as an occupation, does not meet the approval of society as a whole. Third is the necessity to eliminate ancillary crimes that cluster around the profession of prostitution. Fourth, enforcement activity limits the number of contacts between prostitute and client, thus discouraging the transmission of venereal and other diseases through random sexual contacts. These reasons may be subject to debate, but they are the rationale that supports the suppression activities directed toward prostitution.

The profession of prostitution is a sad occupation for the male and female prostitutes. The hope of riches soon gives way to fear, exploitation, and guilt. The prostitute acquires criminal friends, venereal diseases, and eventually the easy way out becomes drug addiction. Drugs and thieves gravitate to the high earnings of the prostitute.

Prostitution, like other vice crimes, is not controlled in a consistent way. The sporadic control exerted by law enforcement will usually be prompted by political cleanup campaigns or as a result of protesting citizen groups. This is frequently done in a manner that proves unreliable and ineffective. Proponents of legalization do not understand the dynamics of this problem, an observation noted in *Organized Crime Task Force Report.*[1]

States and localities should exercise caution in considering the legalization or decriminalization of so-called victimless crimes such as gambling, drug use, prostitution, and pornography. These are known to provide income to organized crime. There is insufficient evidence that legalization or decriminalization of such crimes will materially reduce the income of organized crime. On the contrary, evidence does exist that the elimination or reduction of legal restraints can encourage the expansion of organized activities.

The reasons why legalization or decriminalization may not work with prostitution depend on the underlying reasons for the prostitutes becoming involved in the business. Here are some general reasons:[2]

1. There is a high unemployment rate among young unskilled men and women.
2. The exchange of money and the sex act is a manifestation of social rejection.
3. The prostitute retains differing roles in society, lending credence to the accusation that he or she will in many instances be schizophrenic.
4. The prostitute is usually a social isolate in terms of friends, couples, and normal social life; therefore, many become heavy drug users.
5. The prostitute has a paranoidal distrust of the opposite sex, possibly because of parental deprivation or sexual abuse in childhood.
6. The prostitute has little self-concept so far as lying, loyalties, or violating a trust.

Prostitution, as the term is generally employed by sociologists, social workers, and the courts, refers to the promiscuous bartering of sex favors for monetary consideration, either gifts or cash, without any emotional attachment between the partners.

Prostitution is the practice of offering one's body for indiscriminate intercourse, usually in exchange for something of monetary value. The word "prostitute" is not a technical one, and it has no common law meaning. A woman or man who indulges in illicit sexual intercourse with only one person is not a prostitute. Prostitution is not synonymous with sexual intercourse.[3]

HISTORY OF PROSTITUTION

Prostitutes, honored, scorned, and crucified, have had a tormented background in their struggle to escape the controlling efforts of society.

[1]National Advisory Committee on Criminal Justice Standards and Goals, *Organized Crime: Report of the Task Force on Organized Crime* (Washington, D.C.: U.S. Government Printing Office, December 1976), p. 65.

[2]The conclusions drawn here were taken from law enforcement officer observations over an extended period of years. These observations have no documented basis.

[3]*Corpus Juris Secundum* 224, "Prostitution" Section 1 (St. Paul, Minn: West Publishing Company. 1951).

Sociologists, psychologists, and law enforcement agents all have different theories as to why someone becomes a prostitute. Whatever the causal factor, history indicates that any single control measure will eventually prove ineffective. As society has changed, so have the laws governing prostitution. As the laws have changed, so have the prostitutes' methods of operation.

Prostitution is as old as civilization and appears to be closely related to urban life and mobile populations. Prostitution was recognized and respected in many ancient societies. Parents sold daughters, husbands compromised wives, and religious practitioners engaged in prostitution. The Semites of the Eastern Mediterranean were notorious for their practices. Jewish fathers were, however, forbidden to turn their daughters into prostitutes,[4] and the daughters of Israel were forbidden to become prostitutes.[5] From the biblical teachings, our modern moral code and habits have evolved.

The naturalistic attitudes of the Greeks and Romans were in direct contrast with the teachings of the Hebrews and Christians. In the classical period of ancient Greece, marriage did not attain the same dignity as it did among the Hebrews and the Christians. Women from prominent families and high society often became the playmates of affluent Greek men. As conquests spread, slaves seized as the prisoners of war become their conquerors' prostitutes.

The Romans adopted the Greek attitude on prostitution. The excessive supply of prostitutes from the wars lowered their social position and led to compulsory distinction of their dress, loss of civil rights, and registration of those in houses of ill repute. Eventually, prostitution caused reputable women to become shielded because of tainted blood in marriages with prostitutes. Rigid laws were passed and heavy taxes levied on the occupation of prostitution.

During the reign of the Anglo-Saxon kings in England, antiprostitution laws were severe. Violation meant banishment or death. Later, prostitution was legalized in the London area, and strife over church or civil control brought disrepute and corruption to both the church and the municipalities. As in England, all of Western Europe was in moral turmoil over prostitution control and enforcement. The control was inconsistent, and corruption prevailed. Frequent reform movements were unable to cope with the well-established profession. In the Middle Ages, prostitution was tolerated, the caprice of passions being recognized as a necessary evil. Efforts were taken to control it or at least to keep it within reasonable bounds.

During the Reformation, moral attitudes shifted due to medical necessity. Syphilitic epidemics swept over Europe in the fifteenth and sixteenth centuries and wiped out nearly a third of the population. Fear and disease had done what moral attitudes had failed to do. Major European cities vigor-

[4]Leviticus 19:29.
[5]Deuteronomy 23:17.

ously punished those engaged in prostitution. In the seventeenth century, major cities instituted medical treatment for prostitutes and reverted to the Greek-Roman system of licensing houses of prostitution and punishing private entrepreneurs. The basic form of control remained a common practice through the eighteenth and up to the end of the nineteenth centuries.

At the end of the nineteenth century, British reformers organized antivice organizations. As a result, the Criminal Law Amendment Act of 1885 was developed in Great Britain. In the United States, vice commissions became the popular pastime of civic groups, and the Mann Act of 1910 emerged.[6] Most of the states followed with laws that prohibited third-party profit from the activities of prostitutes.

International control was implemented with the Paris Agreement of 1904. In 1921, the League of Nations established a commission to study the problem of prostitution. Although the League of Nations had little direct effect, it caused the countries of modern Europe to abandon the houses of prostitution and in many instances to offer free medical treatment for venereal diseases.[7]

COMMON METHODS OF PROSTITUTION AND ORGANIZED CRIME AFFILIATION

The problem of prostitution has been studied primarily from the emotional rather than the more objective statistical method. These studies have assisted the sociologist and the psychologist, but have been of little help in identifying the importance of punitive control as a regulatory process. Few studies have been conducted that identify prostitution with organized crime.

Prostitution is identified as an antisocial behavior manifested to meet the psychological needs of the individual prostitute and customer. There is considerable doubt whether enforcement, as it is conducted in Western cultures, has much impact on the professional prostitute's activity. Many psychiatrists and psychoanalysts see prostitution as a more complex problem than do the legislators and law enforcement officials, who often allege that money and unsavory associates are causal factors. Social scientists trace the roots of prostitution to emotional factors. It is therefore generally conceded today that a wide variety of economic, sociological, and psychological factors are involved in the profession of prostitution. Thus, the crime of prostitution awaits control by logical, clear-thinking legislators.

Sociological studies tend to suggest that most prostitutes come from areas with high delinquency and crime rates. In such social subcultures the

---

[6]Title 18, U.S. Code, Section 2421, 2422, 2423, commonly referred to as the White Slave Traffic Act.

[7]*The Encyclopedia Americana* (Danbury, Conn.: Grolier, Inc., 1988), p. 669.

potential prostitute identifies with members of society who are alienated from the ethical standards of a larger society. Thus, these subcultures live with, tend to accept, and adhere to many of the mores of the underworld.

> Drug addiction has been cited as a growing factor in the recruitment of prostitutes and in keeping them in the trade. The majority of drug addicts are young adults from the underprivileged areas of large cities. They are mainly unemployed and uninterested in employment other than to maintain their drug supply, largely by crimes against property and by prostitution.[8]

Types of Prostitute

A prostitute at some time in her or his career may work within each of many classifications of prostitution. One need only look at the Yellow Pages of the telephone directory to discover the innovative methods employed by independent and organized prostitutes. Some of the more common methods are explained here.

The streetwalker.   Streetwalking is perhaps the most common form of prostitution in which the amateur can become involved. This method is also least apt to have confederations sharing in the profits. In poor neighborhoods, the streets are full of young people who are in the business full time or use streetwalking as a means to supplement other income. In the age of the automobile, the streetwalker is an instant business success. Old professional streetwalkers are on the prowl to find new prostitutes to refer to their customers for a small fee. The old streetwalker, in fact, becomes a madam. These madams can usually show fairly solid business associations with local organized criminals. Young women who become street hustlers often begin their careers by raising a few dollars to make financial ends meet. Their intention is to turn a few "tricks" and then seek other avenues of employment. However, once in the business and under the direction of a pimp, it is difficult for them to return to the work-a-day world.

The call girl/boy.   The telephone offers the prostitute a degree of sophistication in contacting clients. It also offers large organized operations clandestine protection from discovery. The telephone serves to maintain a wide circle of contacts for the prostitute. If discreetly used, the telephone gives a certain degree of security from enforcement. Call girls are frequently a part of organized crime because of referrals and protection offered by pimps.

The working prostitute maintains a "black book" of customers. When the prostitute wants to work, she uses the phone to contact listed prospects.

[8] *Encyclopaedia Britannica*, 15th ed., (Chicago: Encyclopaedia Britannica, Inc., 1987), p. 737.

If the prostitute is a part of a stable, working for a confederation, customers will be referred in a variety of ways. A good black book contains more than the name and phone number of the client. For example, identifying notations may contain a prospective trick's social security number, the wife's first name, the wife's maiden name, the names of children, a physical description, and facts about his business that only a particular client would know. From a black book the prostitute can quickly reestablish a business. Thus, the black book has a high monetary value and frequently is sold by the prostitute before she leaves town or is jailed for any length of time because of illegal activities. Through male partners in the confederations, the black book may pass from one prostitute to another within the organization.

The electronic call girl/boy.   A popular technique for the prostitute is the installation of an electronic answering device. The communication between prostitute and clientele is then screened through the medium of a recording device. This device protects the prostitute if he or she is cautious in accepting customers. This answering instrument also eliminates the possibility of an information leak to the police. Frequently, the phone is installed in a vacant room and the prostitute then takes messages from another location via a tone or automatic response from the electronic device. Willing pimps gladly supply maintenance.

The lonely hearts hustler.   Enterprising prostitutes, with the assistance of confederation members, have always found clever ways in which to obtain new clients. The pages of pulp magazines are full of cases where boy meets girl through the lonely hearts club. The numerous contacts made by a prostitute in this manner are seldom reported, and they very seldom come to the attention of the police. The only control law enforcement has over this type of operation is to purchase lists of girls and boys and endeavor to screen professional prostitutes from the legitimate clients. Most departments, however, simply ignore the problem because the apprehension of this type of hustler is tedious, slow, and expensive. Because of the difficulty of apprehension, the organized criminal element may often operate lonely hearts clubs.

The computer-selected date.   Computerized dating firms are in the business of introducing couples. Illicit operators can take advantage of the situation and contact cash customers through this medium. Prostitutes pay the nominal fee, submit a questionnaire, and let the computer select the customers. This automatic matchmaker not only selects congenial prospects, but categorizes as to financial endorsement. In this setting of cybernetic bliss, the hustler is able to choose a $10,000 or a $50,000 per year client. As of this date, the prostitute still has to make the deals and consummate the transactions.

Computerized dating bureaus are interested in protecting their clients, especially women, from unethical males. They compare the variables on the questionnaire and then make the men's names and qualifications available to qualified women members. For the smart hustler, what better and cheaper way is there to have clients screened? Law enforcement has only one alternative, and that is to begin the slow process of joining the club, getting referred to women with the right personality coefficients, and discovering the professional hustler.

The public relations gimmick. The line between legitimate and illegitimate enterprises is frequently so fine it is not a matter of law, but one of morality. The public relations "action" is so covert and the mating of the male and female so shrewd the customer frequently believes the romance is for love. The sponsoring company paying the public relations firm must have a satisfied client, so the amount of money spent is not a factor.

Some years ago a member of a California hoodlum group spent his entire time locating "nice girls" for public relations firms. His title was respectable and the women were hired as secretaries (if they could type) or as product demonstrators (if they had no business talents). The company would send the women out of town to business meetings or conventions to conduct ethical business. During the evenings the women were entertained in the best places, drank the best drinks, and slept in the softest beds. What they did not know was that the hiring agent knew of their every activity. Photographs and tape recordings were used to blackmail both the woman and client. Once the women were in no position to refuse, they became full-time call girls for the hiring agent.

Call girls were then available for weekend trips with clients referred from the public relations firm and others of financial means. These trips were fully documented. Generally, the women were able to keep their salaries and tips received from the client. Later, the hiring agent would offer to sell photographs and recordings of the weekend to the prostitute's client. Known victims of this shakedown paid sums of $14,000, $10,000, $8,000, and so on. Although this activity was known to police sources, victims refused to prosecute because of adverse publicity. Every city has, in addition to the legitimate public relations firms, a group that is for hire usually through escort services with beeper and credit card imprinter.

The photo studio. Photo studios operate in areas that are liberal in certain types of conduct. In areas around Hollywood, California, the small entrepreneur rents an old house and puts up colorful oversized signs advertising nude models to photograph. He then waits for lonely males to beat a path to the door. In many instances, the models may be legitimate and the photographer may actually take pictures. In other cases, the model uses the posing session to make contact with a photographer who never bothers to put film in the rented camera.

The secretarial service.   Wherever a profession is predominately female, there are bound to be a few professional prostitutes who join the ranks to make contact with male customers. Most secretarial services are legal, well supervised, and render a vital service. Occasionally, however, illicit operators will have business connections and begin contracting secretarial services to unethical clients.

Obscene phone calls and other services.   The latest method of operation for making acquaintances is the special phone number where one-on-one contacts may be made via the telephone. The caller may receive titillating messages for a $2.00 fee or meet other "lonesome persons" who like to chat. This is an ideal cover for an enterprising agency with interested hustlers.

The housewife.   It is not unusual among the ranks of prostitutes to find housewives who supplement the family income. This is fairly common among impoverished minorities who must either assist or entirely support a family. A few years ago a national magazine article revealed that a group of housewives from middle- and upper-income families of Long Island and New Jersey were merchandising their favors for $25 to $100.

The favorite sports for the hustlers were the race tracks and bars. When this amateur activity threatened the professionals, the professionals immediately informed the police, who quickly jailed the trespassers.

The massage parlor.   The most obvious inroad of organized crime into prostitution during the past three decades has been through the massage parlor. Wherever a corrupt government agency can be found, there will shortly follow a colony of fixed massage parlors or the more "mobile variety," each catering to prostitute-client relationships. The massage parlors are multimillion-dollar businesses that point a direct finger at corrupt public agencies.[9] The parlors are often referred to as the poor man's country club and with honest law enforcement cannot survive.

Social Habits and Federal Law

Kinsey report.   Kinsey and his associates found that about 69 percent of the male white population in the United States had some experiences with prostitutes, ranging from those who only visited a prostitute once or twice

---

[9]New Mexico—Governor's Organized Crime Prevention Commission, *Annual Report,* Albuquerque, 1979.

to those who paid regular visits. Kinsey found, however, that the percentage of men who visited prostitutes varied with educational achievement. By the time that they were twenty-five years old, 74 percent of the 5300 men studied, who had not gone beyond grade school, had visited prostitutes; in contrast, 54 percent of those who had gone to high school, and 28 percent with college or university training, had visited prostitutes. Many of the married men had some illicit relations, but only 1.7 percent of their total sex outlet was with prostitution.[10]

Rigid sex standards are obviously not accepted by males in the United States, and this complicates any program for eliminating prostitution.

Federal laws.   In 1910, the Mann Act became a major deterrent to interstate transportation of prostitutes. This federal act, known as the White Slave Traffic Act, prohibits and penalizes as a felony the act of any person who transports, causes to be transported, or aids or assists in transporting any woman or girl in interstate or foreign commerce for the purpose of prostitution, debauchery, or any other immoral purpose. The White Slave Traffic Act covers a broad field. In defining the purpose for which interstate transportation of a girl or woman must not be furnished, the language of the act is broad enough to include practically every form of sexual immorality. The previous character or reputation of the woman or girl transported in interstate commerce for immoral purposes is entirely immaterial. The statute is violated where the defendant has transported, procured, or aided in procuring the transportation of a woman or girl from one state to another for the purpose of inducing or enabling her to engage in the business of prostitution.[11]

Perhaps the most humane way to control prostitution is shown in the British Parliamentary Law of 1959, which prohibits open solicitation but permits the prostitutes to operate in their own homes. It also provides rehabilitation to those who wish to change trades. The law does not attempt to dictate private morals or ethical sanctions, but rather only to regulate offenses that are injurious to another's rights.[12]

The law enforcement officer cannot compromise the law. Every case, however, has to be approached with care and caution. What may appear to be a clandestine case of prostitution could be a legally married couple. The officer may be the subject of a civil suit if a prearrest investigation is improperly or inadequately conducted.

[10]Alfred C. Kinsey, Wardell B. Pomeroy, and Clyde E. Martin, *Sexual Behavior in the Human Male* (Philadelphia: Saunders, 1948). Data have not changed substantially through the 1980s.

[11]*American Jurisprudence,* "Prostitution," Section 11, (San Francisco: Bancroft-Whitney), pp. 268–271.

[12]In Nevada, prostitution operates openly in all but two counties. Local residents favor this type of control and do not choose to abate the activity as a nuisance. It is said that direct airline service from Las Vegas delivers passengers to at least a dozen different established houses of prostitutes. The British law is different but with the same results.

With prostitution, as with many moral problems, there seems to be no definite or final solution because the problem is a recurring one for each individual and for each generation.

Perhaps the strongest argument for the control of prostitution is not from a moral approach, but from one of protection from venereal disease.

VENEREAL DISEASE AND PROSTITUTION

A law enforcement officer, in order to understand the basic philosophy for enacting laws prohibiting prostitution, must be aware of related venereal diseases (see Table 6–1). Although the control of venereal disease is primarily a medical problem, the courts and law enforcement are an integral part of the total process. Most states, as part of their sentencing procedures in prostitution cases, require the prostitute to pass a physical test or be sentenced to jail where he or she will be treated.

There is much disagreement among the experts on how to control venereal disease (VD). It is uncertain whether rigid enforcement drives the illegal activity underground where contacts are not reported, or whether "open houses" under close medical inspection, with more contacts, is better for control of the disease.

Few human maladies have influenced the course of history more strongly. The destinies of empires have been decided upon the ravages of venereal disease epidemics.

Gonorrhea

Egyptian writings refer to and describe the miseries of gonorrhea. Ancient philosophers have referred to the cases of gonorrhea as pleasure excesses, urinary tract ulcerations, and the burning fires of the devil. There are references in writings that in Egypt relief was gained from extracts of certain plants. In Arabia, it was not uncommon to resolve the problem through surgery.

Syphilis

In the history of medicine, no infectious disease has ever been eradicated or completely controlled merely by treating infected persons. Improved transportation methods encourage travel and migration, and a disease may be erased in one country only to flourish in another.[13] Travel and war

---

[13]*Encyclopedia Americana*, (Danbury, Conn.: Grolier, Inc., 1985), p. 669.

TABLE 6-1 Increase in Venereal Disease

Reported Cases of Primary and Secondary Syphilis

		1987	1986	% Change
United States	(Jan.–April)	10,009	7,697	+23.1%
California	(Jan.–March)	1,816	1,222	+48.6%
	L.A. County	970	489	+96.3%
	Orange County	176	195	−9.7%
	Riverside County	25	20	+25.0%
	S. Bern. County	44	15	+193.3%
	S. Diego County	66	50	+32.0%
	San Francisco	48	88	−45.4%
Florida	(Jan.–April)	2,123	1,075	+97.4
New York City	(Jan.–April)	1,229	604	+103.5%

California Syphilis Cases in 1986

	Black	Latino	White	Other
Los Angeles County	57.6%	25.2%	11.5%	5.7%
San Francisco	22.9%	*20%	46.4%	*11%
All other areas	23.8%	49.5%	24.6%	2.1%

Gonorrhea and Penicillin-Resistant Gonorrhea

		Jan.–March 1987	Jan.–March 1986	% Change
United States	Total cases	211,809	223,410	−5.2%
	Resistant Cases	*5,040	2,517	*+100.1%
California	Total cases	25,927	24,160	+7.3%
	Resistant cases	727	179	+306.1%
	L.A. County	436	74	+489.2%
	Orange County	26	2	+1300.0%

TABLE 6-1   *(continued)*

Gonorrhea and Penicillin-Resistant Gonorrhea (continued)

		Jan.–March 1987	Jan.–March 1986	% Change
	Riverside County	2	0	—
	S. Bern. County	9	0	—
	S. Diego County	85	27	+214.8%
	San Francisco	18	10	+80.0%
Florida	Resistant cases	1362	1175	+15.9%
New York City	Resistant cases	1082	497	+117.7%

Sources: U.S. Centers for Disease Control, California Department of Health Services, San Francisco Department of Public Health, Los Angeles County, Department of Health Services.
*Estimated.

seem to have been the companions of the venereal disease called syphilis; it is alleged Columbus brought the disease back from the New World. Also, around 1495 in military campaigns against Naples by Charles VIII of France, the scourge of syphilis is reported to have hit his armies and caused retreats back into France. The disease spread to all of Europe, and by 1500, every major country was victimized. The rise and fall of social sanctions against prostitution can be traced to reactions against outbreaks of syphilis.

For more than 400 years after syphilis first became a problem, progress in knowledge of the disease was slow, halting, and wholly clinical.[14] Thus, the social aspects of prevention and education did not really begin until the twentieth century.

Because there were not adequate facilities and knowledge available, the prevalence of syphilis was related to the contact with the prostitute, which in many cases was accurate. The social struggle to stamp out prostitution and thus the disease has been one of society's long wars. Perhaps the profit factor alone has kept prostitution and its companion, syphilis, much a part of the political struggle between the rights of the individual and the rights of society to approve of certain personal behavior. Civil and ecclesiastical authorities have met in conflict time and again. This disagreement between

[14]*Encyclopedia Americana*, (Danbury, Conn.: Grolier, Inc., 1988), p. 670.

the two most powerful bodies of society has created a vacuum in which organized crime has found it most convenient to move in and control.

After the initial shock of the great syphilitic pandemic of the fifteenth and sixteenth centuries, reformation of the citizen became the order of the day. Out of fear of the disease, prostitution control spread throughout Europe. Medical treatment, and the isolation of houses of prostitution, both under the control of the police, became the standard for the progressive European countries by the beginning of the twentieth century.

The medical inspection of houses of prostitution was never very successful. First, the prostitute in multiple contacts could spread the disease before it was detected. Second, there was a tendency for unethical doctors and police officers to engage in bribery to overlook inspections, so the sanctions were useless. Third, the enterprising prostitute was always ready to bootleg the illicit merchandise. The Criminal Law Amendment Act of 1885 was initiated to curb the international trade in white slavery and, in turn, to reduce incidence of syphilis.

While the author does not hold that the control of syphilis is directly related to the rigid control of prostitution, there is evidence that the reduction of prostitute-client contacts must have an impact on the venereal disease rate. The cities that are noted for tight control of prostitutes generally have substantially lower rates of venereal disease. Obviously if organized crime controls a city, there can be no effective enforcement.

The reported data for California indicates the increase to be a public health concern. California, New York City, and Florida data indicate a need for public concern in the spread of venereal diseases. The control of prostitution contacts and the detection, detention, and treatment of active venereal disease carriers is a vital phase of disease control.

> Adolescents contract venereal disease, (syphilis or gonorrhea) at the rate of 1300 or more each day. Youth 15 to 20 years of age contribute to 56 percent of this daily infection rate. Also, 1300 adults per day fall victim to venereal disease. Unfortunately they seem to be as misinformed about this subject as the teenagers.[15]

Government venereal disease experts contend that even these totals fail to represent the true number of cases because many private doctors do not report the diseases as they should, and because many people who can pass on the diseases go untreated because they do not know they have VD (Fig. 6-1).

In the opinion of Dr. William Brown, chief of the venereal disease branch of the Communicable Disease Center in Atlanta, only one in ten VD cases treated by physicians is reported, and he believes that the actual number

---

[15]Edward Maxwell, "Why the Rise in Teenage Venereal Disease?" *Today's Health,* 1965, pp. 18-23, 87–91. These data are still valid; today, the problem of herpes would be added.

of Americans being treated each year is more than a million. Dr. Brown rates VD as a major threat to the nation's health.

The Objective Symptoms of VD

Law enforcement officers will have occasions to associate with suspected or active cases of VD. Both for understanding the problem and as a medical precaution, the officer should be familiar with the symptoms.

The primary stage is the most infectious stage in syphilis. These germs do not float around in the body as commonly believed, but settle in body tissue. Their favorite locations are the brain, heart, and liver. In this primary stage, the germs enter the body. Their presence can be noted in the blood from ten days to three weeks later. This stage is painless to the infected individual.

The secondary stage still produces no pain. Often the victim will break out in a rash. During this stage the carrier is infectious.

The latent or dormant stage occurs about two years after the initial infection, and no signs are usually present. This stage may last from ten to twenty years. It is during this time that infection from syphilis sets in.

In the terminal stage, the vital organs are so badly deteriorated that death results.

Although law enforcement does not hold the answer to the control of VD, if the vice officer is aware of medical ramifications, it is easier for him or her to understand the reasons behind rigid laws for the control of prostitution.

Acquired Immune Deficiency Syndrome

The sexual liberation attitudes of the 1960s through the 1980s have come to an abrupt halt. Sexual liberation has given way to the attitude among many people that sexual misconduct is sin—and that the wages of sin are death. There has been, since 1984, an awareness that death may lurk as a result of sexual encounters. Homosexual or bisexual encounters carry a risk for AIDS. Being exposed to the blood of a carrier through sexual contact and intraveneous blood transfer from needles and blood transfusions are also risk factors. Not since the Middle Ages plague of the black death has such impact been felt on the occupation of prostitution.

Table 6-2 shows the extent of the worldwide AIDS problem. Prostitution, homosexuality, and intraveneous drug use have taken on a new dimension in enforcement and prevention.

Nationally, the total number of syphilis cases during the reporting period increased by 23%. In the same period, the total number of gonor-

TABLE 6-2   Extent of World AIDS Problem, 1987

	Cases	Population	Cases per 100,000
Worldwide	100,000–150,000	5 billion	2.0–3.0
United States	39,263	239.3 million	16.4
New York City	10,229	9.2 million*	111.2
San Francisco	3,858	3.5 million*	110.2
Los Angeles	3,400	8.0 million*	42.5
Other Countries			
Bermuda	55	56,000	98.2
Uganda	1,138	15.5 million	73.4
French Guiana	58	82,000	70.7
Tanzania	1,130	21.7 million	52.1
Bahamas	86	231,000	37.2
Haiti	851	5.4 million	15.8
Guadeloupe	40	333,000	12.0
Rwanda	705	6.3 million	11.2
Trinidad and Tobago	134	1.2 million	11.2
Switzerland	266	6.4 million	4.2
Canada	1,052	25.4 million	4.1
Australia	523	15.6 million	3.4
Kenya	625	20.3 million	3.1
France	1,632	55.2 million	3.0
Denmark	150	5.1 million	2.9
Belgium	230	9.9 million	2.3
West Germany	1,150	61.0 million	1.9

TABLE 6-2 *(continued)*

	Cases	Population	Cases per 100,000
Netherlands	260	14.5 million	1.8
Britain	870	55.6 million	1.6
Sweden	129	8.4 million	1.5
Italy	840	57.2 million	1.5
Brazil	1,835	135.5 million	1.4
Norway	45	4.2 million	1.1

Source: United Nations Population Statistics, 1987.

rhea and penicillin-resistant gonorrhea cases increased over 100%. This data would suggest that the issue of venereal diseases is far from being resolved as a social problem.

SUMMARY

There are many reasons for law enforcement to be involved in control of prostitution. Society views the crime itself to be wrong; society also views itself as a regulator of morality. Ancillary crimes need controlling, and legal sanctions curb venereal contacts.

Although these reasons are logical and unemotional, it is believed that the enforcement officer needs a strong rationale for enforcement policies. With a more thorough understanding of the prostitutes' historical role in the different cultures, an officer can better appreciate the need for some form of restriction on the prostitutes' activities.

Causal factors range from emotional to economic. Perhaps prostitution, more than crimes of property and crimes of violence, supports the "multiple cause" theory of the social sciences. There are very few empirical studies on the "why" of prostitution; therefore, many observations made about prostitution are purely emotional. Alienation from established values by various subcultures tends to perpetuate this antisocial behavior.

An attempt has been made to identify the role of law enforcement as a possible deterrent to venereal diseases by imposing sanctions that minimize contact between prostitute and client.

Police control of prostitution fluctuates along a continuum from no control to fairly rigid control. The degree of control exerted depends on the legislation of proper statutes, the attitude of the community toward suppressing overt prostitution, and the effectiveness of the enforcement agencies in initiating and maintaining control measures.

Most frequently, a city will have areas that attract certain categories of prostitutes. Poorer areas will have streetwalkers and doorway hustlers, while the better apartment house areas will attract bar hustlers as well as call girls working through cabbies and bellboys. The prostitutes who are most overt in their actions will receive a greater share of police attention.

QUESTIONS FOR DISCUSSION

1. Identify and discuss the prime rationale for police involvement in the enforcement of antiprostitution measures.
2. Because of the controversial role of the police in prostitution control it is important for the police to have a knowledge of the history of prostitution. Why is this so important?
3. Identify at least five ways in which organized criminal groups are involved in prostitution activities.
4. How does the practice of prostitution relate to such crimes as drug abuse, burglary, thefts, and so on?
5. Would you normally expect organized criminals to be involved in more sophisticated prostitution activities than the streetwalker? If so, what kind?
6. What are some of the advantages in using the Mann Act for the prosecution of interstate prostitution rings?
7. If the law is wrong with regard to the enforcement of prostitution, why is it important to change the law rather than have police make a lax enforcement of the law?
8. Does the evidence presented about venereal disease offer a logical rationale for some type of control over prostitution? How does the AIDS epidemic impact on control at the community level?

7

Organized Crime and Drug Traffic

LEARNING OUTCOMES

1. Have an overview of how politics affects international drug enforcement.
2. Develop an awareness of the difficulties in enforcing drug laws at the local level.
3. Understand how drugs flow in international trade and how the money moves from consumer to peddler.
4. Be able to identify the importance of metropolitan enforcement groups.
5. Know the influence of new laws and the applications of civil sanctions against known drug dealers.
6. Connect known peddlers with established confederated groups.

To address effective drug control, whether it be an instrument of organized crime or a private business enterprise, we must deal with the issues of federal political negotiations, of federal activity in law enforcement efforts, and of determining the extent of organized crime involvement in drug trafficking. Organized crime involvement deals only with the securing, transporting, and selling of various drugs. The pathologies of the drug user and the impact of drugs on society are the highly emotional and visible elements of the drug problem. There has been little public concern about eliminating the occupation of the drug dealers and resolving the social problems that lead to the abuse of drugs.

The peddlers involved in drug distribution are members of the confederations as well as groups of people who are not dependent on a central authority. These groups depend on mutual trust based on profit interests and an agreed-upon division of labor. Because of the diverse groups involved in drug distribution, all contingencies cannot be covered. This chapter attempts to show that the involvement of confederations in drug traffic is real. During the past decade, known members of established Mafia families have been identified as drug dealers, and some have been convicted on drug charges. The involvement of confederations in drug distribution and sale is addressed in these areas: (1) a political overview of drug traffic history and organized crime involvement; (2) the role of federal, state, and local government units against confederated drug trafficking; and (3) the state and local role in future drug traffic enforcement.

DRUG TRAFFIC: HISTORY AND ORGANIZED CRIME INVOLVEMENT

The involvement of organized crime in drug traffic is, by the nature of the transaction, a national and international problem. International political alliances, carried on by the Department of State, are keystones to the success of drug traffic suppression. When it becomes apparent that political agreements and treaties are unable to curb the flow of drugs, trafficking problems then become a national, state, and local concern. In the past decade there has been increased federal activity in both political relations and enforcement activities. The primary effort of the State Department has been through the secretary of state's chairmanship of the Cabinet Committee for International Narcotics Control. There have been a number of bilateral negotiations to encourage the United Nations to move actively against drug abuse.[1]

The recent history of drug negotiations has little meaning unless the early history is put into perspective. There is little question that organized gangs were involved in drug transactions prior to the ninth century. In the seventeenth century, Western European traders were reportedly prime culprits in the illegal movement of drugs across borders. In the eighteenth century, when opium became the common tonic for pain relief, it also became a prime commodity of tradesmen who traveled from the Orient to Western Europe. When morphine was developed and became a cure for opium addiction, the processing laboratories of Europe controlled drug flow from the poppy fields to retail merchants in Europe, the United States, and throughout the world. The legitimacy of merchants was not questioned; they were looked on as providing a necessary service. In 1874, the German chemist Dresser found the cure for both opium and morphine addiction in a drug called heroin.

In the United States, the distribution of heroin was regulated by the Harrison Act of 1914. The result was a disastrous rise in heroin addiction. Reportedly, the merchandising was done through established drug outlets. A few years later, foreign production, sale, and distribution were banned by the Narcotic Import and Export Act of 1922. (The domestic manufacture

---

[1]For a comprehensive review of drug trafficking problems, see James D. Stinchcomb, *Trafficking in Drugs and Narcotics* (Richmond: Virginia Commonwealth University, (latest edition).

of heroin was outlawed in 1924.) Since that time there have been various updates of the laws:

Marijuana Tax Act of 1937
Opium Poppy Control Act of 1942
Boggs Act of 1951
Narcotics Control Act of 1956
The Drug Abuse Office and Treatment Act of 1972
Currency and Foreign Transactions Act of 1972
Racketeering Influences and Corrupt Organizations (RICO) Act and Amendments 1970, 1978, 1986, 1988.
Omnibus Drug Bill of 1988
Omnibus Crime Bill of 1990

Since the 1920s, organized gangs have controlled the major flow of drugs into the United States. Basically, the statutes covering drugs are adequate, but they have had no appreciable and lasting impact on drug distribution in the past 50 years.

Recognizing the deficiency of enforcement efforts, the federal government has not been idle in attempting to negotiate accords among nations. The Cabinet Committee for International Narcotic Control has negotiated mutual assistance arrangements with Mexico, Turkey, and France in cooperative efforts against illegal drug traffic.[2] This negotiation was brought about by the United Nations' Commission on Narcotic Drugs, which includes 24 member nations. Through a special fund for drug abuse control, a comprehensive UN plan for action against drug abuse was developed. The objectives of the plan are these:

To expand the United Nations' research and information facilities.

To limit the supply of drugs to legitimate requirements by ending illegal production and substituting other economic opportunities.

To enlarge the capabilities and extend the operations of existing United Nations drug control bodies.

To promote facilities for treatment, rehabilitation, and social reintegration of drug addicts.

To develop educational material and programs against drug abuse in high-risk populations.

The first effort under this program was in December 1971 when the United States, Thailand, and the United Nations agreed to coordinate their efforts in drug control projects. This was preceded by a March 1971 Single Convention on Narcotic Drugs, in which 90 nations adopted the basic in-

---

[2]*Attorney General's First Annual Report* (Washington, D.C.: U.S. Government Printing Office, 1972), p. 266. "Baiting the Trap for Drug Dealers," *Insight,* Dec. 26, 1986. *Los Angeles Times,* Oct. 15, 1987, p. 4.

ternational regulation to control the flow of narcotic drugs such as opium and heroin. In 1972 and in 1987, a United Nations Plenipotentiary Conference in Geneva adopted a treaty that commits 97 nations of the world to a resolution of the drug abuse problem.

The protocol empowered the International Narcotics Control Board to:

> Exercise new authority to curb illicit cultivation, production, manufacture, trafficking, and consumption of opium, heroin, and other narcotics.
>
> Require reduction of production of opium poppy cultivation and opium production in countries shown to be sources of illicit traffic.
>
> Extradite and thus prosecute narcotic traffickers who have taken refuge in other nations.

The Convention on Psychotropic Substances imposed the same constraints on nations producing "mind-bending" hallucinogenic substances such as LSD, mescaline, amphetamines, barbiturates, and tranquilizers.

With these accords, law enforcement agencies are for the first time in a position to make a lasting corrective impact on drug trafficking. The major problems remain how to tie organized confederations into the distribution complex and secure prosecutions against top level dealers.

UNITED STATES INTERVENTION IN DRUG CONTROL

We are now viewing the results of five decades of U.S. involvement in active efforts to curb drug importation. These enforcement efforts are based on two philosophies.[3] (1) to seal the borders of the United States against drug imports and (2) to move into the producing countries and attempt to curb the growth and production of narcotics and other illegal drugs.

Sealing the Borders of the United States

The political decision makers who sealed U.S. borders immediately found there were massive problems. First, the borders, open on four sides, could not be sealed with the personnel available. Second, because of the reduction in the flow of drugs from Turkey, Mexico and then Latin America became the major suppliers to the United States. For at least five decades, organized crime had been making Mexican contacts. Almost overnight, the dealers who had been furnishing modest, low-visibility amounts to American distributors were inundated with volume orders. By 1988 there were over 150 well-established Mexican and Colombian organizations handling the

[3]Marcella S. Kreiter, "Fighting Drugs: A Look At The New Laws and Changed Attitudes." *Current Health*, 13, April 1987, pp. 12–16. Nightly drug stories are run on all major television networks.

transportation of narcotics going north. Where ounces had once been the standard, kilos then tons became the new measure. Mobility and flexibility became the byword of the organizations and the bain of the enforcement agencies.

Curbing Growth and Production in Foreign Countries

When a foreign power moves into a country to regulate any facet of that country's sovereign rights, there is a great risk of offending the host country. Relationships established to control drug growth and production in several countries have apparently met with some resistance. For example, Mexico is glad to take money and equipment to assist in its efforts to curb drug production, but it does not want the United States to tell Mexicans how to run their enforcement machinery. In many Latin American countries the feeling is the same.

The two-faceted philosophy, while theoretically sound, has many deficiencies when pragmatically applied. With open borders on all sides, this country has become a veritable sieve for drugs of all varieties.[4] A review of some of the drug import problems and the American effort in each of the major drug-supplying countries may offer some insight as to why our policies are not working better.

The Mexican connection.   When people cannot earn a living legitimately, they will resort to any means to survive. So it is that Mexico, an agrarian culture, without a market for its products, must find a product with a market. Mexicans have found this product in the tons of marijuana and the kilos of "brown heroin" that are shipped north to the United States.

It is unrealistic to believe that the Mexican farmers are ethically tied to stemming the growth of their only cash crop. They are practical people; if they can sell the "gum," they can eat. These farmers sell their products to a wholesaler, who most probably is a relative or a long-time friend. The drug is then channeled into the distribution pipeline.

In attempting to curb the growth and production of narcotics in Mexico and Latin America the United States has spent many millions of dollars. U.S. bureaucrats agree that the amount of drugs coming into the country has been curbed by this effort. They are also optimistic about further inroads to cut drug growth.[5] The drug problem with Latin America is

---

[4]"The Mexican Connection," *Arizona Republic,* July 22, 1979; "Flood of Cocaine Via Desert Route," *Insight,* January 19, 1989, p. 22–23.

[5]Guy Gugliotta, and Jeff Leen, *Kings of Cocaine,* (New York: Simon and Schuster, 1989). "U.S. Launches Massive Caribbean Drug Drive," *Los Angeles Times,* November 2, 1985; "Latin Nations Uniting in War on Cocaine," *Los Angeles Times,* December 3, 1985; "War on Drugs, Rebels Rage in Peru," *Los Angeles Times,* August 2, 1987.

political. If other nations cooperate, the program is marginally successful. If they do not cooperate, it will be a dismal failure.

The South American problem.   Most countries in the Southern Hemisphere have had some involvement in narcotic traffic. The major contributors to the problem at this time appear to be Colombia and Peru. These two countries have tended to hold the spotlight on drug activity for the past two decades.

Colombia is estimated to furnish about 70 percent of the marijuana that supplies 16 million American users. It is estimated that about 225,000 acres of marijuana are under cultivation. An acre of cultivated marijuana produces about two tons of merchandise per year. A farmer growing marijuana can obtain $3 to $8 per pound for the product, compared to 10 cents per pound for coffee. The economic benefits to the grower and the nation are obvious. It is estimated that 43 percent of the GNP of Colombia is generated through the sale of marijuana. Modern communications systems furnish orders for ship lines and fleets of aircraft that operate all over the world. The Colombian government's concern is that the products escape taxation. This drug problem for the United States will probably not be settled through negotiation.

Peru and Bolivia have been the cocaine connection for the world. The coca plant is grown in the foothills that extend along the eastern slopes of the Peruvian Andes, described as the "eyebrow of the jungle." Here the natives harvest the coca leaf that has grown wild in this area throughout history. It is estimated that the area produces about 80 percent of the cocaine imported into the United States through organized cartels comprising hundreds of persons. Because the initial production of leaves furnishes a cash crop for hungry people, there is little possibility that the problem will be solved through diplomatic negotiation or punitive enforcement.

Of the 30,000 tons produced yearly, only a small amount is used in the legal manufacture of medicinal cocaine and flavoring agents. It has been alleged by some intelligence sources that the government has vast stores of cocaine stored in vaults and that the government is able to control the export supply and thus the price. Because of the impact of the cocaine trade on these countries' GNP, it is unlikely that negotiation is going to affect the amount of cocaine exported.

The Middle East.   Politics has brought new "connections" in the Middle East. It is reported that Pakistan and Afghanistan are replacing the "golden triangle" of Southeast Asia. The proximity of the Middle East to Europe makes it a much more desirable source of supply. Also, because the supply from Mexico is under pressure, new sources through Europe are desirable.

Because of the insurgency and political turmoil in these two countries, international efforts for internal control of narcotics has failed. The amount of drugs reportedly moving from this area rivals the days of the "French connection."

Southeast Asia.   The "golden triangle" will not change as long as there is a market for the farmer's opium crops. When a nation, or a tribe, depends on narcotics as a money crop and there is a user somewhere in the world, there will always be accommodating peddlers to help the distribution along.

U.S. efforts are limited to the governments of friendly countries. These countries border on hostile nations, so the flexibility of grower and peddler is always being tested. For example, in Thailand drug peddlers have their own armies for protection. When the armies are overpowered, they merely move their operations to a neighboring country, where they are unmolested. Any political agreement on drug control is just an agreement. Agreements that cannot be enforced have the same impact as no agreement at all.

Despite efforts to curb "golden triangle" production, a 900-ton crop was harvested in 1988. Khun Sa, an opium warlord, whose opium profits support a rebellion against Burma, profits through the efforts of Thailand and Burma to control poppy growth.

Organized Crime Patterns for Drug Distribution

Through various publications it has become general public knowledge that there must be organized elements involved in order to make a complex business operation like that shown in Figure 7–1 function.

Drug traffic patterns illustrated in Figure 7–4, while authenticated only by intelligence reports, do indicate planning and implementation of intricate procedures, which can be done only by a cohesive confederation.

The evidence of organized crime control is shown in the shifting patterns of drug distribution. In the 1950s, most American heroin flowed from the Middle East through France. After enforcement pressure was applied, Mexico and Southeast Asia became the major drug sources. When the war ended in Vietnam and control of the drug source was lost, Mexico again became the big supplier. By 1975, with a highly concentrated enforcement effort against the Mexican sources, the supply routes were reestablished into South America. With European sources moving back to the Middle East, it becomes apparent that much sophisticated planning and organization has gone into these major shifts.

While we give too much credit to the organization of the drug smuggling groups, the major problem is the lack of organization in the American drug control effort. Following the reorganization of drug enforcement agencies in 1973, there has been little coordinated effort among the big federal

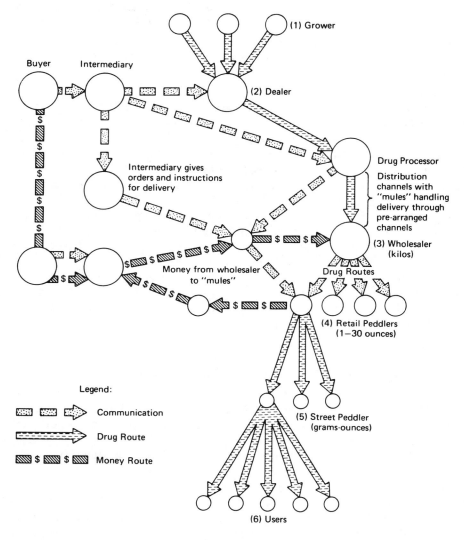

Legend:

▨▨ ▨▨ ⇨ Communication

═════⇨ Drug Route

▨ $ ▨ $ ▨ Money Route

1. Commercial and small growers sell to the dealers in raw materials (opium)

2. Buyer uses intermediary to contact dealer who arranges for processing and distribution.
    A token payment may change hands.

3. Intermediary carries orders and instructions for deliveries. Wholesaler has "mule" deliver to
    pre-arranged location. Sample is tested and buyer has "mule" make payoff to pre-arranged location.

4. Retail peddlers are contacted by the wholesaler with "mules" making all deliveries and contacts.
    Communications downward. Retailer sends money by "mule" to intermediary.

5. Street peddler is contacted by the retail peddlers. Street peddler then deals with the user.
    Communications both upward and downward.

FIGURE 7-1 Drug sale procedures from grower to user.

enforcement units. The information contacts that had been developed over time in the Customs Service Agency suddenly disappeared.

The 1971 conventions also covered the psychotropic substances. While dangerous drugs such as amphetamines and barbiturates are not necessarily an international problem, they became a part of the agreements between governments. Most of these drugs tend to be local and national problems, because they can be manufactured in the bathtub or in small laboratories.

MAJOR DRUG TYPES

Drugs most often encountered in high-volume operation are: (1) opium and derivatives, (2) coca plant products such as cocaine and derivatives, and (3) marijuana and other prohibited or restricted drugs (Fig. 7–2).

Opium and Derivatives

Papaver somniferum, the deadly poppy, has spread its influence throughout the world. It has been recognized, and used, for centuries for its pain killing and addictive qualities. It is the most useful and dangerous member of the poppy family.

From the fields of India (100 metric tons in 1987) where poppies are farmed under government license to the illegal fields around the world comes the gummy residure of alkaloid-rich latex that forms the base for five main derivatives. Some are used legally, many are not (Fig. 7–3).

The latex taken from the poppy hardens into a black gum in about twenty hours. It is then scraped from the pod and may be stored for years without losing its potency. This is opium gum, which may be smoked or reduced to ash and mixed in water for a toddy called Yen she Suey.

Vinegar mixed with gall was offered Christ on the cross (Matthew 27:34). The ancient Hebrew word for gall, *rosk*, means opium. Later medical uses of alcohol and opium included laudanum, a concoction used by medical men as late as 1920. Today, India furnishes about two-thirds of the legal opium used in medicines.

Morphine

This pain-killing opium alkaloid was isolated and called morphine. For acute pain, morphine is unequaled. For trauma victims, such as those with battlefield wounds, morphine is easily and effectively used. It is still a widely used medicine.

	Drugs	Schedule	Trade or Other Names
NARCOTICS	Opium	II, III, V	Dover's Powder, Paregoric, Parepectolin
	Morphine	II, III	Morphine, Pectoral Syrup
	Codeine	II, III, V	Codeine, Empirin Compound with Codeine, Robitussin A-C
	Heroin	I	Diacetylmorphine, Horse, Smack
	Hydromorphone		Dilaudid
	Meperidine (Pethidine)	II	Demerol, Pethadol
	Methadone		Dolophine, Methadone, Methadose
	Other Narcotics	I, II, III, IV, V	LAAM, Leritine, Levo-Dromoran, Percodan, Tussionex, Fentanyl, Darvon*, Talwin*, Lomotil
DEPRESSANTS	Chloral Hydrate	IV	Noctec, Somnos
	Barbiturates	II, III, IV	Amobarbital, Phenobarbital, Butisol, Phenoxbarbital, Secobarbital, Tuinal
	Glutethimide	III	Doriden
	Methaqualone	II	Optimil, Parest, Quaalude, Somnafac, Sopor
	Benzodiazepines	IV	Ativan, Azene, Clonopin, Dalmane, Diazepam, Librium, Serax, Tranxene, Valium, Verstran
	Other Depressants	III, IV	Equanil, Miltown, Noludar Placidyl, Valmid
STIMULANTS	Cocaine	II	Coke, Flake, Snow
	Amphetamines	II, III	Biphetamine, Delcobese, Desoxyn, Dexedrine, Mediatric
	Phenmetrazine	II	Preludin
	Methylphenidate		Ritalin
	Other Stimulants	III, IV	Adipex, Bacarate, Cylert, Didrex, Ionamin, Plegine, PreSate, Sanorex, Tenuate, Tepanil, Crack, Ice*
HALLUCINOGENS	LSD		Acid, Microdot
	Mescaline and Peyote	I	Mesc, Buttons, Cactus
	Amphetamine Variants		2,5-DMA, PMA, STP, MDA, MMDA, TMA, DOM, DOB
	Phencyclidine	II	PCP, Angel Dust, Hog
	Phencyclidine Analogs		PCE, PCPy, TCP
	Other Hallucinogens	I	Bufotenine, Ibogaine, DMT, DET, Psilocybin, Psilocyn
CANNIBIS	Marijuana		Pot, Acapulco Gold, Grass, Reefer, Sinsemilla, Thai Sticks
	Tetrahydrocannabinal	I	THC
	Hashish		Hash
	Hashish Oil		Hash Oil

FIGURE 7-2 Controlled substances. Extracted from U.S. Department of Justice, *Drugs of Abuse,* U.S. Government Printing Office, July 1979. (*Those designated by an asterisk are drugs to reemerge during the 1990s.)

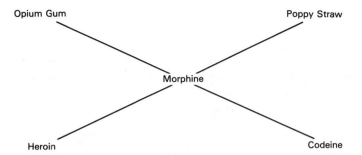

FIGURE 7-3　The poppy and its derivatives.　The entire plant is chopped into a straw from which the alkaloids are extracted.

Heroine

Morphine was modified with acetic anhydride, and its pain killing potential was doubled; this drug became known as heroin. Heroin was a cough and diarrhea preventative offered as a less addicting substance than morphine. Later tests have shown it is more addictive than morphine.

It is estimated that U.S. consumption of heroin is about $4 to $5 billion annually. The mark-up for heroin may be 1000 times the manufactured price. It is estimated that about 50 percent of the U.S. supply comes from the Middle East, 20 percent from Asia, and the remaining amounts from Latin America.

Cocaine and Derivatives

Until a decade ago, cocaine was just another stimulating narcotic, most often used with heroin in "speed balls," but generally too expensive for the heavy users. With sanctions imposed against heroin traffic from Asia and the Middle East, South American cartels established a coca crop clientele in the United States.

The intense euphoric and hallucinatory effects stimulate the nervous system. Within a decade, cocaine became the most popular of all the narcotics. Use of the drug was popularized in the media, and middle and upper class America became an entirely new market. The demand for cocaine made drugs the number one money maker for the Mafia and for the thousands of organized and disorganized gangs who peddled it worldwide.

In 1981, a new, less expensive form of cocaine called "crack" was introduced. Crack is smokable silvers or crystals processed from powdered cocaine hydrochloride through the addition of baking soda or ammonia. The effects of smoking crack are far more intense than snorting cocaine. The use of crack is so addictive and so potent that violence among users is widespread.

Gentle "dopers" of the past have become "gun-toting maniacs" of the 1980s and the drug wars are now being waged in earnest. The occasional killing over drugs has spread to intense wars carried on among gangs.[6] The killings spread from organized gangs to violence among the "socially oriented" street gangs. Criminals exercise territorial rights so rigidly that there are turf wars in nearly every major city in the United States.

The effects of crack have been so devastating on society that remedial measures under the RICO sections of the Omnibus Crime Bill have been undertaken (see Appendix B). Forfeiture proceedings are beginning to be used against the "cottage industry" gangs who are involved in street dealerships. If forfeiture proceedings were strenuously initiated against the inter-city gangs, the control of that drug trade would be noticed immediately. "Rock houses," which operate from behind locked doors and barred windows, have even used sales campaigns and were actually competing against one another for customers on the open market. Brand names, such as "airborne" and "sudden impact," and sealed plastic packages were used to ensure a quality product.

Marijuana

Cannabis sativa has become a mainstay in the drug business around the world. In many states the possession of small amounts of marijuana is a misdemeanor (see Fig. 7–3).

Controlled Substances

There are about 1600 different controlled substances that are known by such monikers as hallucinogens, stimulants, and depressants. Each state has a massive list of these controlled drugs. Most are controlled by prescription, others are cooked up in the bathroom, and several varieties are manufactured by drug companies but eventually end up in the illegal market.

The volume of these drugs may even exceed the profits of the narcotics trade. The users and the market are so diversified, so loosely structured that the organization and control of the market may be vested in unsavory physicians, unethical druggists, motorcycle gangs, street gangs, independent entrepreneurs producing specialty drugs, and novice peddlers who handle a specific kind of drug. The control of these drugs receives a low profile in

---

[6] E. W. Oglesby, Samuel J. Faber, and Stuart J. Faber, *Angel Dust: What Everyone Should Know About PCP,* (Los Angeles: Charing Cross Publishing, 1982). Also see David Blum, "Reality," *New York Magazine,* 21, April 25, 1988, pp. 11–12.

international and national efforts because they are primarily a state and local problem. These drugs, including steroids, are susceptible to control through education and making them socially unacceptable in grade and high schools.

National strategies for the control of drugs has been centralized in a drug czar, and future research efforts may be reflected in the 1989 Department of Education research design, which brings the drug research effort back to where it was in about 1964 when it tended to take a backseat to "crime in the streets." The politicization of the drug problem has created a hodge podge of enforcement efforts. Perhaps the centralization of power at the national level will produce a cohesive effort.

FEDERAL, STATE, AND LOCAL GOVERNMENT UNITS AND CONFEDERATION DRUG TRAFFICKING

Four agencies form the nucleus of the drug control effort by the United States on an international basis. The International Police Organization (INTERPOL) serves as an intelligence and records source. The Bureau of Customs uses intensive searches at ports of entry as part of its enforcement effort. The Department of Defense is a potent deterrent to drug importation in conducting investigations, furnishing intelligence, and maintaining records for drug activity on military posts. The last federal agency in international drug control is the Federal Bureau of Investigation of the United States Justice Department. This agency, in the reorganization of 1982, has been assigned all intelligence, investigative, and law enforcement responsibility dealing with national and international drug control.

With the collaboration of foreign nations, these agencies have conducted operations that confirm that large volumes of narcotic drugs are being financed and imported to the United States, where they are then distributed to major cities. For example, seizures of 300, 400, and 4000 kilos of heroin and cocaine in different international operations indicate that large bankrolls are being risked to promote the entry of drugs into this country.[7]

Although the United States maintains no regular law enforcement liaison with foreign powers, a number of agencies retain contact sources. For example, the Federal Bureau of Investigation, the Internal Revenue Service, and the Bureau of Customs all have intelligence resources that contribute to the enforcement effort. International enforcement efforts to date have not been able to penetrate successfully the tightly woven mesh that organized crime has established abroad because the right of sovereignty is highly respected and jealously guarded.

The next step has been to organize internally so that federal resources can be quickly deployed where needed. Although the "strike force" concept

[7]*Los Angeles Times,* August 5, 1978; February 2, 1987; October 15, 1987; and November 4, 1987.

Cocaine Trafficking Routes

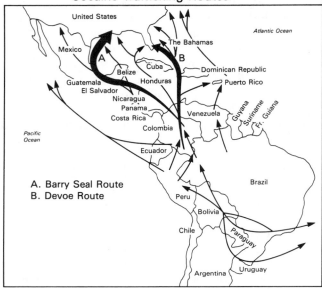

Caribbean Routes Used in Maritime Drug Trafficking

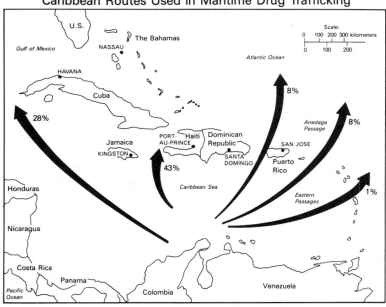

FIGURE 7-4   Distribution routes for South American drugs.

Source: President's Commission on Organized Crime, Report to the President and the Attorney General, *American Habit: Drug Abuse, Drug Trafficking and Organized Crime,* (Washington, D.C.: U.S. Government Printing Office, March 1986), pp. 86–91.

was not designed for drug enforcement per se, the Federal Bureau of Investigation is a participating member in the units now operating. The strike force seems to offer advantages in all types of specialized investigations, and the success of this concept has brought major reorganization to federal law enforcement efforts.

National Drug Control Efforts

The latest published strategies for drug control are the policies formulated by the Strategy Council on Drug Abuse. These strategies are not much different than those formulated in times past. The formulation of policies has been an evolutionary process, one that has changed to fit the ideology of whatever party is in power.

The current three-part strategy is designed around these major efforts:[8] (1) treatment, rehabilitation and prevention; (2) domestic drug law enforcement; and (3) international narcotics control.

The treatment and prevention effort will give priority to those drugs that are pharmacologically most dangerous. The programs will focus on the drug taker rather than on the drug. This strategy follows that practiced by the Bureau of Prisons for many years. It would appear these program planners are treating heroin addicts in much the same manner as they have been treated in the past. Ironically, these treatment programs have not been effective in the long term. Until the hardline or justice model treatment of the heroin addict is followed, the sale of hard narcotics will defy control. Kill the demand and the market will dry up.

The strategy for enforcement within the United States suggests exclusive authority for the Drug Enforcement Administration. It also stresses increased activity on the financial aspects of drug trafficking. If prosecutors at the federal level used all the financial information obtained about major drug dealers, every prosecution could come under the RICO (Racketeering Influences Corrupt Organization) statute, which is Section IX of the Organized Crime Control Act of 1970, 1978, 1986. The Internal Revenue Service could be decisive in the fight against drug trafficking, but it has refused to be involved in prosecutions. Solid application of RICO, as long as the courts will back it, seems to be the surest way to eradicate drug distribution cartels.

The international program is directed to the gaining of international cooperation. If this strategy works, it could be a forerunner of better policies, or it could result in adverse world opinion. Mexico is a classic example; while there may be accolades from a particular government diplomat, the United

---

[8]The Strategy Council on Drug Abuse, *Federal Strategy for Drug Abuse and Drug Traffic Prevention* (Washington, D.C.: U.S. Government Printing Office, 1979). These strategies are still good.

States is still viewed as a meddler in the internal affairs of the Mexican government.

International programs are designed to: (1) reduce illicit narcotic supplies at the source; (2) enhance participation in international drug control organizations; (3) foster cooperation with foreign narcotics enforcement agencies; and (4) develop international drug abuse treatment and prevention programs.[9]

The strategies set forth in the federal programs are designed to make maximum use of intelligence. There is a need to develop financial intelligence so that any international carrier may be prosecuted under RICO. There is a need to automate information programs on peddlers so they are more readily traced and accounted for. Only when this kind of intelligence is refined will the RICO statutes be effective.

The domestic drug law enforcement effort has not changed. The objectives are to reduce the supply of illegal drugs; to control the supply of legally manufactured drugs to avoid illegal diversion; and to achieve the highest possible risk for drug trafficking. This latter objective will lead to prison terms for the violator and the forfeiture of all assets gained from racketeering practices.

The domestic enforcement strategy includes the consolidation of some of the border service agencies, such as Customs and Immigration and Naturalization, into a Border Management Agency. According to the organization within the Justice Department, it would appear that all internal enforcement agencies will be under an associate attorney general. But this type of goal setting and manipulation of agencies is primarily a political ploy; as long as these agencies are staffed with attorneys whose claim to fame is their faithful work for the party, the domestic enforcement effort is in trouble.

Border interdiction, to be passably effective, would take all the personnel of the armed services. As long as the movement of people and products across an open border remains subject to politics, there will be no stemming of the drug tide. The chaotic situation in Florida has been created by bad political decisions, and the cure for the massive drug traffic and the laundering of funds will cease only when civil and administrative sanctions are strictly applied. The new legislation amending the Bank Security Act makes it illegal to transport unreported money outside the United States. If this law is not enforced, the situation will not improve.

Changing a society of drug abusers may be the future of drug abuse control. If the market is unable to absorb the flow of drugs, the drug problem would cease to exist. Nancy Reagan gave support and publicity to the

[9]Ibid., p. 34. Also see International Conference on Drug Abuse and Illicit Trafficking, June 17–26,1987. *UN Chronicle*, 24, May 1987, pp. 44–76.

phrase, "Say no to drugs," which has become the popular cliché of the late 1980s. This approach, while not new, logically must be a part of the eradication or control of the "drug culture" generated in American society for the past three decades. These problems will remain until an aroused public gets fed up with bureaucratic double talk and demands action. Until this is done, the drug import and abuse problem will continue to get worse, not better.

Federal, State, and Local Cooperation

One major weakness of the national drug effort has been the lack of consistent and effective cooperation: the failure of the federal government to assign specific lead agency responsibility; the lack of a plan to bring state and local agencies together in enforcement groups; and failure to integrate intelligence sources.

Assignment of lead agency.   The Drug Enforcement Administration has now been assigned the lead agency role. If properly executed, this coordinating role should eliminate many of the problems caused when representatives of two or three federal agencies and of two or three state and local agencies all show up on the same case. With this change, and the reorganization in the Justice Department, it is possible this problem may be solved.

A second difficulty was the proliferation of task forces, each working independently of the other. DEA should now assume control over all task forces, and the legal specialists can furnish technical staff assistance. Task forces should have the benefit of a legal staff specialist, but an assistant U.S. attorney cannot run a strike force because no one in the strike force has a commitment to answer to him. Field operations should be under the line supervision of experienced investigative personnel with the assigned responsibility for that function.

Plan to bring enforcement groups together.   In the past, individual and agency jealousies have been a disaster for cooperative efforts with local agencies. With the RICO statute to serve as a catalyst, task forces know how to operate; with a realistic law applicable to the racketeering activities of the suspects. The lead federal agency now has more than just money to lend to an investigation. If local agencies can see the advantages of prosecution under the RICO statute, working cooperation can almost be assured.

At this point, some observations should be made regarding the feasibility of using the RICO statute in narcotic convictions. Despite the fact that defense attorneys are slicing at this broad criminal statute, it has withstood several appeals. It would appear that the RICO statute could be easily applied in most drug cases. Unfortunately, since RICO's enactment, these weapons have not been used to their full potential. RICO's provision for civil remedies in particular have in the past been underutilized.[10] This is still true in 1991.

Failure to integrate intelligence sources.   Until information flows up and down the investigative ladder, good cases will not occur. If information gained by federal and local agencies is forced into one system, the "need to know" doctrine can be more clearly determined.

The Drug Enforcement Administration has been a key mover in antinarcotic squads called Metropolitan Enforcement Groups (MEGS). These units have successfully used computer-based data to zero in on street-level peddlers. There is reason to believe they can bring some sensible structure to the enforcement plan for the United States.

Another program begun on a pilot basis has been the Drug Diversion Units based on the strike force concept of bringing together federal, state, and local efforts to obtain prosecutions, revocation of licenses, and other sanctions against those who are exceeding the authority granted by law to get legal drugs into the illicit market. Results from these units indicate gross abuses by legitimate drug manufacturers, druggists, doctors, and private dealers who use various unethical and illegal means to secure otherwise legitimate drugs. These Drug Diversion Units are uncovering evidence that gangs of criminals are in the business of forged prescriptions, obtaining drugs by false representation as well as by burglary and hijacking of drug supply sources.

For the professional druggist and doctor, the abuses uncovered have revealed lucrative profits in the drug dispensing business. The fact that a doctor may often become suspect when administering drugs such as methadone to an addict has caused many legitimate physicians to refuse to maintain drug users as patients. Because of this, a few unethical members of the medical and pharmacological guilds are reaping tremendous profits at the expense of society as well as individual users.

State and Local Roles in the Future of Drug Traffic Enforcement

Local and state agencies will always exert the major effort in drug abuse enforcement. By virtue of numbers, jurisdiction, and physical presence, these agencies are committed to the suppression of drug distribution. The apprehension of middlemen at the state level and the street peddler locally may ultimately offer the surest road to street control.

---

[10]Rudolph W. Giuliani, "Legal Remedies for Attacking Organized Crime," Herbert Edlehertz, Ed., *Major Issues in Organized Crime Control* (Washington, D.C.: U.S. Government Printing Office, September 1987), p. 107. Also see Paula Dwyer, Susan B. Garland, and Aaron Berstein, "Will Going After the Unions Bust up RICO," *Business Week.* May 30, 1988, p. 30. An abstract of the Omnibus Crime Control Act is given in Appendix B.

Because the confederations are not involved locally, we believe that narcotics intelligence and enforcement must move nationally and internationally if there is to be any reasonable control on a large scale. These types of programs are being brought about through federally funded efforts and should have top fiscal priority for a number of years to come. But the idea that national control is ultimately going to prevail if enforcement is effective does not detract from the thousands of cases being made at the local and state level.

Organized criminal groups are being arrested daily. Most of these groups do not owe allegiance to the large drug financiers, but are agents for the men who front with the big money. From a local perspective, the border cities in Texas, New Mexico, Arizona, California, and the nearby port cities of Louisiana can hardly justify organized confederation involvement. There are so many amateurs and semiprofessionals who rush to the border for a few ounces of heroin, a kilo or two of marijuana, or a barrel or two of pills that the professional cannot compete. In major cities inland the story is different, for there the organized group becomes involved simply because a tight distribution network is a necessity.

The nature of a large transaction shows why locals rarely deal with top-echelon peddlers. The financing is always in cash; the plans are made prior to the transaction, so no one knows who sent the shipment; and no one knows who is to receive it. From initial handling through processing to delivery in the United States, "mules" or "couriers" are hired to carry the merchandise. If a shipment is lost, the void in the pipeline can be filled within twenty-four hours. The profit margin is structured to accommodate the losses. Once the drug shipment reaches the point for consignment to the street, local agents can respond. The response at this level is too late. For example, from one kilo (2.2 pounds) of pure heroin purchased for about $70,000 overseas, the heroin is "cut" until there may be 90,000 fixes or more. It becomes an unsurmountable task when local officers must make seizures of grams. At that level, it is impossible to dry up the pipeline.

SUMMARY

In the past decade, the drug dealer instead of the drug abuser has become the main emphasis of enforcement. This switch has resulted from improved intelligence methods, which revealed links between U.S. organized crime groups and between international cartels.

Federal involvement of drug enforcement has been increasing, and broad new anticrime bills have been initiated every two years. The latest anticrime bill of 1991 would authorize the hiring of 2,500 additional federal law enforcement agents and 480 new prosecutors for drug-related offenses and would make drug king-pins eligible for the death penalty. A brief history and pattern of drug distribution have been shown, and the major grouping of drugs has been briefly outlined.

The message about the adverse social and economic impact of drug abuse has finally reached the national political leaders. These impacts have caused the political leaders to commit massive effort into drug control and eradication through the development of better coordinated international intelligence, the crackdown on money laundering, and the taxation and civil recovery of assets gained from the sale of drugs. These actions by the political leaders have resulted in massive drug and money seizures.

Perhaps the most important step in recent years in the drug control effort was the appointment in 1989 of a drug administrator with the authority to coordinate, oversee, and develop new programs in drug eradication. The success of these drug programs remains to be seen.

QUESTIONS FOR DISCUSSION

1. Discuss the difference in enforcing general drug abuse laws and conspiracy laws that relate to confederation participation in drug traffic.
2. Why is it so difficult to gain public support for action against the large drug distributors?
3. Has politics been instrumental in creating a drug trafficking problem? Explain.
4. Discuss in detail the importance of the involvement of international agencies and national government agencies in the drug sale problem.
5. Review the political mandates that now make international enforcement efforts a possibility.
6. Discuss the difference between the old drug control laws and the comprehensive Drug Abuse Office and Treatment Act of 1972.
7. Discuss the UN plan of action against drug abuse. How does this affect enforcement efforts?
8. Identify the significant role of the International Narcotics Control Board.
9. Discuss the two important political accords dealing with narcotics and psychotropic substances.
10. Examine drug distribution and analyze why it is difficult for enforcement officers to secure evidence against important dealers.
11. What are the prime advantages of having a massive federal cooperative effort? disadvantages?
12. Would the seizure of large amounts of drugs overseas indicate that past efforts were successes or failures?
13. Discuss the merits of the strike force concept in both narcotics enforcement and in organized crime enforcement activity.
14. The Drug Enforcement Division has identified ten major systems dealing in drugs. Do you know of any evidence that would indicate organized crime involvement?

15. Discuss new national programs and how these will influence the drug control effort.
16. Will the legalization of drugs eliminate peddler profit?
17. What areas of agreement and disagreement with the authors do you have regarding the local role in drug enforcement?

8

Obscenity and Pornography

LEARNING OUTCOMES

1. Have an understanding of the complexities of enforcing obscenity and pornography statutes.
2. Recognize that organized crime is deeply entrenched in the distribution of obscene materials.
3. Know court decisions affecting the distribution of obscene materials.
4. Be able to apply the four court standards to obscene materials.
5. Know the ways in which action may be taken against peddlers of obscene materials.

Obscenity and pornography are distributed all over the world. In spite of the worldwide scope of this operation, there has been little investigation and research done on who actually controls the markets that distribute these materials. When these investigations are made, the public will find that most of the obscenity and pornography markets will reflect direct control by established, nationally known confederations. At the local level, an investigation will show that many local newsstands dealing in hard core pornography will also be fronting for bookmaking activities. The wholesale pornographic movie and stag show distributors will all relate to the total distribution network established by confederations (Fig. 8–1).

In recent years, there has been an increase in the publication of literary and pictorial pornography. While the problem of obscenity is not new, it is a continuing and critical problem for law enforcement and citizens who are interested in seeing that community morality standards are not established by organized crime. The police role in enforcement of obscenity statutes is akin to walking a tightrope. Each alleged violation is a direct challenge to the rights guaranteed by the First Amendment to the Consti-

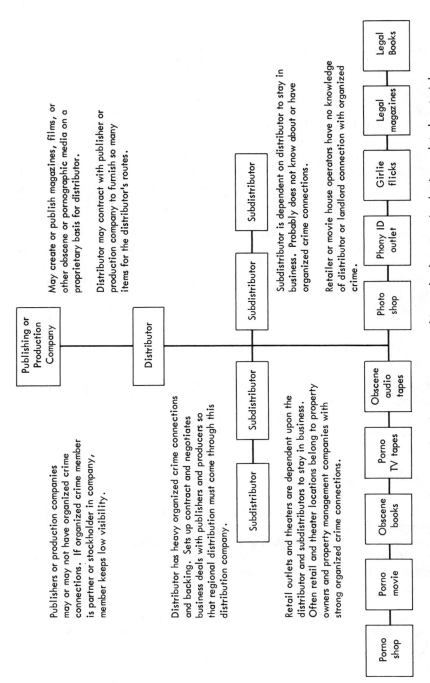

Publishers or production companies may or may not have organized crime connections. If organized crime member is partner or stockholder in company, member keeps low visibility.

May create or publish magazines, films, or other obscene or pornographic media on a proprietary basis for distributor.

Distributor may contract with publisher or production company to furnish so many items for the distributor's routes.

Distributor has heavy organized crime connections and backing. Sets up contract and negotiates business deals with publishers and producers so that regional distribution must come through this distribution company.

Subdistributor is dependent on distributor to stay in business. Probably does not know about or have organized crime connections.

Retailer or movie house operators have no knowledge of distributor or landlord connection with organized crime.

Retail outlets and theaters are dependent upon the distributor and subdistributors to stay in business. Often retail and theater locations belong to property owners and property management companies with strong organized crime connections.

FIGURE 8-1 Typical distribution structure for obscene, pornographic, and other organized crime-related materials.

113

tution.[1] This chapter examines the complexities of the obscenity and pornography issue so that a philosophy for enforcement may be developed by each person concerned with community standards of morality.

Obscenity, according to a definition, is "something offensive to modesty or decency; lewd, disgusting; filthy, repulsive, as language, conduct, an expression, an act." Pornography is defined as "originally a description of prostitutes and their trades; hence, writings, pictures, and other materials intended to arouse sexual desire." Although these definitions are oversimplified, they are adequate for most purposes.

Obscenity is the legal definition that refers to conduct offensive to the public sense of decency. From the point of view of law, it is essentially concerned with publication of indecent written, graphic, or pictorial materials.

In most states, the possession, exhibition, or dissemination of obscene and pornographic material is prohibited.[2] On the federal level, interstate transportation or mailing is a criminal offense. In spite of its widespread prohibition, no other area of enforcement has so many constitutional ramifications. In this chapter, we will look at these aspects of the problems: (1) a moral and political viewpoint, (2) history, and (3) law enforcement.

A LEGAL AND MORAL VIEWPOINT

What ultimately results from the analysis of facts pertaining to pornography and obscene writings is that a person's preconceptions about right and wrong are reinforced by logical arguments presented on several sides of the issue. The main viewpoints are legal and moral.

The Legal Viewpoint

The legal view is split between the absolutists and the conservatives. The absolutist position is this: "Congress shall make *no* law. . . ." It is simple. No law can be passed that would abridge the freedom of speech or press.[3] Another logical argument for the absolutist position is that the Supreme Court has merely assumed "obscenity" was never meant to be protected constitutionally. Conversely, the Court has also created categories of "free

[1]The Supreme Court has held that the state cannot pass laws that violate First Amendment rights. The 1986 Attorney General's Commission on Pornography alleged the court must modify its stance.

[2]In the case of *Stanley* v. *United States*, 393 U.S. 819 (1968), the Supreme Court ruled that possession of obscene materials in one's home is not a violation of the law.

[3]Alan F. Westin, *The Supreme Court: Views from Inside* (New York: Norton, 1961), pp. 173–90. In 1986, the Supreme Court voided a lower court decision in *Hudnut* v. *American Book Sellers* (475 U.S. 1132), calling the law misguided and an unconstitutional limit on free speech.

speech" by completely disregarding all previous standards established and treating "obscenity" entirely differently—as if it were not really speech.[4]

In *Pope* v. *Illinois,* the court held that in a prosecution for the sale of allegedly obscene materials, the jury should not be instructed to apply community standard in deciding the value question. Only the first and second prongs of the *Miller* test—appeal to prurient interest and patent offensiveness—should be decided with reference to "contemporary community standards." The ideas that a work represents need not obtain majority approval to merit protection, and the value of that work does not vary from community to community based on the degree of local acceptance it has won.

> The Supreme Court of the United States has assumed that one of the most basic of all liberties known to man, the freedom to read, write and think what he wants, is not protected by the First Amendment.[5]

This may appear to be a harsh statement, but it is true. The Court has said:

> . . . expressions found in numerous opinions indicate that this Court has always assumed that obscenity is not protected by freedoms of speech and press.[6]

Among the cases cited to justify such a conclusion, Judge Brennan, speaking for the Court, quotes *Chaplinski* v. *New Hampshire*:

> . . . there are certain well defined and narrowly limited classes of speech, the prevention of which have never been thought to raise any Constitutional problems. These include the lewd and obscene . . .[7]

Based on these assumptions and nothing more, the Supreme Court concluded that "obscenity is not Constitutionally protected."[8] As a result of this, the Court has mitigated censorship of both writers and readers.

[4]Larry R. Bass, "Free Speech v. Obscenity: The Only Alternative Is the Absolutists Approach." (Unpublished research report, Kent State University, March 12, 1969.)

[5]Ibid.

[6]*Roth* v. *U.S.,* 354 U.S. 476 (1957). Obscene material is not protected by the First Amendment, which was reaffirmed in the 1973 obscenity case of *Miller* v. *California.* In the case of *Pope* v. *Illinois* (481 U.S. 497), (85–1973), two tests of obscenity were modified.

[7]The cases cited for this were: *Ex Parte Jackson,* 96 U.S. 727, *U.S.* v. *Chase* 135 U.S. 255, *Robertson* v. *Baldwin,* 165 U.S. 275, *Public Clearing House* v. *Coynes* 194 U.S. 497, *Hoke* v. *U.S.* 227 U.S. 308, *Near* v. *Minnesota* 283 U.S. 687, *Hannegan* v. *Esquire* 327 U.S. 146, *Winters* v. *New York* 333 U.S. 507, and *Beubarnais* v. *Illinois* 343 U.S. 250. Brennan is correct; the Court has always just assumed that obscenity is not protected. Among the other reasons discussed was an international agreement that "obscenity should not be restrained." It is interesting to note that at the convention where this was decided, the people spent almost three days attempting to define obscenity. They finally agreed that obscenity could not be defined and then proceeded to outlaw something—even though they did not know what "it" was. Albert B. Gerber, *Sex Pornography and Justice* (New York: Lyle Stuart, 1965), p. 15.

[8]In 1987 the Oregon Supreme Court held that obscene literature is protected by the state constitution.

Also, by assumption, the Court has created categories of speech and has concluded that some speech categories have a "preferred position" and other categories do not. The Court has always held that the First Amendment allows ". . . the widest possible dissemination of information from diverse and antagonistic sources,"[9] and that ". . . Constitutional rights may not be denied simply because of hostility to their assertion or exercise."[10] Also, the Court has said "the idea of imposing upon any medium of communication the burden of justifying its presence is contrary to where . . . the presumption must lie in the area of First Amendment freedoms."[11] The Court has further held that picketing "may not be enjoined . . . merely because it may provoke violence in others,"[12] and that speech may include "vehement" and "caustic" language.[13] However, obscenity was different and enjoyed none of the usual protections, because it had always been assumed that it does not have these or other protections. Later cases have countered these arguments.

The Moral Viewpoint

The absolutist position is opposed by moralist factions, such as church and community groups who believe there is a moral view that should be heard. Obscenity issues from a moral viewpoint are much more important to these people than legal technicalities. Members of the Supreme Court in their 1988 decisions as well as in subsequent cases have been very careful not to alienate the community. They have, however, established national standards to regulate the sale of obscene and pornographic materials. Prosecution is now possible because of the specifics of the law. This change in the law has brought renewed efforts by the community to get enforcement. The great number of X-rated movies and newsstand publications is evidence the absolutists were gaining ground. Into this confusion has moved the power of organized crime. The public sits oblivious to the millions being made while legal actions are stalled in the appeals process.

The public attitude toward sex-oriented businesses and laws controlling these businesses are classic examples of why organized crime is doing so well financially. The National Advisory Committee on Criminal Justice as late as 1976 was unable to connect organized crime to the pornography

---

[9]*Associated Press* v. *U.S.*, 326 U.S. 1 at 20.

[10]*Watson* v. *Memphis* 373 U.S. 251.

[11]*Estes* v. *Texas* 381 U.S. 532 (1965). In Stewart's dissent (joined by Black, Brennan, and White), it is interesting to note that with the exception of Black, the others here have actually put the burden on the "medium of communication" to justify its presence in the obscenity area.

[12]*Milk Wagon Drivers Union* v. *Meadownoor Dairies, Inc.* 312 U.S. 287.

[13]*Rosenblatt* v. *Baer* 383 U.S. 75.

industry.[14] An example of the ties that should have been made by the Task Force was published in the *Los Angeles Times*. In 1975, the Los Angeles Federal Organized Crime Strike Force arrested four persons for attempting to shake down a dummy pornography shop set up by undercover FBI agents. In 1976, this extortionist, who was well known in organized crime circles, was finally sentenced to prison. After two years of appeals, the bond was finally revoked and the person remanded to prison when his appeal failed. In the meantime, this suspect had been indicted on multiple charges relating to interfering with commerce by threat and conspiracy. And this is only one case in one city.

To understand why we are so reluctant to come to a firm decision on the complexities of dealing with obscenity, a brief review of its history should help.

HISTORY

Plato predicted that democracy, of all forms of government, would produce the greatest variety of individual differences. To him this seemed the fairest of organizational concepts for all people. Yet he suggests that it is a state in which liberty can grow without limit at the expense of justice and order. This tends to set the stage for the evolution of obscenity. As freedom has expanded, so have the individual differences of morality with regard to human behavior.

One of the first recorded cases of obscenity in Anglo-American legal annals was that of the drunken drinking companion of Charles II of England. His combination of filthy oratory and urination on the street brought him a conviction for gross indecency. A similar action today would probably produce the same result.

In the early eighteenth century, several books were charged as being obscene. In at least one instance the court ruled the offense was spiritual rather than criminal, so the case should rightfully be tried in an ecclesiastical court. Later in the century, this thinking was overruled, and publication of obscenity was punished as a common law misdemeanor.

In the early American colonies, the common attitude toward obscenity was that it should not necessarily be permitted, but that each man should be held responsible for his own discretions in writing, pictures, or prints.

In 1875 in England, Lord Chief Justice John Campbell secured the passage of the Obscene Publications Act, which provided for the destruction of obscene books by a justice of the peace. The statute was widely and successfully employed. In 1869 in the United States, the case of *Regina* v.

---

[14]*Report of the Task Force on Organized Crime* (Washington, D.C.: U.S. Government Printing Office, 1976), p. 66.

Hicklin gave the law its most enduring definition of obscenity. Chief Justice Cockburn enunciated the famous test in that case:

> I think the test for obscenity is this, whether the tendency of the matter charged is to deprave and corrupt those whose minds are open to such immoral influences and into whose hands it may fall.

From 1869 to 1957, Cockburn's test dominated the law. Regulation of obscenity in the United States had, of course, predated the Hicklin decision. Indeed, the earliest reported case dealing with a book, *Commonwealth* v. *Holmes,* decided in Massachusetts in 1821, was a prosecution for selling Cleland's *Fanny Hill.* Most early prosecutions were, however, based on the common law. The Tariff Act of 1843 was the first piece of federal legislation dealing with obscenity. It was enacted without any challenge on the score that it was inconsistent with the First Amendment guarantee of free speech. The second major statute became law during the administration of Abraham Lincoln. This statute was directed against New York pornographers exploiting the loneliness of Union soldiers by authorizing criminal prosecutions for mailing obscene material and by empowering the Post Office to seize it.

In 1955–56, the Kefauver subcommittee investigations revealed some lucrative business enterprises based on pornography and controlled by organized crime. This subcommittee's findings brought about a series of changes in the laws to combat what had become a racket of gigantic proportions. The laws that evolved covered these areas: the transmittal of obscene material through the United States mail,[15] importation of immoral articles, and importation of merchandise contrary to law,[16] and transporting obscene matter in interstate or foreign commerce (by means other than by mail).[17]

In June 1973, the Supreme Court handed down three new decisions: *Miller* v. *California, Paris Adult Theatre I* v. *Slaton,* and *Kaplan* v. *California.* These cases raised further doubts about establishing consistency between the law of obscenity and constitutional doctrines regarding freedom of speech and expression. The fundamental constitutionality of obscene legislation was again thrown into chaos when the tougher guidelines were laid down and the determination of what is obscene was returned to a form of "local option." The Court, however, in restating the basic definition of obscenity, held that a work is obscene if:

> Sexual conduct is portrayed in a patently offensive way.
>   Taken as a whole, the material does not have serious literary, artistic, political or scientific value.

[15]18 U.S.C.A., 1461, 1463 (Supp. 1963).
[16]18 U.S.C.A., 545 (Supp. 1963).
[17]18 U.S.C.A., 1462, 1465 (Supp. 1963).

Taken as a whole, the material appeals to the prurient interest in sex. Whether the material meets this standard will be determined by the average reasonable adult.[18]

This restatement, which the court now adheres to, is an important modification of the law. In *Pope* v. *Illinois* (1987), the Court opted for a uniform resolution on obscenity. The Court said, "It is not whether an ordinary member of a given community would find (some) value in allegedly obscene material in the material taken as a whole." The value of a work may not vary from community to community based on the degree of local acceptance it has won.

This reaffirms part of the Roth case that said the relevant audience is the average reasonable adult and that the work must be considered as a whole, but it strongly intimates that any more restrictive test would violate the U.S. Constitution.[19]

Following this unrestricted decision, the Federal Communications Commission (FCC) on November 24, 1987, voted to modify their earlier order and permit radio and television stations to broadcast "indecent" programming between midnight and 6:00 A.M., thus nullifying the intended effect of the Pope decision.

Justice Douglas after the 1983 cases indicated the difficulty is that we do not deal with constitutional terms because "obscenity" is not mentioned in the Constitution or Bill of Rights. He further contended that unitl a civil proceeding has placed a tract beyond the pale, no criminal prosecution should be sustained. No more vivid illustration of vague and uncertain criteria could be designed than those we have fashioned.[20] Justice Harlan, in dissenting, indicated that to give the power to the censor as we do today is to make a sharp and radical break with free society. He maintains that conduct that annoys one may not bother another. In all of this we find that no sound legal ground has been assured.

LAW ENFORCEMENT: CENSORS WITHOUT LAWS

The enforcement of laws governing obscenity and pornography is generally a duty of the vice division of a police department. There is a wide area of controversy for certain materials, and there will generally be two major com-

[18]*Pope* v. *Illinois* (481 U.S. 497), U.S. Supreme Court Reports.

[19]*Encyclopaedia Britannica* (1987), 15th ed., (Chicago: Encyclopaedia Britannica, Inc., 1987), p. 615.

[20]In the case of *Pope* v. *Illinois,* the Miller case is modified. In the case of *New York* v. *Ferber,* 458 U.S. 747, the court held child pornography is outside the protection of the First Amendment if it involves scienter and a visual depiction of sexual conduct by children without serious literary, artistic, political, or scientific value.

munity groups in conflict. One group, made up of church leaders and representatives of other community organizations, will lead those who want to draw the dividing line near one extreme. Another group, equally vocal, will have a more diverse membership. It will include people sincerely interested in protecting the right of free speech and the accompanying right of a free press.[21] There will be authors and artists with a sound interest in all work. Some participants will come from groups interested only in the sale of the material in question. This latter group will again be divided, with one part made up of respectable publishers with a fear of excessive and unwarranted censorship and control of their publishing activity. The other group of publishers are those that publish the questionable materials, that make up magazines from press agents' releases, never name authors, and frequently change the name and often the place of publication.

Development of pornography cases is a highly technical and often frustrating experience for those officers involved in enforcement activities.[22] The June 1973 case of *Paris Adult Theatre I* v. *Slaton* illustrates how a civil action causes the filing of the civil complaint. With the judgmental criteria in the *Miller* v. *California* case now modified regarding community standards, those communities now wishing to take action against pornographers can rely on some logical court-decided standards.

An honest accommodation between the requirements of free speech, the hope of legitimate artistic expression, and the simple demands of common decency is being worked out, although it is not yet perfectly realized.

In Oregon's Earl Henry case of 1987 and the case of *Stanley* v. *State* (393 U.S. 819), the Supreme Court ruled that the possession of pornographic materials in one's home is not in violation and does not extend to transportation that is prohibited in 18 USC. 1462.[23]

The Sociological Reasoning Behind Obscenity Enforcement

It is not apparent that obscenity affects behavior. It does, however, dull the social sensitivity of the person's whole personality when it is exposed to obscene materials. Researchers say consumers do act aggressively, especially toward women. However, people usually avoid the real issue. Is there a connection between reading "pornography" and illegal conduct? Whatever

---

[21]The Larry Flint conviction under the Ohio Organized Crime law was the basis for a civil suit by Reverend Jerry Falwell. The civil case was found in favor of Flint in 1988.

[22]Alternatives for direct arrest are often used. Thus, state laws that do not allow for civil redress should be passed by the respective legislatures.

[23]This section has been reinforced by the 1984 Child Protection Act. This will reinforce U.S. Code Title 18 Section 1461 which makes it a violation to *knowingly cause the mails to be used to transport obscenity.*

the connection, if found, it should be beyond a "reasonable doubt." Most studies do not show this. Sheldon and Eleanor Glueck, authorities on juvenile delinquency, did not mention reading among factors that they found to be correlated to youth and delinquent behavior.[24]

Studies have been unable to provide a definite causal link.

In two 1988 texts, the issues of pornography are discussed. From both of these studies the reader is left to draw their own opinion about cause and effect.[25]

In light of findings by Feshbach and Malamath using improved research methodology, it might be logical to conclude that depiction of violence in erotica and pornography could be harmful. Feshbach says:

> The erotic presentation sometimes even approximates a how-to-do-it instructional film. . . . Further, the juxtaposition of violence with sexual excitement and satisfaction provides an unusual opportunity for conditioning of violent responses to erotic stimuli.[26]

The Kinsey study, however, had this to say about pornography and illegal conduct:

> When one reads in a newspaper that obscene or pornographic materials were found in an individual's possession one should interpret this information to mean that (1) the individual was probably a male of an age between puberty and senility, and (2) that he probably derived pleasure from thinking about sex. No further inferences are warranted.[27]

For those who are also convinced that the reading of "pornography" causes an abnormal deviant reaction, Dr. Gebhard indicated that sex offenses do not correlate with the possession of pornography or with the degree of response to viewing pornography.

Thus, there is considerable evidence to show a causal link between "pornography" and illegal conduct. This conduct is not known to the courts, or the researchers, so we must go to the agency that can best evaluate the impact or pornography on society.

A study of sensational sex abuse cases and some serial murder cases would tend to support the thesis that deviant behavior by defendants in these

---

[24]Charles H. Rogers, "Police Control of Obscene Literature," *Journal of Criminal Law*, LVII, 1966, p. 431.

[25]Walter Kendrick, *The Secret Museum: Pornography in Modern Culture*, (New York: Penguin Press, 1987), p. 119; and Edward Donnerstein, *The Question of Pornography: Research Findings and Policy Implications*. (New York: The Free Press, 1987). The 1984 National Commission on Pornography found that today's pornography is made plentiful, more violent, and more accessible.

[26]Seymour Feshbach and Neal Malamath, "Sex and Aggression: Proving the Link," *Psychology Today,* November 1978, pp. 111–22. Arrests in child abuse cases support this idea.

[27]Carol McGraw, "Child Smut Business Going Underground, *Los Angeles Times,* Sept. 16, 1985, p. 3.

cases is closely allied to the obsessive viewing of obscene materials. Since the passage of the Child Protection Act in 1964, investigations indicate that consumers and users of obscene materials are no longer satisfied with selling the materials. Many are involved in the business of selling the children through sophisticated computerized sex bulletin boards that, among other things, organize child sex vacations for pedophiles. Through underground agencies pedophiles can formally adopt foreign children for sexual use, including pornography.[28] The cause and effect argument is much like that associated with the chicken and the egg.

The Police Position

The basic police function in relation to obscene or pornographic material is to receive complaints, as in the case of other offenses, and discover the presence of such material as a part of their regular duties. The next step is to assemble evidence rather than make physical arrests. If there appears to be a violation of the law, evidence should be presented to the proper prosecuting authorities.

The police position, as viewed by the late Frank Dyson, former chief of police in Dallas and Austin, Texas, can be drawn from this speech he gave in 1971:[29]

> A police officer has always been the man in the middle—the umpire in the game of life. He does his best to make judgment calls according to the rules. But, there are times when the rules of the game are not clearly defined . . . and the police are caught between the rock and the hard place. Let me cite an example. We have received many calls from citizens asking why we don't do something about the showing of so-called skin flicks in Dallas . . . why we don't do something about the dirty books that are being sold?
>
> We answer calls of this type with requests for as much information as the caller can provide and then conduct follow-up investigations. If we have what we consider to be a solid case—based on city and state statutes—we ask the City Attorney or the District Attorney to accept a case. Then, it's up to the jury and the courts.
>
> To say that the issue is still somewhat clouded is an understatement. This should give you some idea of how difficult it has been for police agencies, the District Attorney's office and the courts to deal with the pornography problem.
>
> Pornography *is* a problem in Dallas. A report from our Special Investigations Bureau states there are fourteen pornographic bookstores in Dallas. It further states that there are nineteen pornographic theatres and six porno-

---

[28]Paul Shuit, and Paul Jacobs, "Law likely to lead to stronger curbs on pornography," *Los Angeles Times,* April 16, 1986, p. 3.

[29]Speech given by the late Frank Dyson, former chief of police, Dallas and Austin Texas, on television, 1971. These general rules are still applicable in 1991.

graphic lounges, some of which have "live" pornographic stage shows. Fifteen producers and distributors of movies and reading material are located in Dallas or in the immediate metropolitan area.

According to the report, the Dallas-based pornography industry has distribution outlets in cities all over the United States. Several of the Dallas-based pornographic industry distributors and producers have financial backing and direct business connections with larger out-of-state pornography dealers.

The pornography business in Dallas has all of the earmarks of an organized crime operation. We have learned that the organizations in Dallas are linked to an organization which owns and controls the production, printing, distribution and retail sale outlets for pornographic material. This enables the organization to receive profits from all levels of production and sale.

Pornography is a very lucrative business! Figures from *The Report of the Commission on Obscenity and Pornography* state that the cost for production of paperback pornographic books is ten to twenty cents . . . and that the cost for production of magazines of pornographic nature is forty-five to sixty cents. These periodicals sell anywhere from eight dollars to twenty dollars for each copy.

Exploitation films, according to the commission report, gross 70 million dollars annually! An "X" film produced in Dallas—actually filmed in the office of a dealer—grossed over 2 million dollars!

"Mob" tactics have been employed by members of the industry in Texas to achieve their ends. These include thirteen bombings and fires.

The gangland-style murder of Kenneth Hanna—found shot to death in the trunk of a car in Atlanta, Georgia—has been linked to the pornography business. It has been learned that Hanna met with a man known as the "Pornography King" just prior to the murder. At the time that Hanna was killed, he was under federal indictment for interstate shipment of pornographic materials.

Even more alarming to the police department in Dallas are the deaths of two persons in Texas—under very suspicious circumstances—persons who were linked with the pornography industry in the state. Furthermore, we are aware that a Dallas-based pornographic enterprise has—on several occasions—used strong-arm tactics to further their business interests in the state.

As I stated earlier, the pornography business in Dallas is *organized*. We are well aware that the affluent heads of the organization hire others to run their business outlets. And . . . that is why we intend to arrest and prosecute not only the managers, ticket sellers, projectionists and salesmen, but the leaders of the pornography industry in Dallas as well. The heads of these organizations are operating their business outlets and *they* are going to be held to account.[30]

METHODS OF ENFORCEMENT

The police in their enforcement activity should work in close liaison with the prosecuting attorney in any of the following methods.

---

[30]In March 1973, this enforcement policy led to the seizure of the film "Deep Throat" on three separate occasions. These cases were not upheld; this film is still playing in theaters around the country.

Action Against Material

The first method is, in legal parlance, an action *in rem*. In other words, an action against the material itself.[31] This method is a statutory action that provides for the seizure of the obscene material upon court order; for notice and hearing; and for disposition of the material involved by ordering its destruction or ordering it returned to the owner. This type of proceeding is heard before a court without a jury. Applying the community standard, the court sits as the conscience of the community and rules on each piece of evidence suspected of being obscene.

Besides the foregoing advantage, the *in rem* action normally allows more expeditious determinations than are obtained in a trial by jury through criminal proceedings against an individual. It should be noted, too, that once the determination of the obscene character of the suspected material is made by the court through an *in rem* action, there is no bar to further criminal proceedings against the individuals involved in the sale, circulation, and distribution of the obscene material.

Injunction

A second form of proceeding that has been used with success, particularly in the state of New York, is an injunction against defendants enjoining them from the sale, circulation, or distribution of obscene material. The injunction proceedings provide for the seizure of the material, for notice, hearing, and disposition of the material by the court. The U.S. Supreme Court has upheld the legality of the proceeding.[32] A similar purpose may be served through injunction as by the *in rem* procedure. The injunction is an expeditious method of handling a given case where there are several defendants. Here again, criminal prosecution can be instituted after the court has adjudicated the character of the questioned material.

Prosecution

The third and most common method of handling suspected obscenity is by direct criminal prosecution against the purveyors for the sale, circula-

---

[31]See Vernon's Annotated Missouri Statutes, Vol. 38, Sect. 542, 380 to 542, 420. In re. Search Warrant of Property at 5 W. 12th Street, Kansas City, *Missouri* v. *Marcus*, et al., 3344 S.W. 2d 119. Broad civil injunctive relief against pornography-related businesses is barred by the prohibition of prior restraints, regardless of the number of underlying obscenity convictions.

[32]*Kingsley Books* v. *Brown*, 354 U.S. 436, 77 Supreme Court 1325. In 1989, the California Supreme Court ruled it was illegal to use zoning laws to prohibit any firm from doing business. This overturns the finding in *Playtime Theaters, Inc.* v. *Renton* (471 U.S. 1018).

tion, and distribution of the material. With the crowded criminal court dockets of today, this method is time-consuming and necessitates, somewhere in the proceeding, an adjudication of what is or is not obscene or salacious material. Prosecution does not necessarily achieve the ultimate purpose of removing such material from public availability, particularly while waiting for a case to be tried.

SUMMARY

Police receive many complaints concerning the sale or possession of certain magazines, books (particularly paperbacks), photographs, picture playing cards, motion picture films, comic book-type drawings, and various items with an objectionable theme. The police administrator should be aware of the social ramifications and the legal implications that follow these complaints.

There are known groups of organized criminals engaged in the distribution of pornography in all forms. Independent dealers may operate only at the convenience of confederated criminal organizations. This association may be unknown to an independent dealer because the tribute to pay bribes, provide for lobbyists, and other necessary expenses are included in the base price of a document or film. This is paid for by the publisher or producer as a cost of doing business.

There is a wide area of controversy for suspected obscene materials. Generally, two major groups are in conflict. One group, made up of church leaders and representatives of other community organizations, will lead those who want to impose rigid legal interpretations. Other groups will be more liberal in their attitudes. People who are sincerely interested in protecting the right of a free press will favor self-censorship. There will be authors, artists, and teachers with a sound interest in working with no limitations placed on their creativity.

Respectable publishers with a fear of excessive and unwarranted censorship and control of their publishing activity are going to be critical of all censorship. Other groups of publishers will not be so vocal but will use arguments of all groups for their benefit. This will be the organized group that publishes the trash, that makes up magazines from press releases, never names authors, and frequently changes the name and often the place of publication. Their only investment is in the pair of scissors and bottle of paste needed to make up the copy for the magazine. Their resources for distribution have been carefully selected and managed by the confederation.

In the interpretation of obscenity such as the Miller case of 1973, Justice Douglas indicated that obscene material now must meet the three-pronged test: (1) "whether the average person, applying contemporary community standards would find that the work, taken as a whole, appeals to the prurient interest, (2) whether the work depicts or describes, in a patently offensive way, sexual conduct specifically defined by the applicable state law, and (3) whether the work, taken as a whole, lacks serious literary, artistic, political, or scientific value."[33,34] In 1982, the Supreme Court ruled that the interpretation of child pornography was not required, according to state law, to meet the three-pronged test outlined above.

In the final analysis, to keep the police from becoming censors, a number of ways have been suggested to provide for case preparation and presentation of evidence to the prosecuting agencies who then must make the decision on specific material alleged to be obscene. Many police agencies do not concern themselves with the enforcement of obscenity laws simply because the case histories are so vague.

QUESTIONS FOR DISCUSSION

1. Discuss the dilemma for local enforcement agencies when "acting on statute law" and "honoring case decisions."
2. What are some of the merits of the *absolutist* position on obscenity?
3. Why are obscenity and pornography frequently dissociated from protected speech?
4. Identify the three general rules for establishing what is obscene as outlined in the *Miller* v. *California* decision of 1973 (modified by *Pope* v. *Illinois* decision).
5. What impact does the phrase "whether the work taken as a whole lacks serious literary, artistic, political, or scientific value" have on the publication of obscene materials?
6. In the case of *New York* v. *Ferber*, the Court held that the possession of obscene materials does not have to be specifically prohibited by law in the case of children. Discuss.
7. Why will the police position on obscenity enforcement usually split community attitudes that are otherwise quite cohesive?
8. Should there be "national standards" on sexual expression? (See *Pope* v. *Illinois*.)
9. Should content of the material as well as the "business" of peddling smut be considered in obscenity cases?
10. Is there a causal relationship between reading obscene materials and sexual crimes?
11. There are several ways in which the police may proceed against obscene materials. Discuss the merits and weaknesses of *in rem*, injunction, and direct criminal prosecution.

[33]Modified by *Pope* v. *Illinois* decision.

[34]The Illinois Supreme Court in 1977 held that a state may prosecute persons for obscenity even though the kinds of materials describing sexual conduct might not be specifically prohibited. This was reaffirmed in the case of *New York* v. *Ferber* for children. The 1985 Freeman case in California (procuring females to pose in lewd films), the Supreme Court failed to uphold the conviction of procuring for the purpose of prostitution.

12. How does the community disagreement on matters of obscenity benefit organized confederations in the distribution business?
13. Why are obscenity and pornography cited as classic examples of the "double standard" of law enforcement in the United States?

Part III

Other Crimes Related to Organized Methods

This part of the text focuses on business-related crimes and ideologically motivated crimes. The crimes described in Chapters 9, 10, and 11 are subject to control by organized crime groups, although most of them are not committed by the traditional confederations but are instead groups of business entrepreneurs who have developed systems to defraud the public.

White collar and related crimes (Chapter 9) are of four basic types, ranging from individual indulgence in crimes of an organized nature to highly organized groups that own and operate conglomerate empires. Chapter 10 covers some of the business transactions affected by organized criminal groups. There is a shopping list of criminal activities and a typology about how organized crime rips off the commercial interests in a community.

The late 1980s brought about the revelation and the investigation of massive public swindles perpetuated by groups of business persons. These crimes, often perpetrated with political collusion, include Irangate, corporate/military thefts, stocks and futures swindles, and dozens of other business-related frauds. While many of these are not traditional organized crimes, they are an extension of a criminal mentality that pervades some business enterprises that maintain anything goes as long as a profit is shown.

Included in each of the following chapters are cases citing the efforts of the criminal justice system to ferret out and prosecute the criminals.

Many of the crimes are outside the investigative roles of local government agencies, and, increasingly, federal task forces are moving in to investigate these frauds.[1] Entry by organized crime into legitimate businesses and the expansion of business groups into illegal endeavors has increased the investigative roles of state and federal agencies. According to the President's Crime Commission Reports, the entry of organized criminals into le-

---

[1]In January of 1989, six new regional task forces were created in the Justice Department to investigate stock, futures, and loan industry frauds.

gitimate businesses does not diminish the number of illegal enterprises in which they engage.

Of interest in the past year is the resistance that is developing in the business community about federal prosecutors use of the Racketeer Influenced and Corrupt Organizations (RICO) law. The law, sets specific guidelines for federal prosecutors to use (Appendix B).

The *Principles of Federal Prosecution Manual* also is very specific about the crime that the Organized Crime and Racketeering Section of the Justice Department must approve before RICO prosecutions can begin. It appears that Congress intended that RICO was to apply to syndicated gambling, loan-sharking, murder-for-hire, and violent crimes in aid of racketeering activity. Many of the prosecutors appear to have applied the law too liberally on stock frauds and on union activity cases. Future court cases will decide how the law is to be interpreted.

The last chapter in this part discusses a different kind of organized crime, the crime committed because of ideological commitment to a cause and an emotional commitment to the group. These are the reactionaries of the world, organized to meet a common need. In a sense they are dedicated to a criminal activity that requires organization to function. Because of the increased prevalence of militant group crimes and their impact on enforcement activities, they are included here.

9

Organized White Collar and Related Crimes

LEARNING OUTCOMES

1. Develop an awareness of the great number of commercial actions that are susceptible to organized white collar crime control.
2. Identify the ways in which white collar crime penetrates a business.
3. Recognize the social ramifications for a business community controlled by organized white collar crime operations.
4. Determine the impact of white collar crime on the economic stability of a community.
5. Know the general investigative techniques for controlling white collar crime.

Because of the number of violations that concern business enterprises, a large number of crimes have been classified as white collar crimes (see Appendix A). Crimes of a white collar nature may be described as (1) *intent* to commit a wrongful act or to achieve a purpose inconsistent with law or public policy; (2) *disguise* (of purpose); (3) *reliance* on the ignorance or carelessness of the victim; (4) *voluntary victim action* to assist the offender; and (5) *concealment* of the violation as defined by Edelhertz.[1]

In one of the best documents published at the state level on organized crime, the Pennsylvania Crime Commission identified what is commonly referred to as white collar crime affiliation in this manner: "A roster of our 375 legitimate businesses that were involved in the following ways with criminal syndicates: (a) total ownership, (b) partial ownership, (c) hidden interest, (d) use of business for some illicit purpose.[2]

[1]Herbert Edelhertz, et al., *Investigation of White Collar Crime: A Manual for Law Enforcement Agencies* (Washington, D.C.: U.S. Government Printing Office, April 1977), pp. 21–22. White collar crime was defined as "nonviolent" crime for financial gain. Because there is no established taxonomy of crimes, some of the related crimes may include violence.

[2]Pennsylvania Crime Commission, *Report on Organized Crime* (Harrisburg, Pa.: Office of the Attorney General, Department of Justice, 1980), p. 40. There are examples and additional details contained in A Report to the President and the Attorney General, *The Edge: Organized Crime, Business, and Labor Unions* (Washington, D.C.: U.S. Government Printing Office, March 1986).

Whether these crimes are organized will depend on how they are perpetrated. For example, credit card frauds, which are normally a one-person operation, become a type of organized crime if two or more persons get together and develop a scheme to further the criminal conspiracy. The same may be true of any of the categorized crimes in Appendix A.

To delimit and systematize the discussion of white collar crimes, those crimes that most frequently incur physical violence and thus come to the attention of the police have priority here. To orient both the officer and the citizen, the following concepts are considered important: (1) the impact of white collar crime on the social structure, (2) typology of the crimes and techniques of the criminal, and (3) techniques and rationale for investigating white collar crimes.

THE IMPACT OF WHITE COLLAR CRIMES ON THE SOCIAL STRUCTURE

Due to complexity of identifying the deleterious effects of organized crime, we will focus here on (1) general implications on the social impact of organized crime, (2) the economic impact of white collar organized crime, and (3) how business enterprises are penetrated by organized crime.

Social Impact

Salerno and Tompkins most accurately describe the social impact of organized crime and specifically crimes of a white collar nature in the statement that crime is so well integrated into our lives that we often do not notice it moving in or recognize its face when it arrives.[3] The book and the movie *The Godfather* and dozens of other documents have all attempted to point out how the criminal enterprise exists without police awareness, how the operations of an illegal enterprise naturally lead to influence and finally to domination of the legitimate business sector of society. The evolution into legitimate enterprise may be illustrated in this manner:

> A partner embezzles money from his firm to pay for the bets wagered with a bookie, who, in turn, converts much of this cash to wire services, the distribution of which is controlled by a highly sophisticated organization. Then, in order to cover his expenditures of company funds, the partner secures a loan from a loan shark suggested by the bookie. When usurious interest rates cannot be paid, the loan shark becomes a silent partner in the operation and shares in the profits of the company.

[3]Ralph Salerno, *The Crime Confederation* (Garden City, N.Y.: Doubleday, 1969). Losses from organized crime are estimated at $175 billion to $230 billion per year; James W. Coleman, *The Criminal Elite: The Sociology of White Collar Crime* (New York: St. Martin's Press, 1985).

Through the permissive attitude toward the crime of betting, society has sanctioned at least three other types of major criminal activity. Even veteran police officers still do not see the value of enforcing vice statutes. Unless the citizen and the field officer can visualize the connection between the single offender and the crimes of an organized nature, there is little hope of eradicating criminal organizations. Organized crime must be attacked at the street level as well as at the apex of the organization. Criminal confederations cannot be eradicated from the top, simply because authority and responsibility flow through too many insulating layers.

The importance of white collar crime in the social structure has been further described by Edelhertz:

> White collar crime is covert, and not immediate in impact. It is, therefore, difficult to move to the forefront of issues calling for public attention and a place in the priorities for allocation of law enforcement resources. Common crimes always appear more pressing, and no white collar victim clamors for attention. Yet, white collar crimes are serious, and must be investigated and prosecuted promptly. To ignore white collar crime is to undercut the integrity of our society, just as we ignore the safety of society when we fail to cope with common crime. To delay or postpone action is an abdication of enforcement responsibility and not an ordering of priorities.[4]

The difficulty of apprehension and the near impossibility of prosecution make white collar crime a strong ally for regular organized crime activities. A local officer must take the lead in preventing, detecting, and investigating crimes of this nature. These crimes frequently come to light in the investigation of traditional crimes and are presented here for the purpose of making the citizen and the field officer aware of white collar crime. Edelhertz further states:

> The important point to keep in mind is that some wrongful activity, or some aspects of a wrongful pattern of activity are committed by the use of guile and deception, and that there are statutes, methods of analysis, and techniques of investigation which will be particularly appropriate and effective in dealing with them.[5]

In many instances, the so-called white collar crimes will characterize violators rather than violation. Thus, we may be dealing with a person who, singly or with others, derives a living from these activities. More important, in relation to the discussion of organized crime, is the fact that individual crimes of a white collar nature are committed to cover losses incurred

---

[4]Herbert Edelhertz, *The Nature, Impact and Prosecution of White Collar Crime* (National Institute of Law Enforcement and Criminal Justice, LEAA, U.S. Department of Justice, May 1970), p. 1. See James Cook, "The Invisible Empire," *Forbes,* September 29–November 10, 1980 and Roy Rowan, "The 50 Biggest Mafia Bosses," *Fortune Magazine,* November 10, 1986, p. 24.

[5]Edelhertz, *The Nature, Impact and Prosecution of White Collar Crime.*

through affiliation or transaction with the traditional organized crime groups—embezzlement to cover losses on bookmaking activity, the purchase of inferior merchandise forced into a store through illegal pressure tactics, and the purchase of bad stocks and bonds not within the normal channels of government control.

Legitimate businesses must be concerned. Historically, during the more militant phases of labor-management conflict, both sides recruited goons from the organized underworld. As partial payment, a few businesspeople turned over certain commercial enterprises to criminal elements, while some labor officials forfeited union locals. Racketeering infestation intensified in ensuing years.[6] Many businesses have been taken over through factoring (the lending of money against accounts receivable or other asset collateral). This is done most frequently at a high interest rate (30 to 40 percent), and failure to repay in time may result in a partnership with a confederation.

Another illustration of the social impact of organized criminal groups is a case in which a suspect testified that he was the main worker in a $100 million airport theft ring. Thefts included such items as mail, diamonds, and securities that were fenced throughout the country. The securities were also used as loan collateral and security in illicit business deals. The illustrations are endless and increasing at such a rapid pace that local police action is almost totally ineffective (Figure 9–1).

Economic Impact

A number of techniques used by organized confederations have a substantial economic impact on society. These are, to mention only a few:

> The acquisition of massive amounts of money through illegal enterprises, and reinvestment of those funds back into the legitimate business market.
>
> The ability of the labor union to "squeeze" a business through corrupt and illegal tactics thus driving the cost of certain types of labor inordinately high. Therefore, prices are selectively out of proportion to the prevailing economic condition of society.
>
> Prices and interest rates are controlled through anticompetitive pricing.
>
> The use of strong-arm tactics to force legitimate businesses to sell out or come under the domination of confederation management.
>
> The losses to business through organized theft of stocks, securities, merchandise, counterfeiture, and trade secrets espionage.
>
> Bankruptcy fraud, where a company is forced into receivership through various guises.
>
> The retention of lobbyists to ensure that proper legislation is passed.

[6]Chamber of Commerce of the U.S., *Deskbook on Organized Crime* (Washington, D.C.: U.S. Chamber of Commerce, 1969), p. 9. See Ronald Goldstock, "Operational Issues in Organized Crime Control," cited in The National Institute of Justice, *Major Issues in Organized Crime Control* (Washington, D.C.: U.S. Government Printing Office), pp. 85–86.

Type of Business	How Obligations Are Incurred	How Debts Are Paid	Results
Bank, loan or investment company use laundered funds that come through "ghost"	Business experiences cash flow, needs funds for capital improvements, expansion	Company signs for personal or corporate loan, stock; secures options stock	Full or partial ownership in company; blind partnership; may put company in bankruptcy
Land development, real estate, builders	Use of pension funds, use of laundered funds invested back through foreign banks and loan companies, sweetheart labor contracts.	Outright ownership of property; ownership through trusts or relatives, property management companies, or silent partnership	Full or partial ownership of major properties; no strike assurance in construction
Casino gambling	Favorable licensing laws secured through political contacts, assurance of monopoly	Hidden control through stock, monopoly on supplies and equipment, and favors rendered	Hidden control of casinos, buildings, supplies, and equipment; corruption of government officials
Clothing	Money invested through loans; equipment furnished, raw materials supplied, labor contracts arranged or private contractors secured	Distributorships awarded both wholesale and retail; awarding of sewing and supply contracts to "private contractor"	Control of distribution; control of outside job contracts; setting of prices; no quality control; use of slave labor
Entertainment	Money invested through independent producers; "up-front" operators in places of entertainment	Silent partnerships, options on distributorships, retail outlets; use of nightclub talent provided by organized crime	Control of distributorship and retail outlets; use of outlets as fronts for bookmaking and prostitution

FIGURE 9-1 How business and organized crime relate.

The documentation of white collar crime has been steadily improving for the past decade; at least two major government grants have addressed this problem.

How Business Enterprises Are Penetrated by Organized Crime

The Chicago Crime Commission made this observation:

> We recognize the right of a person to choose his associates, but when a business opens its doors to the public, it must accept the correlary right of the public to know with whom it is doing business. . . .
> When a business open to the public is owned or operated by known members of the crime syndicate, keeps among its officers, directors and employees persons who have direct relationship with the syndicate or countenance open meetings of hoodlums on its premises, then we believe that the consumer is entitled to know these facts.[7]

Both the public and the police are entitled to know who these businesses are and how they operate. Although there is no simple way to illustrate how businesses are penetrated by organized crime, these illustrations from the study by Bers may establish some orientation. The reasons for penetration other than pure profit motive are these:

The quest for a safe haven for profits for illicit enterprises.

A desire for legitimacy.

Holdings in business may be viewed as a second base of power.[8]

Types of penetration are described by a number of authors. For example, Cressey cites these two basic forms:

Businesses legitimately purchased "with the fruits of crime" and operated—
Legitimately
Illegitimately.
Businesses illegitimately acquired and operated—
Legitimately
Illegitimately.[9]

---

[7]Copyright © 1979 by CW Communications, Inc., Framingham, Mass. 01701. Reprinted from *Computerworld.*

[8]Melvin Bers, *The Penetration of Legitimate Business by Organized Crime: An Analysis* (National Institute Law Enforcement Assistance Administration, U.S. Department of Justice, 1970), p. 12.

[9]Donald R. Cressey, *Theft of the Nation* (New York: Harper & Row, 1969).

The scope of these operations would include but not be limited to the activities described by Bers.[10]

Legal holding, legally operated.   In addition to profit, this constitutes a base of power and influence for organized crime. For example, liquid assets such as cash hoards, domestic bank deposits, stocks and other securities, foreign bank deposits and other foreign assets, holdings in real estate and other normal business functions shield organized criminal activity.

Predatory or parasitic exploitations.   For example, coercion and extortion such as sweetheart contracts, threat of labor difficulties, loan shark connections and forced purchase of supplies and services. Bankruptcy fraud adds a threat to these techniques.

Monopoly.   The limitation of entry into a business by the destruction of competitors and threats of new entrants. Illegal price fixing such as voluntary or forced collusion.

Unfair advantage.   For example, discrimination in wage and other standards by control and manipulation of labor organizations and pressures from labor organizations. Kickbacks in trade associations. Guaranteed market shares by the intimidation of customers and suppliers securing government contract through corruption. Other means such as the adulteration of goods and failure to observe minimum standards as set by law.

Businesses supporting illicit enterprise and receiving reciprocal support.   For example, business providing outlets for illicit services such as gambling, narcotics, prostitution, and loan sharking. Businesses supportive to organized crime by covering as "legitimate income," through normal profits and through "strong-arm" retainers whose contributions to a business are fictional. Business facilities for hijacking, robbery, burglary; providing outlets for stolen property.

Through the processes just described, there is little chance that any business showing a profit is not going to be penetrated to some degree by elements of organized crime. The ease and magnitude of this fertile field of endeavor is shown in the Bers study. In an economic analysis of figures cited by authorities, about two-thirds of the national elite, in terms of national income, consists of associates of organized crime.[11] If, in fact, these figures are true, $30 billion per year in profits are siphoned off by organized criminal elements. Investments, as cited by the Internal Revenue Service, indicated some 98 percent of 113 major organized crime figures were found to be involved in 159 individual businesses.[12]

Bers further stated:

[10]Bers, *The Penetration of Legitimate Business by Organized Crime*, p. 12.

[11]Ibid., p. 13, updated at $63 billion from narcotics, $22 billion from gambling, $8 billion from other crimes, $50 billion from white collar crimes, for a total of about $150 billion. New estimates indicate the total profits may exceed $230 billion.

[12]Ibid., pp. 14–15.

The total value of industrial and business assets for the national economy is approximately $3 trillion. If organized crime associates control as much as $30 billion, their share is 1 percent. Such a share is far from "takeover," but it is impressive nevertheless. And it would be cause for grave concern on several counts even if the share were half this size, as may well be the case, given the volume of funds thought to be simply hoarded or held abroad, and even if all holdings were in companies currently operated without resort to illegal methods.[13]

Perhaps of equal social impact would be the predatory and parasitic activities normally associated with organized criminal activity. For example, Walsh, in his investigation of corruption at the nation's airports, says:

> The other half of vice on air freight is the teamsters. If the union can get a single master contract with the air freight industry, it could back up future negotiatory demands by shifting down the whole business at will. A nationwide contract would also be a boost to the teamsters' campaign to organize thousands of other non-cargo airline employees with the control of the air cargo industry alone; however, the teamsters would be in a position to close an entire airport, or perhaps all major airports. If that happens, the public can expect to pay more to fly.[14]

This method of operation works well in every industry. For the confederation there is no violation in gaining power, and once power is secured, there is no one in a position to furnish sustained information to gain a conviction and unseat those in power.

The A&P case is another example of the coercive methods used by organized criminals. In this case, a member of the syndicate attempted to force A&P to stock an inferior grade of soap. When the store refused, there was retaliation against both the employee and the store. By not yielding to this pressure and seeking police protection, the store was saved from buying into a partnership with hoodlums.

Still, if A&P represents the scale of enterprise that is necessary to resist such predations, there is little solace in the fact that approximately 55 percent of all industrial and business activity is conducted by firms that are in manufacturing, have less than 250 employees, and make less than $5 million annually. (Thus, they are classed as small businesses.) Approximately 95 percent of all business firms in this country meet these criteria.

Monopolies are so numerous and the schemes so diversified that we

---

[13]Ibid., p. 16.

[14]Denny Walsh, "The 'Second Business' at our Airports: Theft," *Life,* 1971. Later case examples are presented in R.C. Thomas, "Organized Crime in the Construction Industry," *Crime and Delinquency,* 23, 3 (July 1977), 304–11. See James W. Coleman, *The Criminal Elite:* The Sociology of White Collar Crime, New York, St. Martins Press, 1985, for a sociological review of white collar crime. Also see *The Wall Street Journal,* "Scams on the Rise in Health Insurance," July 22, 1988, section 2, p. 1.

can identify only basic schemes (see Appendix A). Thirty-six different frauds are identified in the Battelle study completed in 1977.[15]

TYPOLOGY OF WHITE COLLAR CRIMES
AND TECHNIQUES

To identify criminal activity by function is to oversimplify the interrelationship of one activity to another in the highly sophisticated organizations. The activities described in this chapter are closely interwoven with vice and drugs. In the section discussing loan sharking, we are talking about the manipulation of money and thus the catalyst that holds all organized criminals together in their struggle for power.

These major functional areas are arbitrarily chosen as those white collar crimes with which the police most frequently deal: (1) racketeering, (2) the loan shark business, and (3) black markets.

Racketeering

Gangsterism or racketeering, as it relates to white collar crimes, furnishes the means by which the confederations establish a monopoly or through extortion cause legitimate firms to pay tribute in order to operate.

Racketeering is one of the most pervasive forms of organized crime. Its use against businesses has been an American innovation that is now receiving added attention. Under 18 USC Section 1961–68, the Racketeer Influenced and Corrupt Organizations (RICO) law says that racketeering activity is committed by an individual committing any two of a variety of crimes (24 separate types of federal crimes and 8 types of state felonies) and is subject to severe penalties. The two key elements for prosecution under RICO are these: (1) a pattern of racketeering activity and (2) the existence of an "enterprise" with which the individual has some connection. This definition has broadened the scope of federal prosecutions. While all has not gone well for this law, there have been notable prosecutions and the courts have tended to uphold questions raised about the act.[16]

---

[15]Edelhertz, et al., *Investigation of White Collar Crime,* Appendix C.

[16]J. Atkinson, "Racketeer Influenced and Corrupt Organizations—18 USC Section 1961–68—Broadest of the Criminal Statutes," *Journal of Criminal Law and Criminology,* 69, 1 (spring 1978), 1–18. See also G.R. Blakely, "On the Waterfront—RICO (Racketeer Influenced and Corrupt Organizations) and Labor Racketeering," *American Criminal Law Review,* 17, 3 (winter 1980), 341–65. RICO was updated in 1987. See Appendix B. The courts have upheld hundreds of cases in the past decade. However, see "RICO's Broken Commandments," *The Wall Street Journal,* January 26, 1989, editorial. The indiscriminate use of RICO statutes will bring changes as it relates to stock, futures and commodity trading.

Major racketeering operations have been traced to regional crime families. Their operations, although varying from state to state, accommodate to weakness in local laws but still show common patterns. For example, in Illinois, acceptance agencies can deal in stocks, bonds, warehouse receipts, bills of lading, and other commercial paper. These companies can serve as a cover for disposing of stolen merchandise, the transfer of money between illegal organizations, the manipulation of political bribery, the coverup of loan sharks, and the cooling-off of hot or counterfeit money. "Skimming" from Nevada's gambling casinos proved to be a lucrative sideline for organized elements.

The basic factor of success in racketeering is the exertion of the proper amount of pressure so there is no alternative for the victim. Once racketeers are in a position to exercise pressure and force, they are able to extort levy and tribute. Reckless identified two types of racketeering: the *simon-pure* and the *collusive agreement.* An example of the simon-pure involves one individual who can levy power with a minimum of organization and affiliation. The collusive agreement, however, is an interlocking conspiracy. This type of racketeering operates like wheels within wheels, which makes it difficult to expose.[17] Political action committees become the wheel's hub.

Rackets are further reduced to two fundamental subtypes, monopoly and associations. The monopoly is the simplest type that employs the aid of politicians. In this example, the racketeer places himself as a necessary middleman. The association type approximates the collusive agreement among businessmen, labor leaders, and racketeers for the purpose of fixing prices and preventing undercutting. In this fundamental type, the racket is one in which tradespeople or shopkeepers are forced to join and pay dues for protection against violence to their persons and property. Furthermore, the criminal enterprise is able to dictate terms of doing business and the control of prices of commodities. In discussing the rackets, functions frequently overlap these classifications, and many criminal enterprises may be identified as belonging to both classifications.

The monopoly.   Criminal monopoly is the use of criminal means to destroy competition.[18] It may be by the levy power with little affiliation or the collusive association bordering on extortion. The curtailing of competition by threat or by force has been a common method of operation that may take in both definitions by Reckless. Weston and Wells describe how the confederations have gained and retained their power:

[17]Walter C. Reckless, *The Crime Problem* (New York: Appleton-Century-Crofts, 1961), chap. 15. James W. Coleman, *The Criminal Elite,* expands on this classification into organizational and occupational crimes.

[18]Paul B. Weston and Kenneth M. Wells, *Criminal Investigation: Basic Perspectives* (Englewood Cliffs, N.J.: Prentice-Hall, 1980), p. 431.

The object of the syndicate (confederation) is to get protection from competition when the law will not allow it or legal techniques cannot be used to achieve it. The syndicate (confederation) members learned the technique of curtailing competition in their black market areas of prostitution, gambling and narcotics through strong-arm methods that originated in the beer and whiskey-selling days of Prohibition. Strong-arm tactics are also used to bulwark the operation of one of the syndicate's (confederation's) firms to buy solely from syndicate suppliers. Linen and laundry services, sale of food products, and placement of vending machines are businesses in which this tactic has been used. A legal business, illegally operated by strong-arm methods, can be a profitable enterprise under organized crime.[19]

The association.   As identified by Reckless, the association is probably organized crime's most potent ally for gaining control of activities that will eventually lead the confederations into legitimate businesses. These associations include such organizations as trade and labor unions, and other organizations in which access to business is through a third party. Activities may include the price-fixing of merchandise. For example, a criminal cartel may exist if the garment trade eliminates cut-throat competition by an agreement on prices and wages, hiring thugs to enforce the agreement.[20] This may or may not violate a federal regulation or statute, except that coercion to enforce such agreement may lead to a crime.

The associations serve as a clearing house to get organized criminals into a trade where cheating may be more easily conducted. For example, in the bar business, who knows how many drinks are served, how many are given away as business favors and bribes, how much liquor is brought in the back door (not invoiced from the regular sources), and how many employees are hired thugs not related to the conduct of the business?

Labor racketeering.   Organized labor's control of the work force through hiring hall practices has been a sad exploitation of human dignity. Both overt and subtle abuses involving the hiring halls have included but are not limited to the following abuses:

Unethical local union officials cause blackmailing of contractors through the withholding of labor forces unless certain special conditions are met such as overtime, attachment of wages to payoff, hiring hall bookies and gamblers who are kicking back to union leaders.

Loan sharks, with the cooperation of crooked union management, maintained officers at the hiring hall, and the hiring was not done unless loans were paid up, usually at a bonus rate in addition to the already usurious rate.

---

[19]Ibid., p. 432. Also see U.S. Department of Justice, *Report to the Nation on Crime and Justice,* (Washington, D.C.: U.S. Government Printing Office, 1988), p. 9.

[20]Thomas C. Shelling, "Economics Analysis and Organized Crime," *President's Commission on Organized Crime,* (Washington, D.C.: U.S. Government Printing Office, 1967), p. 117. Also see G. Robert Blakely, *Definition of Organized Crime in Statutes,* (Washington, D.C.: U.S. Department of Justice, 1985).

Raises, acquired through pressure tactics of the hiring hall, may be siphoned off into flower funds and other special projects not in the regular union dues.

Concessionaires, peddling lottery tickets, stolen merchandise, and other side businesses, find a mecca about the hiring halls. All pay a fee for the right to service the workers.

Arrests made by local officers in the vicinity of the hiring halls are compromised and settled out of court through union pressure tactics. Lower fines negotiated through the hiring hall representatives never show on court documents. The loyalty of union managers pays well.

The President's Commission on Organized Crime reported that more and more businesses were turning to organized crime for their competitive edge. Business executives are increasingly being involved in laundering illegally gotten money; lawyers and union leaders either share in these and other illegal activities or look the other way. Rudolph Guiliani, the U.S. prosecutor for southern New York, predicted in 1988 that there would be greater efforts toward the investigation of the Teamsters' Union. Many experts have predicted that the use of RICO in trying union members would probably render the Act useless.

The Loan Shark Business

Loan sharking may be defined as a financial transaction at usurious or exorbitant rates of interest, usually without collateral and with the fear of physical force to guarantee payment.

Shylocking, or money lending outside the regulation of government, has persisted throughout history. Ancient Rome had its money lenders, and English history identified many famous shylocks. Not until the past four decades, however, has organized crime moved in to make it a lucrative nationwide business. Many major cities rank loan sharking as the number one moneymaker for the confederations. The dollar amounts are estimated nationally at $350 million to over $1 billion.[21]

The economic impact of loan sharking and the ultimate cost to the general public are undoubtedly substantial. Through loan sharking, professional criminals siphon off significant resources from the legitimate economy to finance additional illegal activity. Loan sharking is the fifth-ranking crime in terms of financial cost to the public; adding the cost of government ef-

---

[21]President's Commission on Law Enforcement and Administration of Justice, *Task Force Report: Crime and Its Impact: An Assessment* (Washington, D.C.: U.S. Government Printing Office, 1967), p. 53. Newer scams include swindles through boiler room solicitations, property crimes, and computer-related crimes in bank and stock market operations.

forts to combat the problem, the total price to the public becomes a matter of concern to every person, whether a victimized borrower or not.[22]

Loan sharks depend on the comfort of the confederation affiliation when force is necessary in collecting payments. It is also natural that loan sharking be affiliated with the organized groups, because many of the loans are made to cover confederation-sponsored gambling losses. Loan sharking, of all organized criminal activities, is the linchpin that controls every other segment of organized crime.[23] Through proper manipulation, the shylocks are in a position to encourage business takeovers, to cover gambling losses, to encourage burglaries by giving loans against merchandise that will go through a "fence" for stolen goods, and keep loan recipients obligated through usurious rates and through loan contracts that cannot be paid off. When a person is in control of money, his influence is enhanced. The flow of illegally acquired money through loan sharks destroys the continuity for tracing such funds. Because of transactions through loan sharks, economists' and accountants' estimates on the amount of money involved in organized crime are a combination of guess and speculation.

In his research into the shylock business, John Seidl defines three common elements for loan sharking:

> The lending of cash at a high interest rate.
>
> The borrower-lender agreement which rests on the borrower's willingness to pledge his and his family's physical well-being as collateral against a loan with its obvious collection implications.
>
> . . . a belief by the borrower that the lender has connections with ruthless criminal organizations.[24]

Based on these elements, a multimillion-dollar industry has evolved. Actual field operations do not necessarily dictate violence as a means of collection, nor are all debts collected. Often a bad debtor will be pressured by threats and intimidation; when these methods fail to work, the debt is forgotten. This type of settlement, however, is not the type of image that is good for organized crime confederations. If the citizen has an honest police department, district attorney, and court to depend on, there is usually little to fear from the loan sharks of organized crime. The *fear* of reprisal is organized crime's greatest collection tool.

---

[22]An update on contemporary loan sharking can be found in R. Goldstock, "Controlling the Contemporary Loanshark—The Law of Illicit Lending and the Problem of Witness Fear," *Cornell Law Review,* 65, 2 (January 1980), 127–289.

[23]Much of the loan shark industry is conducted by individuals not allied with any organization. This book is concerned with the organized segment.

[24]John Michael Seidl, " 'Upon the Hip'—A Study of the Criminal Loan Shark Industry." (Ph.D. Dissertation, Harvard University, December, 1968), p. 30.

Unfortunately, it is not always an individual who must do business with loan shark operations. Business firms borrow funds from "money lenders." Companies that finance a product in production and prior to sale are often controlled by questionable groups who lend at usurious rates. A business that must borrow this kind of money may find itself with perpetual high interest rates. The detailed operation of business lenders has been described by the Institute of Defense Analysis. In another study, shylocking was described as a multibillion-dollar guaranteed annual income for the confederation.[25]

The flow of money through the illegal operators is practically impossible to trace (Figure 9–2). The method of operation of the individual engaged in the business will vary according to geographic location and the clientele.

How the loan shark operates.   Money coming into the confederation will be pushed into circulation through the hierarchy and ultimately through the street loan shark. The street shark usually pays from 3 to 4 percent interest per week for syndicate money. He, in turn, will loan it to "street friends" for 5 percent per week (approximately 260 percent per year). Deals generally occur through acquaintances who become known to the street loan shark, or referral through friends. Because of the nature of the business, a loan shark may be involved as a receiver of stolen property. Furs and diamonds at 10 percent actual value can often cancel a debt.

Loan activities are basically of two types: (1) "vigorish," which provides for weekly payments of interest only, payments on principal being made when "convenient" to the borrower; and (2) "pay down," which provides for weekly payments of interest and principal for eventual liquidation of the entire debt. The first is most harmful to borrowers because it commonly results in their having paid much more than the initial loan, while still owing at least that entire principal amount.[26]

Black Markets

There are basically two forms of black market operations in which organized criminals are involved: (1) the black market commodity, and (2) the black market monopoly. Activities such as narcotic sales will cover both categories because it is the monopolizing of an illegal commodity.

The black market commodity includes a vast number of consumer goods and services. Illegal transactions, pornography, and all contraband

[25]Institute of Defense Analysis, LEAA, *Task Force Report: The Courts* (Washington, D.C.: U.S. Government Printing Office, 1967), p. 3.

[26]"Loan Sharking: The Untouched Domain of Organized Crime," *Columbia Journal of Law and Social Problems,* pp. 94–95.

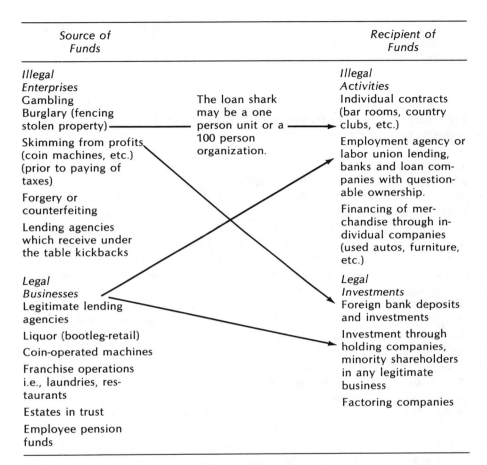

Source of Funds		Recipient of Funds
Illegal Enterprises Gambling Burglary (fencing stolen property) Skimming from profits (coin machines, etc.) (prior to paying of taxes) Forgery or counterfeiting Lending agencies which receive under the table kickbacks	The loan shark may be a one person unit or a 100 person organization.	*Illegal Activities* Individual contracts (bar rooms, country clubs, etc.) Employment agency or labor union lending, banks and loan com- panies with question- able ownership. Financing of mer- chandise through in- dividual companies (used autos, furniture, etc.)
Legal Businesses Legitimate lending agencies Liquor (bootleg-retail) Coin-operated machines Franchise operations i.e., laundries, res- taurants Estates in trust Employee pension funds		*Legal Investments* Foreign bank deposits and investments Investment through holding companies, minority shareholders in any legitimate business Factoring companies

FIGURE 9-2 Flow of money into and through the loan shark industry. Money from legal or illegal enterprises may be channeled through legal or illegal recipients.

are prohibited by law, as are reselling tickets above purchase price (scalping) and wartime control on restricted items. The second party to these transactions will usually be aware of their illegality.[27]

The black market monopoly occurs when the marketeer enjoys a protected market in the same way that a domestic industry is protected by a tariff. The black marketeer gets automatic protection through the law itself from all competition unwilling to pursue a criminal career.[28] For example, a labor racket is a local monopoly. A second party is frequently unaware the transaction is illegal until it is too late.

[27]Commission Report, *Organized Crime,* p. 116.
[28]Ibid., p. 117.

These classifications are important only in that they clearly illustrate the complexity of prosecutions at the apex of an organization. Frequently, it is the crime itself that must be attacked if organized groups are to be eradicated.

TECHNIQUES AND RATIONALE FOR INVESTIGATING WHITE COLLAR CRIME

The suggestions offered here are for the orientations of the field officers who will have an opportunity to investigate white collar crimes. What does the field officer look for in detecting and seeking out criminals and criminal activity that may be affiliated with organized crime of a white collar nature?[29]

The officer should review crime reports and study newspaper stories of stock market manipulations and "suspect business transactions" for names and locations of persons living in the district who are involved in activities that may be unethical, although not necessarily illegal. A loose surveillance by the district officer on suspected persons frequently reveals good intelligence information on many varieties of white collar crimes.

Frequently, in the investigation of business burglaries, robberies, and other crimes, there will be attempts to cover shortages of partners and associates. For example, at a burglary scene, where checks were taken, an officer investigating the check ledger for missing checks was notified by a secretary that a loan company received checks from the business at weekly intervals in round number amounts. Subsequent intelligence and investigation work revealed the loan company was a collection agency for a syndicate bookmaking operation. In a second case, the discovery by an employee of a large number of stock certificates in a business safe that had been burglarized led to the solution of an interstate burglary and embezzlement gang. Both the field officer and the citizen, if properly trained and reasonably alert, can be effective contributors to the intelligence process.

The patrol officer and the businessperson in street contacts should listen for hints that embezzlement, corruption in government, extortion, labor racketeering, and dozens of other crimes may be occurring. Prostitutes, cab drivers, and bartenders are notorious for knowing what goes on. The field officer is in daily contact with these people and should be encouraged to submit simple intelligence information reports as part of daily reporting activity.

---

[29]Weston and Wells, *Criminal Investigation,* p. 425. The concept of "wraparound" is important to the investigation of confederation operations. This means organized criminals trade off in every business of organized crime until the operation is wrapped around every possible means of making money.

For example, a prostitute in one case was able to identify the "torch men" for a maverick labor union effort to unionize restaurants. This information came to a uniform field officer from the informer because he made his patrol work a challenge rather than just routine patrol.

The uniformed officer is frequently a liaison between specialized units in large city departments and departments in rural areas. He or she deals with field situations that may cross specialized lines such as narcotics, homicides, burglaries. If proper procedures are not established to debrief this officer, valuable information will not be gathered, compared, and evaluated. Roll call training sessions, when conducted regularly and properly, may bring this type of information to light.

The field officer should know his or her district and the knowledge should be put to work for a department. Investigators who desire information on a particular person or place over a long period of time should be forced to sit down and review cases that might be generated from some intelligence collection. Investigators, who are conducting an investigation, if the investigation will not be compromised or endangered, should be required to sit down with officers who are assigned to a district. All too often, investigations are ineffective simply because "secrecy" preempts logical investigative procedures. All too often, the "need to know policy" imposed by investigators at all levels of government is detrimental to an investigation. Uniformed patrol officers should be trained to render such aid, and liberal use should be made of their knowledge and contacts in a district or precinct.

In gaining an overview of white collar crime, the field officer must see how governmental processes are subverted through corruption, how business enterprises are penetrated, and how prosecutions are thwarted.

SUMMARY

In this chapter it has been pointed out that organized criminals are deeply involved in business ventures. This involvement may come about through a number of monopolistic and coercive practices. These practices are highly refined techniques designed to avoid the publicity that may associate a business venture with confederated crime organizations. Because publicity is avoided, the public will frequently be active participants in street level crimes that support the organized criminal hierarchy. In citing the elements of white collar crime it has been shown how easily business enterprises are penetrated, why this association is desirable for the organized group, and how each criminal enterprise operates within these classifications: (1) legal holding, legally operated, (2) predatory or parasitic exploitation, (3) monopoly, (4) unfair advantage, and (5) businesses supporting illicit enterprise and receiving reciprocal support.

Three major subcategories of white collar crimes have been identified. Racketeering has been discussed first because through monopoly or association, the confederations are able to exert control over any business. In labor racketeering, the coercive forces of an unethical or illegal act by a union can spell life or death for a business. The loan shark has been shown to be a vital and dynamic part of organized criminal power. Money manipulators through the loan shark make the confederations cohesive and powerful. Black markets, although normally associated with wartime shortages, also include products that are illegal or in short supply. Many organized criminal groups receive protection from the law while holding exclusive control over a business franchise such as city bus lines or ambulances.

Because of the variety of violations, how a crime is investigated will depend on the criminal methodology of an individual or group.

QUESTIONS FOR DISCUSSION

1. Identify and discuss those businesses in a community that may be subject to organized criminal influences.
2. Do the citizens of a community support an activity such as bookmaking? How may this relate to subversion of business?
3. Do city political figures know who hold their franchises? Are there past histories of criminal records that show a common pattern?
4. Are the public services, such as airports, bus, and train stations, subject to large theft losses?
5. Do the crime rates of theft and burglary indicate that merchandise is being fenced?
6. Are businesses controlled by permit or some other form of regulation? Are complaints against firms that fleece the public thoroughly investigated?
7. Who owns the coin-operated machines?
8. Who may control local labor unions, and is coercion through strikes and stoppages a common method of operation?
9. Are there an unusual number of harassment activities against businesses in the community? How is RICO used to harass legitimate businesses?
10. Are bids let by public agencies to questionable contractors for poor work?

10

Organized Crime: Frauds and Thefts

LEARNING OUTCOMES

1. Know how the confederations actually control and manipulate different businesses in the community.
2. Develop an awareness that some businesses in the community are more susceptible to organized crime control than others.
3. Understand in some detail how securities, including credit cards, are used to defraud.
4. Identify key elements of special frauds, including use and abuse of computers.
5. Recognize how political contributions from businesses affect organized crime.

There are more than 100 identified crimes closely affiliated with organized groups. It is fair to say that any transaction or any activity that requires trust may be subject to dishonest manipulation by an individual or by an organized group. In addition to the three categories listed in Chapter 9, there are these: (1) business acquisitions by racketeering, (2) manipulation and embezzlement of stocks, bonds, and credit cards, and (3) special frauds, swindles, and thefts.

BUSINESS ACQUISITIONS BY RACKETEERING

Officers at every level of the enforcement hierarchy will see business maneuvers, exchanges, and transactions for which there is no apparent reason. Officers will see organized crime figures engaged in almost every legitimate business enterprise. Businesses, such as the bars and restaurants, offer quick turnover and accounting methods that are easily manipulated. Thus, confederations are attracted to these businesses. Legitimate businesses are particularly susceptible to manipulation and coercion by organized criminal groups. Activities such as the following are only illustrations of events that are occurring in hundreds of locations each day of the year. Gangster infiltration of legitimate business through racketeering methods may be done in many ways.

The Coercive Contract With Public Agencies

An effective way to gain government contracts, for example, can be found in a San Diego County, California, case in which an organized crime member, with union assistance, moved in to force independent hauling contractors into joining the union or losing the right to work on a multimillion-dollar state highway project. When the independent operators were squeezed out, the organized crime member moved in as a prime subcontractor and with leased equipment did millions of dollars worth of contract hauling simply because he was able to eliminate the independent contractor as a competitor. In addition, in 1987, New York City building construction bids and food services were arranged for a 1% commission.

Strong-Arm Tactics

This method is still in popular use. It can bring a business into a cooperative arrangement in a swift fashion. For example, if a confederation decides a particular business location would be desirable for a bookie spot, lottery office, or pornography shop and the owner refuses to cooperate, a number of techniques are used.

Usually, the confederation will first try to "buy off" the business. They make the initial offer so attractive that it is difficult for the owner not to cooperate. If a cooperative agreement fails to materialize, a few threats against the owner's family may bring concessions.

If the owner will still not cooperate, mob-controlled distribution monopolies will not deliver services. For example, a restaurant depends on food supplies, garbage services, and miscellaneous services such as waiters, dishwashers, linens, glassware. The loss of any of these services will bankrupt a business. As a last resort, the business may be picketed, burned out, bombed, or other strong-arm tactics such as beatings or kidnappings may take place.

Often these actions take place without police knowledge. Even when brought to the attention of the police, nothing is usually done to protect the citizen. There is a very fine line in determining whether we are dealing with methods that may border on competitive business practices rather than criminal activities.

Legitimate business takeovers through racketeering tactics in such areas as coin-operated machines, loan and other fiscal operations, and the deceptive expenditure of public funds through public official and gangster association are but a few of the methods of business acquisition by outright acquisition, by corporate control, or by the corrupt use of employees already in the organization. The infiltration by whatever means includes "mom and pop" stores as well as stockholder influence in many of the nation's conglomerates.

MANIPULATION AND EMBEZZLEMENT OF STOCKS, BONDS, AND CREDIT CARDS

This section concentrates on some financial manipulations that constitute less than complete control of a business. These manipulations of the financial strength of an organization can have a disastrous impact on the operation of a business. When organized crime, through fiscal manipulation such as manipulation and embezzlement of stocks or bonds, can control the operation of that organization, it is then easy to maintain a cover for other illegal operations.

When asked about organized crime involvement in the theft and counterfeiting of stocks and bonds, the late FBI Director Hoover made this reply:

> I would not credit La Cosa Nostra or the other elements of organized crime with all the thefts on Wall Street, but quite frequently either members of La Cosa Nostra or their close associates turn up in our investigations.
> One . . . case involves eight separate thefts totaling about $17 million in which we have made a number of arrests and recovered many of the stolen securities. One of the persons we arrested is known to us as a member of La Cosa Nostra and additional arrests are pending. Before we were called into the case, the subjects were able to realize in the neighborhood of $1.8 million.[1]

In other multimillion-dollar cases, spurious covers were developed for laundering stolen and counterfeit securities. Brokerage firms had agents prepare phony documents to show prior ownership of stolen securities. This laundering process, when completed, filtered clean documents back through various corporate structures, and the monies were then fed into legitimate businesses.

Other common crimes perpetrated against businesses are illegal leveraged buy-outs, needless bankruptcy frauds, including the scam of planned bankruptcy and fraudulent concealment, where assets are concealed in anticipation of insolvency. Another popular fraud scheme is the *boiler room,*

---

[1]J. Edgar Hoover, "The Bull Market in Stock and Bond Thefts," *Nation's Business,* March 1970, p. 30. Updated in James Cook, "The Invisible Enterprise," *Forbes,* September 29–November 4, 1980. Also see R. Foster Winan, *Trading Secrets: Seduction and Scandal At The Wall Street Journal.*, (New York: St. Martin's Press, 1986).

which involves the use of telephone solicitors to sell securities, solicit donations, and so on.[2]

Securities Manipulation and Theft

The illegal use of securities, such as stocks and bonds, has come of age
since the President's Crime Commission failed to address the problem in
depth.[3] The massive movement of "hot paper," which has been the subject
of theft or counterfeiting, has been operating without adequate sanctions
to protect the public. Several reports suggest that multimillion-dollar corporations can be set up instantly through the use of paper to be counterfeited
or not yet stolen. Either alternative gives certificates that are sufficient for
brokerage to the public. Some estimates by government officials in the
Securities and Exchange Commission indicate that these types of fraudulent
transactions may be as many as 300 million per year.

The U.S. Chamber of Commerce states that a majority of the securities
that find their way into organized crime can be used in these ways:[4]

1. Sold to a bargain-hungry investor for 30 cents on the dollar.
2. Offered to banks as collateral for loans to finance underworld enterprises.
3. Rented to dishonest businessmen, who will include the securities as assets that
   will appear on certified balance sheets.
4. Dummy companies sell Financial Guarantee Payment Bonds to those in need
   of bank loans. When the loan is granted and the borrower defaults, the bank
   is left with worthless paper.
5. Dummy corporations issue notes or other paper to purchase assets of other
   corporations.

A major problem in any of the areas listed is that no federal agency
has either sole jurisdiction or the people to cope with the massive amounts
of paper securities that are accumulating. Several subcommittees are attempting to work out new, more secure methods of handling stocks. Under the
present system, an unethical stockbroker can use the same securities for any
number of transactions without an owner being aware of illegal manipulations.

There are any number of ways for confederation members to
manipulate stocks. For example, it is not unusual to find a marginal business

---

[2]Herbert Edelhertz, *Investigation of White Collar Crime:* A Manual for Law Enforcement
Agencies (Washington, D.C.: U.S. Government Printing Office, April 1977), pp. 298-299.

[3]The 1972–73 Equity Funding case in New York is an example of fraudulent manipulation to benefit the stock exchange at the expense of the public.

[4]Chamber of Commerce of the United States, *Deskbook on Organized Crime* (Washington,
D.C.: An Urban Affairs Publication, 1969), p. 51.

organization with stolen or counterfeit stocks and bonds in its portfolio. It is not uncommon to use these documents as a basis for credit for inventory buildup, for expansion of facilities, or as a basis for floating legitimate stock on the open market.

In businesses owned by the confederations, it is easy to hold hot documents until they cool or through intercorporation transfer get the hot stocks out of the country so they can be traded or negotiated for new money that may then be returned to this country without taint.

It is not unusual for a case of stock theft on the West Coast to be consummated on the East Coast within a week. Again, the speed of transmitting stolen documents exceeds that with which the police are able to transmit information that will curb such practices.

In the bond business there are a number of ways in which organized criminals have been involved. There are two common methods of operation. (1) Forgery of an owner's name on a registered bond is a common activity of the confederations. (2) Some big operations have involved unregistered bonds. These thieves simply add a name and the bond is cashed through normal channels. By the time the theft of the bonds is discovered, the salesperson has vanished. Women are often used as passers in this type of activity.

The manipulation of stocks and/or bonds within a company has become an important moneymaker for the confederations. They purchase an old defunct corporation and through loans secured by using stolen stocks or bonds as collateral, members of the confederations are able to form new corporations and eventually put company stock on the public market. Once the public has subscribed to the legal limit, the confederation drains off all the liquid assets and declares bankruptcy.

There is serious need for new and better methods to control the paper transactions of a company. There are a few states where practically no binding law exists for the control of corporations. In such states the "fly by night" operators are busily fleecing stockholders from throughout the world. One of the best illustrations of how intricate business operations are open to unethical and illegal manipulation was the 1987 Rizetello case in Los Angeles where he conspired to sell public improvement bonds stolen from Manufacturers Bank of New York in 1983. In a 1988 indictment, E. F. Hutton employees were charged for converting suitcases of cash for tax exempt bearer bonds.

The Futures Market

Another phase of stock market operation that is highly susceptible to manipulation by both confederation and unethical business groups is the investment in futures stock. The quick turn-around in this high-profit (or loss) operation makes it attractive to professionals who may need a tax shelter for their income. Although one would expect the fluctuation in prices to be responsive to economic and other conditions, frequently it is the manipulation of large amounts of money that makes the investment in futures desirable.

Because most speculators never see the commodities in which they are investing, their participation is the buying and selling of papers. Thus, these investments are subject to many abuses.

Many companies, and especially those owned by the confederations, "lay off" by purchasing futures on their own products. This type of hedging opens doors for many types of deceit and fraud. For example, a business with a large inventory of marketable products can negate its loss on its cash stock value by investing an equal amount of the product in the futures market. Many questionable companies are "selling short" in such schemes. In such instances it is the consumer who ultimately pays.

This type of maneuver can work in reverse. For example, a farm coop may have orders that exceed its stock on hand. It buys futures contracts equal to the extent of its orders. If the price of the commodity goes up, the price of the futures contract will also increase by a similar amount. Even though the coop may have to purchase a quantity of a commodity and sell at a loss, the rise in the futures contract still generates a profit. If this type of practice is the order of business, a consumer must eventually be the economic victim.

Credit Card Frauds

Organized groups are a natural for this crime. Through thefts, burglaries, and the manufacture of illegal cards, organized groups thrive on volumes of business and weak verification of credit card holders.

Many petty thieves and professional burglars steal credit cards in the normal course of their work, and these they pass through fences. In turn, the fences sell the cards to shoppers who make fraudulent identification to match the card and present the card for the purchase of merchandise. The merchandise, in turn, is peddled back through the fence for about 10 percent of its original value. Other credit card abuses securing cards under false names or with false statements with no intention to pay. Prosecutions of these crimes may be had under state theft, forgery, or federal mail fraud statutes.[5]

SPECIAL FRAUDS, SWINDLES, AND THEFTS

Fraud of the Elderly

One of the big swindles of modern America has been with elderly victims. They are susceptible to hard-sell gimmicks on radio and television.

[5]Edelhertz, *Investigation of White Collar Crime*, p. 287.

Pharmaceutical dispensers, auto repair operators, and dozens of businesses patronized by the elderly are first to swindle the elderly. In 1968, the Subcommittee on Consumer Interests of the Elderly identified schemes that were swindling the elderly of billions of dollars. Schemes for home repair, new cures for old age illnesses, and fad diet foods are all sold to the elderly. Health insurance, cemetery lots, and inflated burial contracts are all part of the swindlers' game. Whereas all these crimes may not be the forte of the better-known organized confederations, there are enough in these businesses to classify them as organized operations.

Although most crimes of an organized nature that directly affect the elderly cannot be identified separately, they are important to mention. For example, the garage operations probably fleece more elderly victims of more money than all the commonly recognized crimes such as burglary and robbery. Being fleeced by the unethical and frequently confederation-owned garage operator is so common that most persons accept the gouging without complaint. The poor and the elderly are prime victims for such ads as "complete motor overhaul $89.95," with "if engine condition permits" in very small print. Once in the garage the vehicle owner must sign to have the vehicle worked on. If the vehicle owner is not careful, he has signed an open-ended contract that permits the garage to do the work it deems necessary. In any event, after a vehicle is dismantled, the "engine condition" rarely allows a $89.95 overhaul. The garage will then contact the vehicle owner and advise him that his engine is in such poor shape that it will require a $539 overhaul job. When the victim says he does not have that kind of money, the friendly garage indicates it will accept the $89.95 as down payment and float a loan, frequently at a usurious rate of interest. An alternative to going along with the garage is to pay a reassembly fee. This fee is generally from $35 to $50. If both offers are refused by the victim, the garage dumps the parts in the vehicle and stores the vehicle, usually for a high fee, until an independent tow truck can retrieve it. The nature of the small garage operation makes such businesses attractive to the confederations. For example, stolen vehicles can easily be converted to spare parts, and control over garage mechanics can be exercised.

Welfare and Medical Swindles

Swindles in the welfare programs are basically one- or two-person operations and would not normally be classed as organized crime. However, when a number of persons conspire to steal welfare, pension, and other checks from mail boxes and to engage in a concerted effort toward other crimes, the organized crime title is appropriate. For example, a news release from New York City indicated how such crimes are perpetrated. Obviously, New York is not unique in these types of swindles. For example, four men were accused of donning a variety of disguises and faking credentials to bilk the state of $300,000 in unemployment insurance over a five-year period.

The most common targets of todays organized crime entrepreneurs are the health clinics and health laboratories.[6] The culprits are not necessarily from the organized crime groups but are self-made entrepreneurs who have consolidated their business techniques to take advantage of the mass movement toward universal medical treatment.

Two common methods of extracting money from legitimate sources are to extract as much money as possible from the underwriter insurance company over a prolonged period of time. A second method is to undercut legitimate underwriters or third-party administrators so that a business owned and operated as third-party administrators by organized crime can have a larger share of the market.

Doctors and legitimate businesspersons who are looking to cut costs and extend their profits are prone to succumb to a business association that does not necessarily benefit society or their patients. The collusion between business operators, including doctors, became a part of the scheme by handling patients friendly to organized crime.

Excessive tests and treatment, false claims, kickbacks for referrals, charging excessively for services, and coercion to belong to specific medical plans are all methods used in these swindles.

Prescription frauds carried on between doctors and pharmacists through hidden corporate ownership have yet to be fully investigated. Drugs prescribed through a "prescription physician" tend to find their way into the illegal drug channels.

Investigations into medical fraud cases are complex and lengthy. The emphasis on the sale of the medical insurance by insurance companies takes precedence over the investigation of fraud.

Political Contributions

How corruption pervades the political picture may be shown in this example, A federal grand jury indicted President W.A. "Tony" Boyle of the United Mine Workers union on charges of embezzlement, conspiracy, and unlawfully contributing $49,250 in union funds to political campaigns.

A special panel investigating tangled affairs of the miners' union charged that Boyle, in conspiracy with other UMW officials, embezzled $5,000 in union funds and gave, among other contributions, $30,000 to the presidential campaign of Democratic nominee Hubert H. Humphrey in 1968.

Political action committees.   PACs have legitimized organized crime involvement in the election processes. The PACs were created by the Federal

[6]Kenneth P. Walton, "Organized Crime and Medical Fraud," *FBI Law Enforcement Bulletin.* Washington, D.C., October 1986, pp. 21–24.

Election Campaign Acts of 1971, 1976, and 1979 and were intended to purify the big money campaigns of political candidates. Through PACs, campaign funds can be broken down to individual contributions and gotten to the candidates of their choice. In light of the ABSCAM trials where congressional candidates were shown stuffing $100 bills into their pockets, perhaps political action committees are the lesser of two evils. While legislation creating PACs set limits and documentation on contributions over $100, it is filled with loopholes that even the "honest politician" can crawl through. PACs in their affiliation with political parties and unions now control member fees who have no choice in the candidates they support.

The abuse of provisions in the Election Campaign Acts are exceeded only by the loopholes found in the Ethics Bill of 1978 by which influence peddling of departing government employees has become standard fare.

The Regulatory Commissions

Partisan politics and political favoritism are the two major factors that allow organized crime to retain a controlling interest in the vital regulatory functions of federal, state, and local government.

In recent years, commissions have become increasingly important in the conduct of government as they relate to the regulation of businesses. The efforts of government commissions, although active in revealing some symptoms of organized crime, have not had the resources or the expertise to adequately perform their assigned responsibilities; thus, guilty parties have been allowed to shrug off allegations and continue as before. The failure of the commissions to generate interest in acting against these crimes is reflected in this example. In fiscal year 1971, the Federal Trade Commission referred only one case to the Department of Justice for prosecution, and this was for failure to respond to a subpoena. Three cases were referred to the Department of Justice for violation of the truth-in-lending provision of the Consumer Credit Protection Act. Twenty cases of antitrust violations were sent to the Justice Department in the past two years for criminal prosecution.

This failure of the regulatory agency to perform points up a lack of interest in prosecuting certain regulatory violations.[7] To offset this disinterest, consumer protection committees have been established in many cities throughout the United States. These committees function as a coordinating body between federal, state, and local government organizations involved in consumer protection. These committees include members of the Federal Trade Commission.

[7]Attorney General's First Annual Report (Washington, D.C.: U.S. Government Printing Office, 1972, pp. 502–503. Also James W. Coleman, *The Criminal Elite,* Chapter 4. Also see Alan A. Block, and Frank Scarpitti, *Poisoning for Profit.*

Another important commission that deals with the control of organized crime in the areas of fraud and theft is the Federal Communications Commission, which under the authority of statutes 18 U.S.C. 1302 (broadcasting lottery information), 18 U.S.C. 1343 (fraud by wire or radio), and 18 U.S.C. 1464 (broadcasting obscene language) has the opportunity to regulate organized crime's use of the communications system. In addition, this commission investigates unauthorized interception and divulgence of law enforcement radio communication (Section 605 of the Communications Act). The entire spectrum of communications, as it supports organized crime, needs more active enforcement.

The Civil Aeronautics Board (CAB) is important to the control of thefts involving organized crime. By the nature of its law enforcement activities, the CAB regulates such activities as unauthorized air transportation (tour groups). Under the Fair Credit Reporting Act, credit terms offered to airline consumers must be fully disclosed.

Savings and Loan Frauds

At this time massive investigations are continuing into the financial collapse of a group of failed savings and loan institutions including some of the largest in the nation. The Federal Home Loan Bank Board testified before Congress that fraud was involved in about 25 percent of the failures. According to national news services, 284 failed or failing savings and loan companies with $11.4 billion in losses are involved.[8] The Federal Savings and Loan Insurance Corporation will be required to cover losses in many of these cases. As these investigations unfold, these thefts may turn out to be the crimes of the century in terms of monetary losses.

These cases point up the fact that the Federal Deposit Insurance Corporation is a vital link in controlling organized crime manipulation involving internal banking operations of all financial institutions. Special types of organized criminal activities, by necessity, must be housed in a bank or savings and loan organization. These institutions can loan vast amounts of money on property and securities. They can negotiate for and cover for stolen securities, launder drug money, and set the control for the financial development of a community.

Burglary

Although many professional burglars operate as independent agents, they are tied to organized crime through the sale of merchandise to fences

---

[8]"GAO Cites Fraud in Failure of S&Ls," *Los Angeles Times,* January 14, 1989, p. 1.

or receivers. Frequently, stolen goods, such as automobiles, will be fenced directly to a drug dealer, who, in turn, will make a profit on the sale of the drugs. Professional burglars dealing with organized groups are most apt to be in the business of stealing jewelry, furs, small business machines, and securities.

The life blood of the professional burglar is to have a fence. There would be no commercial jewel thieves if there were no fences. The burglars are interested only in cash, not the jewelry. Thus, the fence or receiver of the stolen property is an integral part of the organized groups who engage in burglary. Closely allied with the fences are the "chop shops," who receive stolen vehicles, strip them for parts, remove numbers, and restore the vehicle, and secure registration indicating it has been resurrected from the boneyard of wrecked vehicles. This is a specialized multimillion-dollar activity. The variety and magnitude of fraud and theft are shown in Table 10-1.

COMPUTER CRIMES

Many crime experts predict that one of the big white collar type crimes of the future will be that involving computer technology. This technology has begun to regulate our movements and direct our lives. Computer systems control the flow of $35 trillion per year between member banking and financial institutions. Thus, most major businesses depend on the communications and information networks that make up the computer industry.

Because of the rapid growth of machine technology, the application of the system has not been subject to tight administrative control in the installation or operation of the systems. The weaknesses of the systems are attracting criminals, who usually work in a position of trust and often with an accomplice. As the complexity of the computer systems grows and the scope of the operations increases, the next logical step would be to see organized crime move into computer frauds.

In a December 1979 *Reader's Digest* article, author Nathan Adams, writing about California, indicated that the confederations have major investments in the banking industry, the garment industry, and electronics. From these combined investments, about $6.3 billion per year is being stolen from the citizens of California. Many of the industries mentioned in this article are heavily computerized. Obviously, many of the operating and controlled industries of organized crime are already computerized.

Computer crimes are becoming so prevalent as to constitute a new security industry. Some schemes are innovative, some are simple, and many so sophisticated they have gone undetected. During the past decade, the most prevalent form of fraud has been the "hacker." These electronic pirates commit pranks, thefts, and the placing of misinformation, all of which are expensive amusement. The computer virus became the topic of investigation

TABLE 10-1   Federal White Collar Crime Convictions

Offense	Convictions	
	Percent	Number
Fraud	100	5,972
Tax	20	1,204
Lending and credit	9	540
Wire and mail	24	1,428
Other[a]	47	2,800
Embezzlement	100	1,753
Bank	48	842
Government	10	173
U.S. Postal Service	18	313
Other[b]	24	425
Forgery	100	2,014
U.S. Government documents	79	1,594
U.S. Postal Service	8	152
Securities	13	254
Other	1	14
Counterfeiting	100	503
White collar regulatory offenses	100	491
Import and export[c]	26	127
Antitrust	23	114
Transportation	23	113
Food and drug	17	84
Labor	8	37
Agriculture and agricultural materials	3	16
Total white collar convictions	100	10,733

Note: Data include cases brought by U.S. attorneys and the Criminal Division of the Department of Justice.

[a]Includes false claims and statements; government program fraud; fraud concerning bankruptcy, commodities, securities, passports, or citizenship; and conspiracy to defraud.

[b]Includes labor organizations, Indian tribal organizations, and other federally protected victims.

[c]Includes customs violations and export of restricted defense materials and information; does not include drug offenses.

Source: U.S. Department of Justice, *Report to the Nation on Crime and Justice,* (Washington, D.C.: U.S. Government Printing Office, 1988).

in 1989 when over 300 networks were infected by a single "hacker." Other innovative thefts of the past decade are: data alteration, including false orders which are expensive headaches for business. Counterfeiting of bar codes has created costly lessons for grocery and other merchants. Information manipulation, from the Department of Justice down to the local doctor who falsifies medical billing, has cost consumers billions of dollars. False information or propaganda has caused elections to be lost. Malicious manipulation of data has been the basis for the sale of billions of dollars in goods. Inside information that gave competitive advantage has been found in the stock market, in real estate, and hundreds of other enterprising applications. Point-of-sale crimes account for billions in lost dollars to merchants. The list is limited only by the criminal's imagination.

There are many areas of interest for the law enforcement officer in the computer field.[9] Several new books deal only with computer fraud investigation. For the purposes of this text, we will look at three areas: (1) laws that control computer abuse; (2) computer uses by organized crime; and (3) the potential for future use of the computer network by organized crime.

Laws That Control Computer Abuses

Computer networks span the world, so to maintain integrity in the security of the system there will have to be international standards of construction and operation. It would appear that the American enforcement agency in international operations will be the Federal Bureau of Investigation. The Computer Securities Act of 1987 gave the National Bureau of Standards control over computerized government files except those containing national security information. The National Computer Security Center, an arm of the National Security Agency (NSA), will retain ultimate international intelligence control. *Computerworld* magazine identified the major effect the law has on enforcement agencies.[10]

> When federal jurisdiction "exists concurrently with state or local jurisdiction," federal law enforcement officers, in determining whether to exercise jurisdiction, should consider among other things,
>
> 1. The relative gravity of the federal offense and the state or local offenses.
> 2. The relative interest in federal investigation or prosecution.
> 3. The resources available to the federal authorities and the state or local authorities.

> The bill defines the computer as a device that performs logic, arithmetic, and storage functions by electronic manipulation and includes any property and communication facility directly related to or operating in conjunction with such a device. Misuse of home computers, automated typewriters, and handheld calculators is a matter for state jurisdiction.

> State laws to control computer fraud are being modeled after the federal statute. California became the fourth state to have such a law. Penalties under the federal statute call for fines of two times the amount of loss or $50,000, whichever is higher, and/or five years in jail.

[9]In a 40-hour training course held in computer fraud and countermeasures sessions at Long Beach (CA) City College, 21 areas of training were presented. In the six-week course offered by the Federal Bureau of Investigation, dozens of different areas are included.

[10]"The Federal Computer System Protection Act," *Computerworld*, November 19, 1979, p. 2. In late 1988, Codercard's ARGUS computer system was approved by the Treasury Department for use in high-risk areas (see Fig. 10–1).

Until the political question of making adequate laws is settled, those involved in computer type crimes are being prosecuted under the different theft and fraud statutes of state and federal governments.

Computers and Organized Crime

Computer crimes may be described as computer abuse, computer fraud, computer-related crime, and automatic data processing crime. By whatever title, there are a great number of ways to use the computer in committing criminal acts.

Perhaps the most important computer fraud, and a different kind of crime than we would normally contemplate, but of great value to organized crime, would be the case cited in one congressman's *Newsletter*. In this letter the congressman said: "The day after my motion to expell Charles Diggs from the Congress failed by just eight votes, I found out that one of those listed as voting against my resolution was in Chicago, Ill., at the time of the vote." Despite his absence from Washington, D.C., the offending member of Congress was recorded by the House Computerized Voting System as having voted not once but *six* times that day. *Members of Congress are not allowed to vote by proxy.* This problem was resolved with the installation of a new computer system.

The billion-dollar Equity Funding case of several years ago has faded from memory as the biggest corporate swindle of all times. False corporate assets were manipulated to create one of the decade's fastest growing conglomerates. After Security and Exchange Commission investigators finished their investigation, it was said the only thing straight in the corporation were the shafts driving the computers. The next big swindle was the Los Angeles Security-Pacific Bank theft of $10 million. This crime was committed by a systems analyst who knew how to manipulate the system and transfer funds to other banks. The culprit was subsequently sent to jail and Security-Pacific stands to lose $1 million from the theft. While this was not a typical organized type crime, it certainly sets the pattern for future schemes.

In November 1979, in Tulsa, Oklahoma, the Organized Crime Task Force spent nine hours deciphering a minicomputer code to crack a bookmaking ring making $181,000 per week, on a $15,000 machine. If the programming had been slightly more sophisticated, law enforcement would not have broken the code. This is probably a forerunner of the future for numbers and bookmaking outfits.

Parker reports on two cases of organized crime being directly involved with a computer operation.[11] In one case, a janitor associated with the Mafia was running embossing machines during the operators' lunch break with

---

[11]Donn B. Parker, *Crime by Computer* (New York: Scribner's, 1976), pp. 269–70.

blank credit cards and authentic names and account numbers; these produced duplicate cards that would avoid computerized rejections when used for purchases. The criminal was caught and agreed to help authorities catch others in the organization.

In another case in the Midwest dealing directly with organized crime, during raids on football betting establishments FBI agents discovered computer printouts listing scheduled and betting odds. The name of the paper company and the page serial numbers were printed on each page. The paper was traced back to the central computer center and a case was made for prosecution. It would appear that with proper programming and coding, this type of crime would not be solvable.

There are indications that many forms of organized crime have already sought the shelter of the computer. Coded messages, impervious to police penetration, can move nationally and internationally via telecommunication systems. If we extrapolate from the cases cited here, we can see that confederations may succeed in a crime while individuals fail.

The Potential for Future Crime

Approximately 50 percent of the GNP is related to data processing and communications. In 1975, there were about 71,000 large-scale computers and 200,000 minisystems. In 1984 the general use computers of the Justice Department and other enforcement agencies were accessed by Internal Revenue computers so that all activities now become subject to IRS scrutiny. It is predicted that by 1995 there will be 12 million terminals in government, business, education, and the home.

Very few law enforcement agencies are even partially trained or equipped to recognize, process, and prosecute computer crime cases. Systems analysis, accounting, and auditing operations are not normally areas of study for local, state, or federal criminal law enforcement investigators. Thus, most known crimes involving computer technology are neither investigated nor prosecuted, as one Senate subcommittee noted.

1. Only 1 percent of all computer crimes are detected.
2. Of the 1 percent, only 15 percent are reported.
3. Of the 15 percent, only 3 percent are convicted.
4. One computer criminal in every 22,000 is detected and convicted.

The attraction for organized crime must be obvious. The areas of susceptibility of a system are shown in Figure 10–1.[12]

[12]Bill Colvin, "Computer Crime Investigators: A New Training Field," *FBI Law Enforcement Journal* (July 1979), 9–12. In the Privacy Act of 1984, computers tied into the Internal Revenue Reporting System. The Deficit Reduction Act of 1984 stated that individuals must be notified their records are subject to review by the Internal Revenue Service.

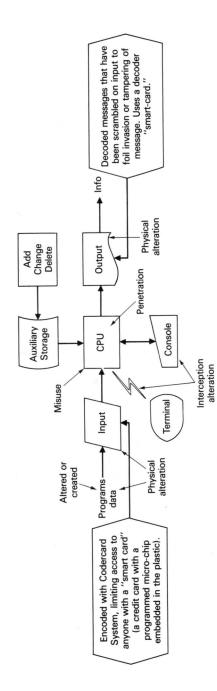

FIGURE 10-1 Vulnerability of computer systems.

According to Colvin, the data entry specialist is the least skilled person and the area with the greatest number of people assigned, while the systems analyst is the most skilled, with the fewest personnel assigned. The culprit may operate internally or externally. Because of the nature of the systems, it is rare that a crime is committed against a computer system without inside assistance.

Identification of the suspect in part depends on a study of the processes of the organization. One investigator has established a formula for factoring key positions in an organization that may be susceptible to computer fraud. While it is only a guideline, it enables an investigator to zero in on certain critical areas. For example, a simplified approach to suspect identification is included in this formula.

CF_p = Probability of being a computer fraud victim
(Rating 0.0–1.0)
D = Honesty factor (0–10 rating)
O = Opportunity factor (0–10 rating)
M = Motive factor (0–10 rating)

$$CF_p = \frac{D \times O \times M}{1000}$$

$$CF_p = \frac{10 \times 10 \times 10}{1000} = 1.0 \text{ (probability of 100\%)}$$

This is an interesting approach; it shows that to catch a crook requires a basic understanding of systems and systems routing operations.

Computer crimes have varied from box cars to gambling, and it is not likely that organized crime will pass up an opportunity to make an easy dollar. It would appear that computers are beginning to appear in many areas where organized crime has been active in the past. The situation can only be worsened because there are serious problems of gathering and presenting evidence. The complexity of computer crime can tie up a court for months or perhaps years.

SUMMARY

Business acquisition by racketeering may occur through coercive agreement or by force. Both types of acquisition may be so subtle that control of an organization may move from legitimate to illegitimate without the principal administrators of a business being aware of the transaction.

Many business schemes today may be merely unethical and some may be illegal; yet they are so numerous and covert that they seldom come to the attention of law enforcement agencies. In many cases, local enforcement agencies do not have the geographical authority to deal with such crimes, and federal participation is limited because of the vastness of the problems.

Special frauds and influence in criminal activities such as those against the elderly, people on welfare, use of political contributions, computer frauds, and others illustrate the fine line between fraud and honest participation.

QUESTIONS FOR DISCUSSION

1. From your own experience, cite businesses in your community that are subject to control by organized crime elements.
2. What areas of the public domain are most susceptible to inroads by confederation members?
3. Control of many crimes such as the embezzlement or theft of stocks, bonds, or credit cards must be vested in the business domain, not in law enforcement. Explain.
4. The use of stolen documents as collateral against legitimate loans is a direct link to the establishment of fixed interest rates. Explain.
5. Why are present regulations inadequate for persons dealing in market futures and how can the manipulation by "money interest" crime confederations affect small investors?
6. What are some of the dangers of filtering law through administrative regulations to be administered by regulatory commissions?
7. Describe how organized fencing operations provide employment for street-level burglars.
8. Describe ways organized crime can use computers to aid in circumventing the law.
9. Are computer crimes easy to identify? Are they easy to control? Why or why not?

11

Militant Groups: A Force in Organized Crime

LEARNING OUTCOMES

1. Relate the problem of militant group objectives to confederation activities.
2. Have knowledge about the groups and how they relate to functional organized crime control.
3. Identify select groups and observe reported actions of these groups.
4. Determine what enforcement tactics are best suited to counter tactics used by covert militant groups.
5. Be able to help develop strategies that counter the political manipulations of militant groups.

In reflecting over the past two decades of group violence in the United States and all over the world, there is little question that many of these radical activities fall within the definition of organized criminal acts. Many of these acts have been addressed by local, state, and national law enforcement as an organized crime problem. The militant groups cited in this chapter are criminal activists, political radicals, social reactionaries, and plain criminals who just happen to have organized into groups. All pose a severe problem for law enforcement. The basic differences between these groups and traditional confederations are their motives and methods of attack. But even these motives and methods are often similar to those of traditional confederations. Mass demonstrations and bombings have given way to kidnapping, murder to maintain control, and direct assault on society.

Los Angeles County data indicate that gang members, in and out of prison, have been responsible for 2700 murders up to this time.[1] The con-

---

[1]Office of the Attorney General, *Criminal Information Bulletin,* Sacramento, Calif., 1989, page 1.

Extreme Situations	Approaches	Endemic Conditions
Total institutions	Biologism	Deviance
Mass terror	Economism	Discrimination
Genocide	Psychologism	Rationalization
Thermonuclear war	Social psychologism	Alienation
	Sociologism	

FIGURE 11-1   Social problems and pathologies that assist in identifying the causes of militant behavior.

ditions that nurture militant causes have been documented by social scientists. In the broadest perspectives, Rosenberg, Gerver and Howton identified the major problems in the classifications shown in Figure 11-1.[2]

Few other kinds of crime have so many ramifications or so little hope for control by punitive means. Thus, this text identifies the problem but offers few solutions. Traditional police methods are not going to be the solution; however, the police are charged with intelligence gathering and controlling these groups. If criminal activities by militant groups are to be curbed or controlled, local police are going to need national resources such as military intelligence. Whether one likes to admit it or not, local police forces are inadequate to deal with the necessary gathering of intelligence and the deployment of forces in the face of major confrontations with organized militant groups.

TYPOLOGIES OF CRIMINAL GROUPS

Many of the groups discussed in this chapter are dedicated revolutionaries whose ultimate goal is the overthrow of our present form of government by force. Some groups may be merely idealists. These organized groups and their objectives are known through intelligence information; therefore, a police agency cannot ignore them. Basically, these groups consist of (1) international conspiracies, (2) national conspiracies, and (3) splinter groups. All of these groups' objectives are to disrupt and destroy the established social system.

---

[2]Bernard Rosenberg, Israel Gerver, and F. William Howton, *Mass Society in Crisis* (New York: Macmillan, 1971). Also see U.S. Department of State, *Patterns of Global Terrorism 1988*, (Washington, D.C.: U.S. Government Printing Office, 1989).

---

1. May 19th Communist Organization, Prairie Fire Organizing Committee, Armed Forces of the National Liberation, Communist Party, USA

2. Cuban National Liberation Front, FLNC (Cuba)

3. Abu Nidal, Hizballah and 15 May Organization

4. IRA Provisional and Republican Army (Northern Ireland)

5. Basque Homeland and Liberation Movement Army (Spain)

6. South Moluccan Extremists (The Netherlands)

7. Turkish People's Liberation Army (Turkey)

8. EPB-Macheteros, Republic of New Afrika/New African Freedom Fighters

9. Armed Proletariat Nucleus (Italy)

10. Japan's Yakuza Gangs

11. Vietnamese Mafia (similar to old Italian Mafia)

12. People's Revolutionary Army, ERP (Argentina)

13. Black Panther Party, Aryan Nations, Fuqra, National Alliance, The Covenant

---

FIGURE 11-2 International militant groups. Even though some of these groups are politically motivated, all engage in terroristic activities to achieve their goals.

INTERNATIONAL CONSPIRACIES

Terrorism is the ultimate weapon of international revolutionaries. In terrorism, revolutionaries have found a coercive weapon that meets their specific needs. Coercive terrorism by organized crime has been used in the United States for the past century. It has been used for decades in urban guerrilla warfare in Latin America. Reactionaries in Northern Ireland and the Quebec Province of Canada have kept the spark of "patriotism" alive for many years. The tactics used by these reactionaries range from kidnapping, hijackings, and bank robberies to bombings. The domestic problem with these crimes was addressed in a 1976 report by The Private Security Advisory Council.[3] Organizations such as the International Communist Party and Weather Underground factions are examples of the national and international groups dedicated to the overthrow of the current system and the installment of governments that follow their ideologies. Some of the major groups are shown in Figures 11-2, 11-3, and 11-4.[4]

[3]U.S. Department of Justice, *Prevention of Terrorists Crimes: Security Guidelines for Business Industry and Other Organizations* (Washington, D.C.: U.S. Government Printing Office, May 1976).

[4]The October 1987 issue of the FBI Law Enforcement Bulletin is devoted to the issues of terrorism.

Position: U.S. branch of the international Communist Party. Policy comes directly from Moscow.

Leadership: May vary from year to year.

Location: Headquarters, New York City; membership estimated at between 12,000 and 13,000.

Character: Predominantly white adults.

Brief History: Founded in Chicago, Illinois, September 1, 1919. Poverty and the U.S. depression helped strengthen party during the 1930s. It polled 100,000 votes for its presidential candidate in 1932. Hitler-Stalin Pact of World War II, preceding the German invasion of Russia, caused many U.S. members to drop out of the party. After the war, CP-USA went underground to escape the 1940 Smith Act, which made it a crime to conspire, advocate, or teach the violent overthrow of the government; and the 1950 McCarran Act, which required registration of members. By mid-'50s, Senator Joseph McCarthy had died; the Smith Act was "gutted"; the McCarran Act registration requirement was ruled unconstitutional. The party returned to its open activities.

Although the Moscow brand of communism is considered reactionary by much of the New Left, party membership has increased about 25% since 1960. In 1968, the party had an official presidential candidate on the national ballot for the first time in 28 years. July 1968, Zagarell reported that "the student unrest on the college campuses and the anti-draft demonstrations have been helped along by the Communist Party." The party's youth group, the W.E.B. DuBois Clubs, had less than 100 members in March 1969, but party officials claim much of their own new membership consists of young people. At the May 1969 national convention, Hall cautioned that "it is not yet time to organize armed struggle;" but the party's Commission on Black Liberation approves "cooperation" with BPP [Black Panther Party].

FIGURE 11-3   Communist Party—U.S.A. (CP-USA)

Source: Published with permission of *U.S. News and World Report. U.S. News and World Report,* Chapter 1.

The reactionaries discussed in this book may or may not be associated with any international apparatus. It should be made clear that there are two distinct kinds of international groups in operation. One is ideologically tied to Marxism, the other is ideologically tied to a utopian concept of government where human values replace the traditional machine orientation of capitalism. Frequently, the two will merge in common interests.[5]

---

[5]This text is not about international conspirators, but they are discussed to show how relationships may be established with national militant groups.

Other International Groups

Acts of terrorism have dominated the headlines in the past few decades. Aerial hijackings have necessitated an entirely new intelligence and security system for U.S. law enforcement. Bombings, skyjackings, kidnappings, and other forms of political terrorism have become the way to gain media attention for terrorist groups.

The acts of international terrorism are a means to an end, the end being the destruction of a free society. Thus, the terrorists have always tried to provoke repression to hasten the collapse of authority. The media may have been their greatest aid in this endeavor. Poor intelligence and underreaction by the civil police may have been the terrorists' greatest ally.

Communist Party in the United States

The Communist Party holds a unique position among subversive groups and requires extensive intelligence and police type investigations at the national level. Few local agencies have the expertise to maintain extensive intelligence activities against this group.

Whether these international terrorists are freedom fighters or criminal terrorists depends on who is doing the interpretation. After years of siege, many nations are now willing to class these groups as international criminals. The acts of violence they commit have become common crimes rather than a form of political expression.

Palestine Liberation Organization (PLO). Viewed by many as Third World shock troops. This group has organized political factions throughout Central Europe and engages in coordinated efforts in hijackings and bombings.

Popular Front for the Liberation of Palestine (PFLP). This group maintains liaison with the PLO and is also active in Western Europe. Both groups have become famous for their commando raids and their willingness to die for a cause.

United Red Army (URA), in Japan, *The Italian Red Army,* and the spanish group known as *GRAPO* are all active throughout the world and are all identified with the Marxist philosophy.

The Federal Bureau of Investigation noted in 1987 that the PFLP carried out a great many joint operations with the BAADER-Meinhof Gang and the Japanese Red Army. They also have ties with Irish, Iranian, and Basque guerillas. "Carlos," the most famous of all terrorists, worked with this group.

FIGURE 11-4   International terrorist groups.

At the local level, however, intelligence officers of major cities are charged with assimilation of data on suspected Communists. This information becomes a part of the intelligence file and is made available to federal agencies. The role of the local officer in Communist Party subversion basically ends at that point.

NATIONAL CONSPIRACIES

Many hard-core militants emerged from campus demonstrations of the 1960s (Figure 11–5). Others emerged from ethnic frustrations regarding equal rights, and still others developed from prison populations. Many of the militant groups are dropouts from the competitive economic system and find

During the 1980s, about 125 terrorist acts were attributed to U.S. militant groups. In addition to these acts, there have been hundreds of murders related to the drug dealing groups in cities throughout the United States. Much of the terrorist investigations of the late 1980s can be attributed to a multitude of black, Mexican, Jamaican, and Haitian gangs in their disputes over the distribution of "crack" cocaine and other drugs.

Domestic groups' activities tend to be cyclic; one group may dominate for a period and then emerge under a different banner. Many of the activities of the 1960s and the 1970s have given way to new causes. While nationalism was the prime cause in recent history, internationalism now prevails. The posture of the United States in world affairs has created terrorist-motivated activities from the Middle East, South America, and the Orient.

According to the Federal Bureau of Investigation, major problem groups in the United States today are: *Aryan and Ecologically oriented groups.* These groups have received a great amount of publicity because of assassination attempts and because of bombings and murders that have been attributed to them. *FALN* — a left wing Puerto Rican group in the *Macheteros* has been organized to ferment revolution and chaos in the Caribbean and in the United States. The *Oriental Networks* including Japanese, Chinese, and Southeast Asians have gained headway, especially along the West Coast. The major problems in controlling these terroristic activities are the people's suspicion of government and their failure to cooperate in prosecutions.

FIGURE 11–5 Contemporary national groups. The ideologies of political groups are of little interest to law enforcement. The law enforcement concern is with the acts of terrorism, murders, and other crimes committed by members of these groups.

The groups that commit terrorism are far from being eliminated.[6] Most active during the 1980s has been the *Order,* an offshoot of the Aryan Nations. Puerto Rican leftists have been active as has black groups such as *El Ruhns,* of Chicago, the *Ahamddiya Movement* (AMI), and *Fuque,* of Detroit. Black gangs such as the *Bloods* and the *Crips* and Mexican gangs from the Western United States are active. Right wing groups such as *Aryan Nations, The Covenant, The Sword, The Arm of the Sword,* Jewish extremists, and dozens of other groups present problems for the public and law enforcement.

Prison-related groups such as *La EME, Nuestra Familia,* the *Aryan Brotherhood,* and the *Black Guerrilla* group have evolved in California, and some of these groups have filtered into other states. La EME, the Mexican Mafia spawned in metropolitan centers, is the largest of the four groups, with 200 to 600 associate members. This group is engaged in rivalry with *Nuestra Familia,* a group from the farms, and the *Black Guerrilla,* which represents the blacks in prison. La EME maintains a working relationship with the *Aryan Brotherhood,* who are white neo-Nazis.

FIGURE 11-6   Splinter groups. Criminal activities, not ideologies, are the reason for law enforcement involvement with these groups.

satisfaction in forceful retaliation against what they see as an alien society. Whether Americans want to recognize the facts or not, they have created armies of militants who will struggle for the downfall of the system simply because they believe the present system is not responsive to their needs. Every police agency in this generation will feel the impact of the militant groups. The acts perpetrated by the extremists are going to be criminal activities and will be subject to the same police investigations as other types of traditional and organized crime.

SPLINTER GROUPS

In addition to the political radicals and other militants, there are many groups who identify with neither cause (Figure 11–6). Groups of ideological believers have taken up practices that are in conflict with laws of the nation and the individual states. One example would be the religious cults, where violence and torture frequently become part of the code of conduct. For example, in *The Bible of the Church of Satan,* nine points of the cult's philosophy cite a ritual in torture. The same book orders members to vengeance rather than

[6]*Criminal Justice Digest, Special Report on Terrorism,* 2, 7 (July 1974), 2.

Intelligence files bulge with information on hundreds of gangs formed around ethnic heritages, beliefs, and friendships. The following are cited as examples:

Groups such as the *Hells Angels, The American Indian Movement, the Crips,* a black Los Angeles gang, *The Whiters* and the *Longos,* who are basically Chicano groups, all contribute to crime and political corruption in the community.

Oriental groups on the West Coast have in many instances gained a reputation much like that of the Italian Mafia in the early 1900s. These groups include Korean, Vietnamese, and Japanese engaged in extortion for protection. The Chinese groups tend to identify with six families or companies from mainland China. These six companies tend to exercise control over the fraternal guilds or *tongs.* There are three predominate tongs in California: the *Bing Kung,* the *Hop Sing,* and the *Suey Song.* The enforcement groups for these *tongs* belong to the guild but are somewhat under the control of the *Wah Chings,* which has emerged as the most powerful Chinese gang. Other groups, however, under a peace agreement exercise control over their own turf and operate under the direct control of the six companies.

FIGURE 11-7   Other militant groups.

to turn the other cheek. Followers of these cults believe in and practice such activities. These practices are violations of statute law and, as such, must be investigated and prosecuted. Another example would be the California People's Church, where drugs and ideologies of social vengeance led to senseless murders. Other groups are formed around ethnic identification (Figure 11–7).

COMMON MILITANT GROUP STRATEGIES

To establish proper intelligence and enforcement techniques, enforcement officers need to know what they are up against.[7] The following list of activities gives some of the more common group methods. When an organized group begins establishing a target area, it will:

1. Identify the geographical target area. Pending elections, ethnic composition of the community, and economic conditions are common determiners.
2. Make contact with people who have vocally or in written form expressed a desire to achieve the common objective of the confederations or militant groups.

[7]John W. Harris, Jr. "Domestic Terrorism of the 1980s," *FBI Law Enforcement Bulletin,* October, 1987, pp. 5–13.

3. Move some into a target area, if no contact people are available. Schools serve as a convenient instrument in retaining flexibility of contacts.

4. Have contact people train a group to implement a plan for obtaining objectives. This technique is regularly used by the Black Panthers, the Muslims, and other groups.

5. Ensure that this group is easily influenced by contact people. For example, the Black Berets maintain contact with jail inmates through the distribution of "care" packages.

6. Have contact with people who will influence the power structure. This is especially apparent in minority pressure groups.

7. Have an organized group that will influence the average person and some organizations through confrontation efforts.

8. Pick a volatile subject to pursue, such as skirmishes with the police, labor disturbances, and student unrest.

9. Have an organized group make demands of public agencies. May be in the following order, depending on the subject pursued:
   A. Public schools—for media visibility
   B. Churches or other public gatherings—for media visibility
   C. Post-secondary educational institutions—media visibility and societal pressure
   D. Public-supported service organizations
   E. City and/or county governments
      1. Law enforcement agencies
      2. Courts
      3. Jails and other retention facilities
      4. Welfare agencies
      5. Fire fighters
      6. Others
   F. Private enterprise
      1. Coercive threats
      2. Boycotts
      3. Physical damage

10. Have an organized group bring charges because all demands are not met.

11. Have an organized group create physical disturbances to bring more pressure to bear and revitalize media visibility, as well as the creation of unstable and sympathetic attitudes within the community.

12. Bring pressure to bear in the following ways:
   A. Court injunctions
   B. Hearings before special commissions, such as the Civil Rights Commission

The splinter groups have begun to organize. When national social situations create a vacuum, these groups move in to promote ideologies that may be contrary to popular thought using illegal methods. It is only the latter that interests the police. If law enforcement does not maintain an adequate intelligence network within these groups, the same violent scenes of the past will be repeated across this country for the next decades.

How much intelligence must be gathered from these groups and how it is obtained will become a political question of the future. Unless Congress and courts establish adequate legal guidelines, good law enforcement will become a political footnote and the losers will be the average citizens who need protection from this form of organized criminal activity.

SUMMARY

There is a large number of groups whose ultimate goal is the violent over-throw of the present form of government in the United States. Other organized groups seem more interested in personal aggrandizement and money collected from constituents than in a cause. Whatever the purpose of these militant groups, there is need for an approach to comprehensive intelligence gathering on the part of law enforcement agencies. There is little question that intelligence on these mobile groups is far too vast an undertaking for local law enforcement. Thus, it has been suggested that cooperative military, federal, and civilian intelligence are necessary to get the job done.

Today, most local law enforcement agencies are committing themselves to the termination of terrorist acts without adequate intelligence on the different groups. Politicians have found it expedient to play down domestic intelligence in the name of civil rights. In the late 1980s this trend on intelligence gathering was reversed to gain gang-related intelligence. For example, in mid-1988, the California legislature authorized wire-tapping to gain intelligence. At about the same time, the U.S. Supreme Court ruled that evidence may be secured from a garbage container once that container is set in the public area for collection. These are steps that a civil liberterian would not advocate, but the vocal public has become disgusted with the continual presence of gang activity in the community and in this country.

Internationally, the antiterrorist activity of the United States is not highly regarded. However, after the bombing of Libya, there has been a dramatic decrease in terrorist activity. It is easy to be critical of a policy, or lack of policy, that rely on huge preemptive strikes against terrorists, but power and violence are the only authority understood by dedicated radicals. When dealing with terrorists, there are very few ways to succeed and thousands of ways to fail. If an administration is too patient with terrorists, they are accused of being soft. If an administration is too harsh, they are branded as killers. Terrorism leaves little neutral ground for negotiation.

QUESTIONS FOR DISCUSSION

1. What are some of the qualities of militant activities that cause them to be classed as organized crime?
2. What are some of the basic pathologies that cause militant behavior to be unresponsive to punitive control?
3. According to many militants, there is a fine line between a Marxist philosophy

and a philosophy where human values are placed above those of capitalism. Explain.

4. Intelligence gathering, especially in the area of political philosophies, is done for the purpose of protecting the innocent as well as for the prosecution of the guilty. Explain.

5. Is it important to understand the heritage of an organization in relation to its militant activities? Explain.

6. Local participation in intelligence gathering has increased dramatically with the evolution of militant groups. Explain.

7. What are the reasons for the dramatic rise in drug imports despite the national war on drugs?

8. Law enforcement is reactive in its investigation of terrorism, thus, it is the criminal act that is important, not the group's ideology. Discuss.

9. What are the major causes for the dramatic rise in local murders and assaults associated with the distribution of drugs?

Part IV

Internal Agency Operation

This part of the text addresses organizational, administrative, and communications problems encountered in enforcing the law against organized crime. In addition, some general principles for enforcement methods are discussed.

The organizations of the multilevels of governments have been major reasons organized crime has been able to establish a foothold throughout the United States. For many years, the Federal Bureau of Investigation refused to acknowledge the existence of organized crime as a national problem. Thus, national syndicates expanded across state lines without any organized or coordinated opposition. In the past two decades, this trend has been reversed and the Federal Bureau of Investigation and other federal agencies have played important roles in coordinating state and local intelligence and enforcement coordination. The federal effort, in addition to being actively engaged in enforcement, has furnished staff and operational intelligence through the National Crime Information Center (NCIC) and the organized crime dossiers maintained at the University of Michigan.

In May 1988, the official government approval of the expanded use of the military in *direct organized crime law enforcement* brought new dimensions for curbing the thousands of kilos of drugs now being shipped yearly to this country. Whatever form this aid may take, it will involve many thousands of people. Thus, the tasks of organizing and coordinating viable, legal activities become more complex.

In the past decade, the movement into coordinated strike forces has lent a significant punch to local and regional law enforcement activities. Huge seizures, of up to four tons of cocaine, have been registered by these task forces. Drugs are also being seized by local law enforcement units who are waiting for better intelligence and coordination from those levels of government whose jurisdiction extends internationally.

The hidden agenda for every effort to curb organized crime is not merely to apprehend the criminal but to eliminate the desire for organized crime products and services.

12

Organization and Management Problems for Organized Crime Control

LEARNING OUTCOMES

1. Establish an overview of key problems involved in organized crime enforcement.
2. Know the difference between the federal and local response to organized crime enforcement.
3. Be aware of the key issues of management for enforcement agencies.
4. Identify the different organizational structures that bring about more effective management of enforcement units.
5. Begin to develop an individual philosophy about enforcement strategy and ethics.

Organizational structure and management processes are of paramount importance for effective enforcement. Although the types of crimes and manner in which they are committed may be fairly consistent throughout the nation, organizational techniques for enforcement are not consistent enough to limit these crimes. To arrive at effective organization and management procedures, we must regard organized crime violations as a problem with national priorities. There must be a high degree of state participation, and identification of individual crimes from a local perspective so that appropriate laws, policies, and procedures may be planned. Organized crime is a concern for all levels of government and must be recognized as such if proper policies and procedures for enforcement are to be developed.

To study the best methods for organized crime control, we will discuss the following concepts: (1) planning for organizational efficiency in controlling organized crime, (2) policy development for organized crime enforcement, and (3) special administrative problems for more effective control of organized crime.

PLANNING FOR ORGANIZATIONAL EFFICIENCY

Two diverse philosophies should be reconciled prior to planning. Local law enforcement is geared toward the *violation-response* approach; the federal effort is geared toward the *attrition* approach.[1] Both are proper concepts because each performs a necessary function at the level of use; therefore, enforcement organizations at all levels must be made to accommodate both methods. As criminal structures are created with layer upon layer of leader insulation from criminal acts, methods must be devised that will literally rip the criminal organization at all levels of activity. No single method will be successful.

Organized crime is a combination of variables, some of which exist as fact and some of which are created as diversionary activities; thus, the enforcement organization to counter such activity will vary from city to city. For example, two important variables are illegal markets and the type of law enforcement exerted.[2] Logically, one will influence the other as to the amount and type of enforcement needed. Other variables may be the types of criminal penetration into legitimate business and sociopsychological factors associated with the individual criminal. The form and function of the organization engaged in organized crime will be guided by the interaction of these and other variables.

Organizational methodology, structure, and function depend on which variables are selected by the enforcement administrator as being most important. The following suggestions identify factors that influence organizational structure and processes.

The organizational concept of accountability is paramount. The separation of power through "checks and balances" is an excellent method in making an enforcement organization responsible for its sphere of apprehension and prosecution. For example, in many states no higher unit of government is accountable for seeing that the lesser units of local government perform. Thus, there is little or no accountability for seeing that laws are adequately enforced and prosecuted.

[1]Annelise Anderson, *Organized Crime: The Need for Research,* Organized Crime Programs Division (LEAA, U.S. Department of Justice, Washington, D.C., 1971), p. 2. The *attrition* approach reflects a concern with organized crime as an institution rather than a collection of individual violations. *Report of the Task Force on Organized Crime* (Washington, D.C.: U.S. Government Printing Office, December 1976). Also *Report to the Nation on Crime and Justice,* 2nd, U.S. Department of Justice (Washington, D.C.: U.S. Government Printing Office, 1988), pp. 8–10.

[2]Nowal Morris and Gordon Hawkins, *The Honest Politician's Guide to Crime Control* (Chicago: The University of Chicago Press, 1970), p. 211.

The identification of ecological factors as they relate to organized criminal activities is also important. For example, the geographic, political, and cultural environment serve as indicators for the level of enforcement activity required.

In enforcement agency structures, there are built-in organizational safeguards that can increase the degree of efficiency and minimize the presence of corruption. Enforcement policies must be developed within the organization that will allow for the enforcement of statutes within imposed limitations. This type of planning should be projected through policy and procedure manuals.

There are fairly standardized techniques of management a department should strive for to obtain the maximum enforcement effort sanctioned by community sentiment. These techniques should be stated in writing, and employees should be oriented to their proper use. The techniques for managing an organized crime unit are, in most instances, contained in general principles of administration. There are, however, some unofficial techniques that must be passed from one generation to the next. Training programs for this should be planned and implemented.

The complexity of the various state statutes makes planning difficult. The large numbers of statutes make it impractical to cite each violation in determining how to plan for an efficient organization. Federal, state, and local statutes will have different wording and different court interpretation. Organizational processes will vary from state to state. In many instances, what one state permits another prohibits. In the law, the elements of organized crime are neither singular nor nationally accepted, but are an unstructured mix of ingredients based on the formal and informal pressure groups at the state and local levels. This problem will be somewhat alleviated when states begin to adopt model laws similar to the statutes in the 1986 Omnibus Crime Control Act (see Appendix B).

An important factor in structuring an enforcement organization is the types of crimes committed by the criminal confederations. Obviously, an investigation into securities will differ from one dealing in vice crime and will call for a different degree of sophistication in personnel and organizational structure. An organization structured to emphasize civil action will be different from one oriented toward criminal prosecution.

Several important methods for pursuing organized crime now apply. An example is double or triple damages in suits by victims of organized criminal activities. Identifying whether the criminal engaged in organized crime can be enticed to testify if guaranteed safety and economic security is another. Research is needed on postprosecution results; it may produce evidence that will show a need for enforcement organizations of a substantially different nature.

The factors that influence planning grow as new techniques are developed. The organizational structures in this chapter are offered as examples for organizations moving into more active enforcement.

Structuring the Organization

When structuring an organization to conduct investigations relating to organized crime, certain control measures may be initiated within an organization to make it more efficient. Obviously, not all control techniques will apply to all organizations, because personnel management ideologies and community needs are unique and diverse. Basically, within the organizational structure there are built-in safeguards that can increase the degree of efficiency and minimize the presence of corruption. Fairly standardized management rules and techniques have been developed to provide a degree of internal "checks and balances."

The Federal System

The Justice Department contains the nucleus of agencies that exert pressure on organized criminal activity. Each of the divisions and bureaus holds a key to a coordinated national effort, and no single agency can be successful without the cooperation of every other agency. The administrative interrelationship among the agencies is shown in Figure 12–1.

In a 1987 reorganization, the President expanded the federal coordination role by establishing a new communication and drug intelligence center, to be operated by the Customs Service at March Airforce Base, near Riverside, California. Politically, this gave Customs the lead-agency role in the interdiction of drug shipments at the nation's borders. By giving Customs a lead role, it was hoped that greater coordination would be secured among the various enforcement agencies who are spending $800 million yearly on drug control.

The machinery established at the national level has been built around the "strike force" concept, with several departments of government represented on each of the strike forces. In 1988, sixteen task forces were in the process of prosecuting 2200 cases. About 38 states have special units for the investigation of organized crime cases; they are part of the state attorney general's office.

As the federal strike forces are pressed into service, local forces are organized to assist in the follow-up investigations that result from task force prosecutions. Local task forces specializing in burglary rings or drug operations have been very successful in their operations with the federal strike forces.

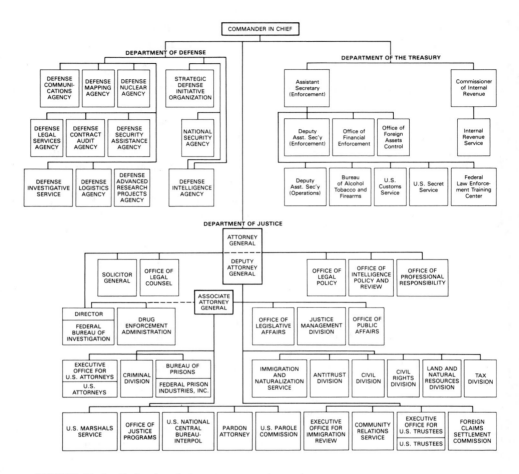

FIGURE 12-1 Federal enforcement agencies.

Source: U.S. Government Organization Manual, 1989–1990, Washington, D.C.: Office of Federal Registrar, National Archives and Research Administration, 1989), p. 372.

Regional Systems

One of the passing dinosaurs of the past decade has been the multistate compacts. As soon as the federal funding stopped, so did the multistate idea. This concept was full of political and operational pitfalls and never lived up to its potential.

Federal strike forces under the direction of the U.S. Attorney for the various districts have replaced the multistate plan. These programs were well funded and politically in tune with administration policies. The strike forces have made some massive seizures of drugs. For example, in May of 1988, about 45 tons of marijuana and hashish were seized from a tugboat in San Francisco Bay. This load had a wholesale value of $162 million. See Figure 12–2 for reorganization of the Department of Justice strike force nucleus.

State Plans: A New Role

The states have such diverse laws and differing political ideals and philosophies that the multistate compact idea has now become an ideological dream. About the only thing that now brings states together in their efforts against organized crime is a common communications network and information system at the federal level, the informal communication among state attorneys general, and the overlap of state jurisdictions within the federal judicial districts. After 1984, with the establishment of the Department of Justice Assets Forfeiture Fund, there has been great pressure for state and local agencies to interact in the federal enforcement process. The evolution of this process is shown in Figure 12–3.

The role of forfeiture in state enforcement.   Illegal assets from the traditional organized crimes have become a significant income factor in major departments where active forfeiture procedures are initiated. The huge money seizures administered through the Department of Justice Assets Forfeiture Fund for forfeiture under customs laws have provided millions of dollars for local agencies who have shared in the enforcement activities in major cases.

Forfeiture processes take time to allow for persons who have an interest in the property to make a claim. Seized property is normally kept from 6 months to 1 year before being declared forfeited. Contraband or materials that are illegal per se, such as drugs, are disposed of relatively quickly.

Regional Metropolitan and Intelligence Groups

The same information exchange system is used in several states, such as Michigan and Ohio. California maintains this information coordination

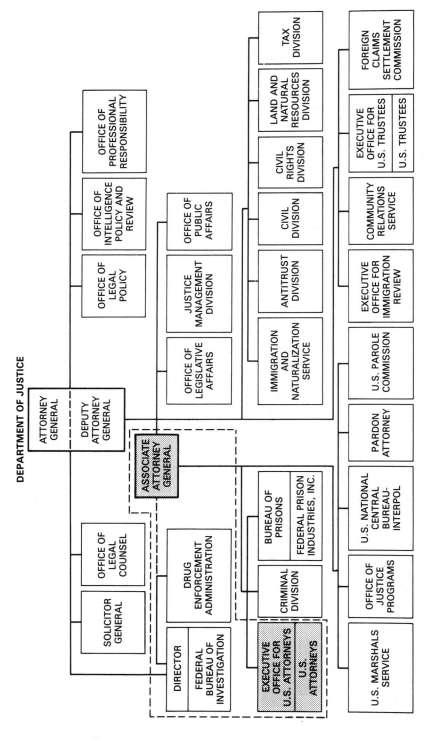

FIGURE 12-2 Executive Office for U.S. Attorneys—with 94 offices (Strike Force Nucleus).

Source: U.S. Government Organization Manual, 1987–88. (Washington, D.C.: Office of Federal Registrar National Archives and Research Administration, 1987).

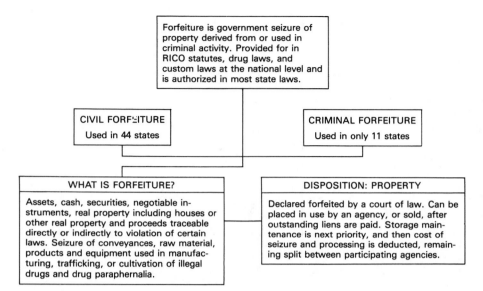

FIGURE 12-3   The evolution of the forfeiture process.

Source: U.S. Department of Justice (Washington, D.C.: U.S. Government Printing Office, 1988).

through its Criminal Information and Identification System and New York, through New York's State Identification Intelligence System.

Within a state, the most viable enforcement organization has been developed through a regional concept—the consolidation of efforts within the major metropolitan areas to include satellite cities. In 1981, the director of the FBI announced that the entire ruling hierarchy of the Los Angeles organized crime family was convicted of racketeering and extortion charges. This was the result of cooperation among regional units. The assignment of U.S. or district attorneys for legal assistance has made this type of organization a potent force against organized crime.

In the metro squad concept, the district attorney, the sheriff's office, and local bedroom cities furnish people to pursue organized crime investigations that cross boundaries. This cooperative approach eliminates problems frequently encountered with groups moving out of the city limits when the "heat" is on in the city. Figure 12-4 illustrates the organizational structure of this concept.

The multicounty concept has some inherent problems because it places the district attorney in an enforcement as well as a prosecutorial position. Investigators are assigned to the unit from a local agency. This places the district attorney in both a supervisory and prosecutorial role, thus minimizing conflict with the traditional enforcement attitude toward prosecution.

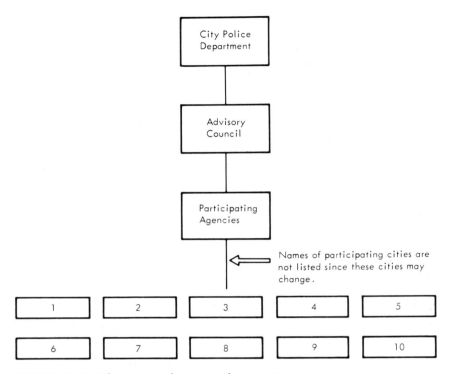

FIGURE 12-4   The metropolitan squad concept.

However, this concept does violate the separation of power principle. The organizational structure is shown in Figure 12–5.

One advantage of this system is that a multicounty area comes under the jurisdiction of the district attorney and the organized crime unit. This concept expands the "metro squad" into a regional unit and enhances exchange of information, coordination of investigations, and the ability to move beyond city and county limits to combat crime that inevitably springs up in the suburbs when enforcement pressure is exerted within the city.

POLICY DEVELOPMENT

Merely because enforcement becomes regionalized or national in scope does not remove the threat of corruption. As law enforcement activities extend from the executive branch to the judicial branch and into the elective process, the likelihood of corruption increases. When identifying efficiency within local police systems, an important organizational key lies in the overlapping of enforcement units that serve as a "check and balance" for other units of

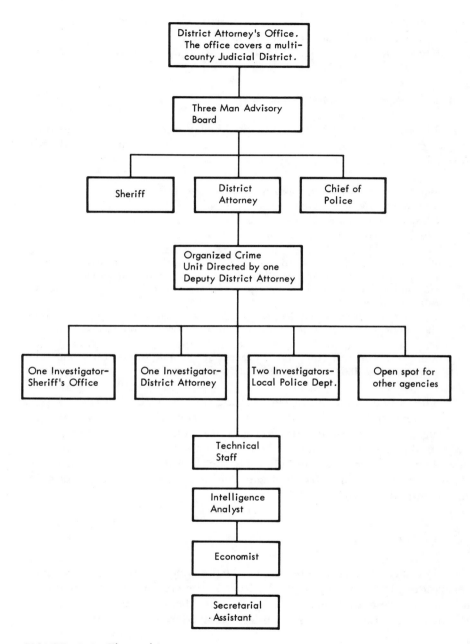

FIGURE 12-5 The multicounty concept.

the system. For example, an internal security, internal affairs, or personal unit overseeing the conduct of officers is necessary if a department has been lax or has failed to investigate organized criminal violations.

Determining Community Needs

In the formulation of broad policies, the law enforcement administrator should carefully assess many factors in determining a community's needs. A few basic guidelines are cited here:

What is the character and makeup of the community with reference to economic and industrial development?

What is the extent and type of organized crime in the community?

What is the community sentiment; do public and official goals coincide to offer guidelines for a sound policy?

What is the past history of enforcement for vice and other crimes of an organized nature in the community? Political structures rarely make vice reform a continuing process; political corruption is rarely investigated at the local level of government.

What are the physical facilities available for organized crime enforcement; does the physical plant include equipment necessary for complex investigations?

How can personnel needs be met and fiscal support found? Organized crime units are frequently considered unnecessary expenditures. Political factions can eliminate all organized enforcement effort through budget manipulation.

The police chief can, in part, dictate the degree and effectiveness of enforcement through the administrative structure of the department. Although a chief of police may delegate the authority for vice and other organized crime enforcement tasks, the ultimate responsibility for the success of an enforcement policy belongs to the chief. The police administrator should have rigid policies regarding the enforcement of all statutes pertaining to organized crime.

Use of Personnel

Formal and informal pressures make the allocation of personnel a matter of administrative judgment. Organized crime enforcement, while using all the basic organizational techniques, must also make special provisions to ensure that the following criteria are considered.[3]

All violations, with particular emphasis placed on vice violations, should be strictly enforced.

[3]Changes to emphasize organized crime instead of vice have been made.

Intelligence officers should be oriented to the political dangers inherent in the job, community, etc.[4]

Organized crime violations should be an enforcement function of all officers.

The techniques of enforcement should be within the rule of law.

Sensational or emotional crimes are no justification for deviating from the laws of legal arrests and procedures.

An officer enforcing organized crime statutes cannot moralize. The statutory laws are explicit and serve as a guide for strict enforcement.

A policy of personnel transfer in and out of organized crime units may be desirable. Although this may appear to create inefficiency, this should not be the case in a well-organized unit.

All violations reported to a department should be in writing.

All investigations made by a unit should be recorded in writing as the investigation progresses.

Records should be protected but should not be so secretive as to render the information useless. This problem is discussed in Chapter 13, where reference is made to the policies of the SEARCH Committee.

Not only supervisors, but the operating organized crime investigators must know the reasoning behind a policy. If the officers understand the policy and the reasons behind its formation, they will be better able to accept responsibility for rigid enforcement.

The organized crime investigator is primarily an independent operator while in the field; therefore, special instruction on department policy toward this type of enforcement is mandatory. Many departments recognize this need and actually have supervisory ranks operating in conjunction with or in direct control of one or two officers.

Policies for Expense Accounting

Intelligence officers are, as a general rule, supplied money from official sources to conduct investigations. Most organized crime prevention operations are supplied with funds to pay for information. The expenditure of this money requires that for every dollar spent there must be (1) a signed receipt from the expending officer, (2) a designation of the amount spent, (3) the reason for the expenditure, and (4) a record of any complaints, arrests, or other case dispositions made as a result of this expenditure.

In most agencies at the local level, the informer will be paid on a "piece basis." In state and federal agencies, the informer may be employed on a full-time basis. This type of expenditure runs into thousands of dollars, but in most instances will be more effective in securing organized criminal intelligence.

Unit commanders usually have some latitude in determining how the money is spent. The policy governing the expenditure of "secret service

---

[4]Intelligence functions are the backbone of the organized crime unit. Some departments may have special units designated as an organized crime unit and use intelligence as a staff service.

money" by a department or agency must be closely audited. Political office seekers are quick to audit the expenditure of these funds.

The example of such an accounting system presented here is adopted, in part, from a memorandum from the Law Enforcement Assistance Administration, Department of Justice, addressed to operating organized crime units:

> Confidential expenditures will be authorized for subgrants at the State, County, and City level of Law Enforcement.
>
> The funds authorized will be established in an imprest fund controlled by a bonded cashier.
>
> The Agent or Officer in charge of the investigation unit to which the imprest fund is assigned must authorize all advances of funds up to $500.00 to Agents or Officers for the purchase of information. Payments in excess of $500.00 must be approved by the head of the law enforcement unit to which the subgrant is made. Such authorization must specify the information to be received, the amount of expenditures, and assumed name of the informer.
>
> There must be maintained, by the investigation unit, confidential files of the true names, assumed names, and signatures of all informers to whom payments of confidential expenditures have been made. To the extent practicable, pictures and/or fingerprints of the informer payee should also be maintained. A sample signature of the informer will be obtained and attached to the informer identity sheet.
>
> The Agent or Officer shall receive from the informer payee a receipt of the following nature.
>
> On 25 percent of the contacts, when payments are made, a second Agent or Officer will appear as the witness to the transaction.
>
> On 10 percent of the meetings, the Agent or Officer in charge shall be present to verify the payment to the informer.
>
> The signed receipt from the informer payee with a Memorandum detailing the information received will be forwarded to the Agent in Charge and/or the Supervisor of the Unit.
>
> The Agent in Charge and/or the Supervisor of the Unit will compare the signature on the receipt with the signature on the informer identity sheet.
>
> The Agent in Charge and/or the Supervisor will evaluate the information received in relation to the expense incurred.
>
> A certification of payment to the cashier will be made on the Purchase Voucher form and will be approved by the Agent in Charge and/or the Supervisor on the basis of the report and the informer payee's receipt. Final approval before submission will be by the Chief of the Criminal Law Enforcement Division, i.e., Project Director.
>
> The Agent in Charge and/or the Supervisor will prepare a quarterly report showing the status and reconciliation of the imprest fund and itemizing each payment, name used by informer payee, information received and use to which information was put. This report will be furnished to the Director of the Agency or Chief of the Department upon request.
>
> All of the above records necessary to support, document and verify expenditures are subject to the record and audit provisions of the concerned agency/department with the exception of the true name of the informer.

For practical implementation and application within the bounds of these guidelines, the following procedures will also be in effect in the disbursement of confidential funds.

Usual procedures as outlined will be followed in applying for reimbursement. This procedure shall consist of:

Explanation and breakdown on Weekly Activity Report.

Detailed investigative or Intelligence Report and/or a Memorandum "keyed" to the expenditure, along with an additional Memorandum explaining in detail the expenditure involvement.

The submission of a signed Purchase Voucher form.

The completion of and submission of an informer identity sheet "coded" to the informer's identity.

The Commander of the Division or Bureau will approve the expenditures involved by signing the appropriate Purchase Voucher.

The Agent or officer in charge of the Unit will then approve these expenditures by signing the Purchase Voucher as approved by the Supervising Agent. The Purchase Voucher will then be submitted to the Chief of the Agency or Department for his approval prior to being forwarded to Accounting. The Purchase Voucher will reflect the expenditure number and the appropriate budgetary unit as assigned by the Accounting office.

Filing Procedure—Adequate files will be maintained and are to include:

Weekly Activity Reports reflecting activity and expenditures.

Monthly Mileage Reports reflecting miles traveled.

Travel and/or Per Diem Travel Record.

Informer Identity Sheet (coded and complete as practical).

Informer Signature Card.

Accounting Ledger to be maintained by the Unit Accountant reflecting all expenditures in detail by name, date and key code number, adequately cross indexed in order to readily provide a full justification and/or explanation of expenditures involved.

One copy of the Purchase Voucher will be filed.

The informer receipt will be maintained in the informer's file.[5]

SPECIAL ADMINISTRATIVE PROBLEMS

A few key administrative problems have been selected for discussion. The five cited here are issues that arise in most law enforcement agencies when dealing with organized crime. They are (1) the structure of administrative subunits to ensure lines of authority, responsibility, and channels of communication; (2) supervisory responsibility in planning operations; (3) informal groups within the formal organization; (4) goals for the officer; and (5) the violator and officer relationship.

---

[5]The policies cited were originally established from the General Accounting Office policies for organized crime control units. They have been changed and updated with fiscal policies of several major police agencies to etablish what the author believes to be an adequate system of accounting.

The Structure of Administrative Subunits

The personal philosophy of an agency head will dictate how to organize an agency for effective control. The illustrations given here are only four of many variations that may exist in the organizational hierarchy of a department.

The chief of police in small and medium departments may have intelligence officers and supervisors reporting directly. This line of command is shown in Figure 12–6. In larger departments, this authority is usually shared with the division or precinct commanders, as shown in Figures 12–7 and 12–8. If this authority is delegated, the chief should have one or more units to ensure that the policies are being carried out. The organizational structure of a department helps to ensure policy compliance. In Figure 12–9, the overlapping of unit jurisdictions serves as a check on other units enforcing laws dealing with organized crime.

Supervisory Responsibility in Planning Operations

While most activity will result from individual action, there are times when large-scale activities become necessary. These operations must be carefully planned and coordinated, and minute details must be given to participating enforcement officers. An important facet of an investigation is to assign overall responsibility to one person.

The political ramifications of an action should be anticipated and all possible loopholes closed. Special attention must be given to the safety and conduct of officers when a large group operates. A plan detailing where each officer will be stationed or positioned during every phase of an operation is important. The location, physical features, numbers, and types of suspects anticipated, as well as special evidence to be seized, should be discussed before the entire group of investigating officers.

The importance of expertise in organized crime investigations man-

FIGURE 12-6 Small centralized vice and intelligence unit.

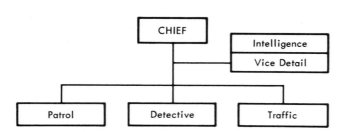

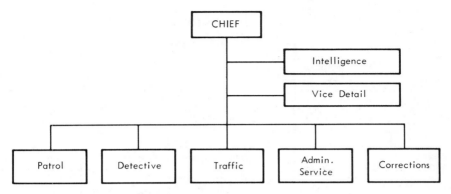

FIGURE 12-7   Large centralized vice and intelligence unit.

dates an ability for informal leadership. Planning and the stimulation of personal and professional pride are the criteria for a successful supervisor.

Informal Groups Within the Formal Organization

No other work or assignment will so readily create small cliques within any formal organization as vice and organized crime enforcement. Two or three working members of a unit will evolve into a working team unto themselves. This type of informality may enhance the individual's morale, but,

FIGURE 12-8   Large decentralized vice and intelligence unit with separate organized crime unit.

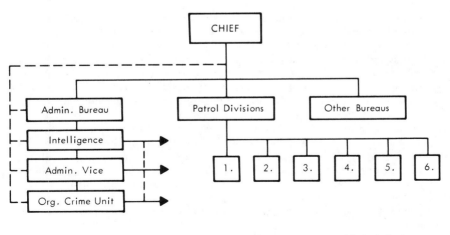

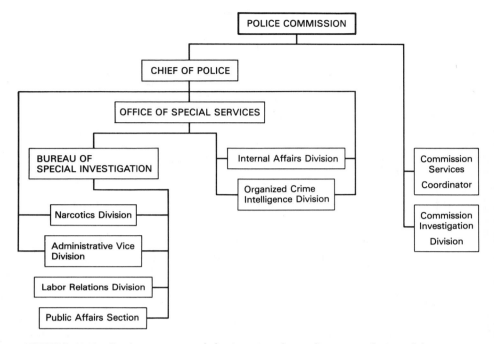

FIGURE 12-9 Basic structure of the Los Angeles police units designed for organized crime control.

in the long term, it destroys discipline and the formal operational structure. The supervisor of these units should be aware of these situations and keep all members of the unit working in close cooperation by:

> Making sure all information coming to the intelligence or organized crime unit is made available to every member of the unit, unless revealing it materially interferes with the investigation.
>
> Having current investigation findings in written form on complaints so that information may be made available to all investigators assigned to the case.
>
> Being sure, through staff meetings, that current knowledge possessed by the entire unit is disseminated to every other unit of the department working on organized crime.
>
> Providing shift overlap for units that are organized into day and night shifts. This will bring the crews going off duty into contact with those coming on duty.
>
> Being a group leader in brainstorming sessions on how to execute difficult investigations. Generally, a fixed location where activities are being conducted is known to some unit members. They can detail approaches, warning devices, and means of entry to a location.
>
> Determining whether past information may also support probable cause for arrest.

Assuming the role of a training officer. With court decisions, department policies, and division enforcement techniques constantly changing, training should be a daily function of the supervisory officer.

Directing the staff in establishing the tempo of the investigations, establishing debriefing techniques and coordinating the information that will go to staff and into a national system. The supervisor should be sure that interpersonal contact and contact with the public is maintained for the good of the agency and the public it serves.

Goals for the Officer

The most logical approach for effective organized crime control is to work on the apex of the confederations. It must be realized that the intelligence or organized crime unit officer at the local level is restricted in scope. The local officer usually finds little difficulty in identifying and arresting individual gamblers, bunco artists, and drug users. It is when he or she attempts to climb the ladder of the criminal hierarchy that he or she encounters difficulty. As the "small violator" becomes a "big violator," much more time is required for the investigation, more money is necessary for undercover work, and avenues of investigation will close because of influential contacts by the individual being investigated. Although it is desirable to apprehend the "big violator," the pressure of making cases just to maintain a semblance of control restricts the number of "big cases" on which an organized crime unit can work.

Violator and Officer Relationship

The relationship between an organized crime member and the officer is usually congenial and friendly because each feels dependent on the other for mutual assistance. A congenial relationship does not imply deals and collusion; however, many officers have found they are unable to keep the relationship on a friendly yet professional basis. The criminal violator is most anxious to encourage close relationships because this necessitates a trade of information. Frequently, that trade of information may be detrimental to the investigation. The officer must be cautious of what he or she tells an informer or criminal acquaintance. The officer should get information, not give it.

The vice, intelligence, and organized crime unit officer will spend years on the borderline of semilegal associations. The bookie, bunco artist, loan shark, and racketeer of all descriptions will be daily contacts. Without these contacts the officer will be ineffective. However, the problem of association is one of selection and of administrative transfers. Records of corruption and dishonesty in enforcement agencies will show that these acts are preceded by lax policies that permit these associations to continue over long periods of time.

DEVELOPING A PHILOSOPHY FOR ORGANIZED CRIME CONTROL

The ultimate goal for establishing policy and organizational concepts is to arrive at an enforcement philosophy to which a department may subscribe. The development of a sound philosophy should precede the development of policy and organization. However, with organized crime enforcement, there has been no pragmatic philosophy established.

The individual concerned with vice control and other organized crime violations must identify and establish his or her own philosophy. Whether an officer recognizes it or not, every person concerned with control of this type of human criminality has a philosophy on which he or she relies in doing the job. It is neither systematic nor integrated. Most frequently, it is illogical, inconsistent, and contradictory. What one reveals outwardly is likely to be inconsistent with the philosophy he or she uses in practice. There must be some logical coordination between the dynamics of these activities and the philosophy of the individual in the enforcement of organized crime.

There are many reasons why an officer's philosophy and practices are illogical and inconsistent. Organized crime personnel deal with complex problems in complex surroundings. As many critics have pointed out, the enforcers cannot be completely rational about their actions because it is impossible in this type of control to solve all the conditions of rationality. It is impossible for them to know all the facts about the situations they face. They cannot conceive all the ramifications that may result from situations they must deal with from day to day. They are not usually aware of the vast range of alternatives to be given consideration. Their knowledge of the goals to be achieved is limited, and that lack of knowledge for the ultimate results is critical to a compatible solution.

If the law officer is to deal adequately with complex organized crime problems, he or she must simplify them, put them in logical contextual frameworks of understanding, and relate them to a system over which he or she has some degree of control. He or she must analyze the problems in terms of ideas and of values that are significant to him or her. To do a good job, the officer must depend on a philosophy. This section is an effort to assist the officer in understanding that personal philosophy by presenting a broad group of ideas on which the individual may then base a systematic enforcement ideology.

A person may use the term "philosophy" in any one of its many meanings. For the purpose of this text, it has been viewed as "a system of ideas" that does two things. First, it attempts to define what is true—when certain crimes are legalized, the inevitable decay of society will result; or legalized gambling corrupts the whole of society. What our philosophy alleges to be true may not be subject to empirical proof, and sometimes it may be wrong. Yet it is important to describe the complex nature of reality in these terms.

Second, a philosophy should attempt to determine what questions are important, ask them, and rule out others. This is a decision the individual officer must make. Frequently, the officer must decide on the basis of indecisive rules of law and group pressures. Of course, not all questions have equal value for the individual. "Natural law" students, who think it is important to ask what values the moral order of the universe would impose on them, or a causist, who might ask what precedents existed for handling a situation, will arrive at different conclusions from a given set of facts. To evaluate each crime situation, and even more accurately the general concepts of organized crime control, this chapter has covered a broad spectrum of ideologies. Not all have been adequately treated, but they should serve to help the individual develop a set of values in making decisions. Each reader must establish, develop, and implement a personal categorical set of values. For example, an officer must reconcile in his or her own mind that contracting with a street bookmaker is, in fact, contracting with a national organization. The officer must carefully weigh evidence that shows labor union influence in settling issues repugnant to his or her own viewpoints. When an officer finds political and legal corruption, does he or she become a participant, or does he or she follow an individual code? The questions, of course, remain unanswered until the problems present themselves.

A citizen is faced with the same challenges. If citizens are weak, corrupt, or indifferent to organized crime, they can hardly expect law enforcement, judicial officers, and political officers to be different. The criminal justice system is a reflection of the people it serves.

SUMMARY

Dynamic management processes are keystones in the effort against organized crime. Correct planning processes have been avoided until recently simply because no one took sufficient interest in the "victimless" crimes. When comprehensive planning comes into general use, a number of organizational concepts need to be studied and expanded. For example, there must be established a clear accountability in law and management procedures for all levels of control. In addition, ecological predictors will indicate the amount of enforcement for organized crime in local areas. An important organizational task is to refine the policy and procedures manuals using accepted management practices. There is need for the standardization of laws simply because criminals move across state lines.

Local option, if there is to be effective control, is a dead issue. There is a need to structure the organization around regional units, and to devise special strategies for organized crime control based on strategies outlined in the President's Commission Report of 1986. Key policy issues in organized crime enforcement are expense accounting, basic unit structure supervisor responsibility for planning, and the control of informal employee groups. Each officer must establish goals and a philosophy as he or she works in the enforcement of all laws and in association with violators.

QUESTIONS FOR DISCUSSION

1. Organized crime prevention units have unique organizational problems that deserve special attention. Identify them.
2. Do the two philosophical approaches to organized crime control (violation response vs. attrition) influence the organization and operations of an enforcement unit?
3. Does the precise identification of variables that influence organized crime in a particular area of the country dictate the type of enforcement needed?
4. Why is "accountability" such a critical factor in the organizing process?
5. The basis on which effective organizations will be established on a national scale will be consistency in law. Can the 1970 Organized Crime Control Act serve as a model?
6. Discuss the concept of "checks and balances" and identify how effective organizational structure makes it function.
7. Identify the advantages of the multistate compact; the disadvantages.
8. Discuss the importance of the state role in organized crime control.
9. What are the strongest arguments for making organized crime units regional?
10. Identify five key administrative problems that must be solved for the operation of an effective organized crime unit.

13

Intelligence Gathering and Dissemination

LEARNING OUTCOMES

1. Gain an overview of the need for domestic intelligence gathering.
2. Understand the complexities and the processes of intelligence gathering.
3. Know the legal and social ramifications of loosely controlled intelligence systems.
4. Develop techniques to perfect intelligence-gathering methods.
5. Recognize analysis as a necessary ingredient of an intelligence collection system.

The heart of any program designed to control organized crime is the intelligence-gathering process.[1] How these processes take place under constitutional safeguards poses special considerations for enforcement agencies. The intelligence-gathering processes have a different significance at each level of enforcement. A modular system must be developed to deal with this difference. The requirements of an effective system first and foremost must guarantee individual confidentiality and rights as well as the rights of society. With the growth of effective data processing intelligence-gathering systems, there are few physical limitations for collecting information. In reality, the data-gathering capability of present systems is far greater than that needed and desirable for an effective enforcement network. To illustrate practical intelligence-gathering processes, the following areas are considered: (1) ethical considerations in data gathering, (2) intelligence records organization, and (3) common methods for data collection.

[1]Intelligence may be defined as information that has some degree of verification. For a complete discussion of agency intelligence, see Don R. Harris, *Basic Elements of Intelligence*, (LEAA, U.S. Department of Justice, September 1976).

ETHICAL CONSIDERATIONS

Mass civil intelligence gathering in the late 1960s and the early 1970s brought to light a dramatic need to evaluate carefully who should be in the business of data compilation and the type of data needed to ensure public safety without violating the freedoms and rights guaranteed the individual under constitutional government.

Civil intelligence collection quickly takes on many aspects of military intelligence gathering. This poses many philosophical, legal, and ethical problems for the law enforcement officers who must ultimately do the field intelligence work. Methodology for intelligence investigations, no matter how clearly spelled out, is subject to ethical oversights, abuses, lack of administrative direction, and legal questions.

In an article in the *Saturday Review,* Ralph Nader illustrated in "The Dossier Invades the Home" how privacy is being invaded and how information that is being collected is abused. He showed that by selecting bits of information from hundreds of sources, information systems are thus developing a pattern of life style. The privacy of the individual has vanished. There is no question that good intelligence does precisely as Nader says. Some form of control must be implemented for both civilian and government intelligence networks. We need an intelligence-gathering capability that will protect society and its members.

Because intelligence gathering is modified by individual values and priorities, an attempt is made here to cover the broad general approaches of standardized intelligence gathering as outlined by statute and as practiced by operating agencies. These basic procedures must be followed to establish national computer capability. For example, standardized coding forms must comply with those from the National Crime Information Center, and all data gathered should be coded to conform to the format shown in Appendix D. Data collection must also conform to the requirements of the Electronic Communications Privacy Act of 1986 (ECPA).

To safeguard automated records, a national committee entitled Systems for Electronic Analysis and Retrieval of Criminal Histories (SEARCH) has developed comprehensive guidelines for use in information and intelligence gathering. This system has been implemented through the Interstate Organized Crime Index.

General Guidelines of the SEARCH Committee

The most carefully thought-out guidelines regarding the problems of publicity and release of information have come from this federally sponsored group for civilian data gathering. The objectives in the report published by the project staff are threefold and still serve as guidelines in 1989.

1. To construct a fundamental working document that enumerates potential security and privacy problems and presents solutions for the guidance of participants using Project SEARCH guidelines.
2. To provide a dynamic framework of essential elements of security and privacy for a national system developed as a result of Project SEARCH.
3. To outline the kinds of security requirements and self-imposed disciplines that participants have, by their own initiative, levied on themselves and their colleagues in Project SEARCH.[2]

The issues identified regarding security and privacy are these:

1. Unintentional errors. From typographic errors to mistaken identities, there is always the possibility that the data finally stored in the system will be incorrect, without any intent to make it so.
2. Misuse of data. Information can be used out of context or for purposes beyond the legitimate criminal justice functions, by persons who are actually authorized access and by those who acquire the information without authorization.
3. Intentional data change. The data maintained can be destroyed or modified to accomplish the same objectives as described under misuse, or to restrict the proper and effective performance of criminal justice functions. It has been suggested that organized crime may attempt to penetrate the system for this purpose.[3]

In identifying these issues, the committee implemented a number of recommendations and established national guidelines in the following areas:

A code of ethics
Development of model administrative regulations
A resolution to limit the information
Content of the central index
Acceptance of the principle of postauditory evaluation and feedback
Education and training for participants

These guidelines show how state and local agencies have standardized to provide information flow back and forth to all agencies. There is reason to believe some federal agencies will not be committed to this system in theory or in fact. These guidelines point up reasons for believing that "hard core" intelligence information will still be transmitted from person to person by those engaged in law enforcement. In spite of weaknesses that may exist in a computerized system, it is still the only hope for developing an adequate system for information retrieval and dissemination.

---

[2]*Security and Privacy Considerations in Criminal History Information Systems* (Sacremento: Project SEARCH Staff, California Crime Technological Research Foundation, 1970), p. 1. Changes conform to the Electronic Privacy Act of 1986.

[3]Ibid., p. 5. These concepts are still viable and serve as guides for an evolving criminal justice intelligence network. SEARCH offered basic guidelines, and the systems that have evolved throughout the country follow the pattern it recommended.

During the development of an intelligence-gathering system, all persons, both civilian and government, have been kept informed of the security and privacy problems associated with massive data gathering. The SEARCH committee drew up guidelines that have served as a model for the development of a data-based system.

Security and Privacy Recommendations

These policies on data content have been recommended by the committee and can serve as guides for a department and for the field officer. *Data included in the system must be limited to that with the characteristics of public record.*[4] In substance, these would be:

> The fact, date and arrest charge; whether the individual was subsequently released and, if so, by what authority and on what terms.
> The fact, date and results of any pretrial proceedings.
> The fact, date and results of any trial or proceeding; any sentence or penalty.
> The fact, date and results of any direct or collateral review of that trial or proceeding; the period and place of any confinement.
> The fact, date and results of any release proceedings.
> The fact, date and authority of any act of pardon or clemency.
> The fact and date of any formal termination to the criminal justice process as to that charge or conviction.[5]

These recommendations pertain only to public records. Data not falling in this category will be discussed later in this chapter.

If these data are to be part of the public record, the intelligence system should be:

> Recorded by officers of public agencies directly and principally concerned with crime prevention, apprehension adjudication, or rehabilitation of offenders.
> Recording must have been made in satisfaction of public duty.
> The public duty must have been directly relevant to criminal justice responsibility of the agency.[6]

Participants using the system have adopted a careful and permanent program of data verification, in the following manner:

> First, any such program should require participating agencies of record to conduct systematic audits of their files, in a fashion calculated to insure that those

[4]*Public Access to Criminal History Record Information*, U.S. Department of Justice, NCJ–111458, Washington, D.C., November 1988. Also see "The Electronic Communications Privacy Act: Addressing Today's Technology." *FBI Law Enforcement Bulletin*, April 1985, nn.

[5]*Security and Privacy Considerations*, p. 16.

[6]Ibid., p. 11.

files have been regularly and accurately updated. Periodic programs of employee re-education should also be required, so that every record custodian and clerk is fully conscious of the importance and necessity of faithful, conscientious performance. Appropriate sanctions, as described later in this chapter, should be available for those whose performance proves to be inadequate.

Second, where errors or points of incompleteness are detected, the agency of record should be immediately obliged to notify the central index (if the change involves data stored in the index) and any other participating agencies to which the inaccurate or incomplete records have previously been transmitted.

These procedures will be conducted by systematic audits. The agency of record shall maintain a file of all participants to which the inaccurate or incomplete records have previously been transmitted.

The agency of record shall maintain a file of all participants that have been sent records. Within a state, a record shall be kept of all agencies to which the System's data has been released.[7]

The Fair Credit Reporting Act, effective April 1971, imposed restrictions on the release of information. In addition, all known copies of records with erroneous or incomplete information are to be corrected.

Purge procedures shall be developed in accordance with the Code of Ethics. Each participating agency shall follow the law or practice of the state of entry with respect to purging records of that state.[8]

The purposes of these procedures are:

To eliminate information that is found to be inaccurate or at least unverifiable.

To eliminate information that, because of its age, is thought to be an unreliable guide to the subject's present attitudes or behavior.[9]

How such procedures are initiated is still being researched. Model state statutes for protecting and controlling data in the system have been adopted by participating states. How these statutes will evolve is still a part of the ongoing SEARCH Project. Basically, the system is assigned a governing board that has the authority to:

Monitor the activities of the participating state agencies.
Adopt administrative rules and regulations for the system.
Exercise sanctions over all agencies connected with the system.[10]

[7]Ibid., p. 20
[8]Ibid., pp. 11–12.
[9]Ibid., p. 20.
[10]Ibid., p. 35. Types of communication exempt from Electronic Communications Privacy Act of 1986 include publicly accessible radio communication, tracking devices, radio portions of cordless telephone communication, and tone-only paging devices.

Other general guidelines used in the intelligence system are as follows:

Direct access to the system should continue to be restricted to public agencies which perform, as their principal function, crime prevention, apprehension, adjudication, or rehabilitation of offenders.[11]

Under the general standards described above, the following classes or public agencies are permitted direct terminal access to the data system:

Police forces and departments at all government levels that are responsible for enforcement of general criminal laws. This should be understood to include highway patrols and similar agencies.

Prosecutorial agencies and departments at all government levels.

Courts at all government levels with a criminal or equivalent jurisdiction.

Correction departments at all government levels, including corrective institutions and probation departments.

Parole commissions and agencies at all government levels.

Agencies at all government levels that have as a principal function the collection and provision of criminal justice information.

Definitional questions as to users are presented for resolution to representatives of all the participating states in the system. To limit access, the following restrictions are made:

1. Participating states have limited the number of terminals within their jurisdiction to a number they can effectively supervise.
2. Each participating state has built its data system around a central computer, through which each inquiry must pass for screening and verification. The configuration and operation of the center provide for the integrity of the database.

Participating agencies have been instructed that their rights to direct access encompass only requests reasonably connected with their criminal justice responsibilities. Requests from outside the criminal justice community to examine data obtained through the system should be honored only if the receiving agency is authorized access by local law, state statute, or valid administrative directive. Efforts have been made to limit the scope of such authorized access. The security and privacy staff have studied various state "public record" doctrines and initiated appropriate exemptions from these doctrines for the system's data.

The use of data for research involves the following restrictions:

Proposed programs of research acknowledge a fundamental commitment to respect individual privacy.

[11]Ibid., pp. 12–15. After *Paul* v *Davis* (1983), many of the states have gone to open record statutes so that all intrastate information is public record.

Representatives of the system fully investigate each proposed program.

Identification of subjects is divorced as fully as possible from the data.

The research data are shielded by security system comparable to that which ordinarily safeguards system data.

Codes or keys identifying subjects with data have been given special protection.

Raw data obtained for one research purpose are not subsequently used for any other research purpose without the consent of system's representatives.

Security and data protection requirements are included in any research contract or agreement.

Nondisclosure forms are required and the system retains rights to monitor and, if necessary, terminate any project.

The following are minimum requirements for control of data dissemination:

Data received through the system are marked and readily identifiable as such.

Heads of agencies receiving information sign a copy of an appropriate recommended nondisclosure agreement.

Educational programs have been instituted for all who might be expected to employ the use of the system data.

Users are informed that reliance on unverified data is hazardous and that positive verification of identity should be obtained as quickly as possible.

Users are informed that careless use of data represents unprofessional conduct and may subject the user to disciplinary actions.

The central computer within each state, through which all data inquiries pass, screens all inquiries to exclude those that are inconsistent with system rules.

Rights of challenge and redress include the following:

The citizen's right to access and challenge the contents of his or her records forms an integral part of the system consistent with state law.[12]

Civil remedies are provided for those injured by misuse of the system as provided for by state law.

Organization and administration include these points:

The system participants operate with a board of directors (governing body) to establish policies and procedures governing the central index operation.

The system remains fully independent of noncriminal justice data systems and is exclusively dedicated to the service of the criminal justice community.[13]

[12]The Freedom of Information Act has not brought government records from behind closed doors, as was originally intended. There are nine categories of exemptions for disclosure, and these have been sufficient to protect law enforcement files from disclosure.

[13]Information of a noncriminal nature is frequently the most important strategic intelligence. If the system is to perform as a comprehensive data system, methodology to assimilate noncriminal data must be verified, analyzed, and placed in appropriate files.

A permanent committee or staff has been established to consider problems of security and privacy and to conduct studies in that area.

The permanent staff undertakes research to identify differences among the states in procedures and terminology, and disseminate information concerning these differences to all participants.

A systems audit is made periodically by an outside agency.

From the guidelines that have been presented here, the law enforcement officer is in a position to analyze those procedures that are acceptable and ethical.

Publicity and Release of Information

Organized crime information gathering, if not rigidly regulated, is subject to much valid criticism. The investigations surrounding organized crime produce information on persons who have high community visibility and political influence. Basically, two different approaches serve to control and regulate the dissemination of intelligence information. First are those persons who are interested in keeping intelligence gathering rigid and dissemination legal, factual, and ethical. Second are those who stand to benefit from a minimum amount of information being revealed regardless of how legally and how ethically the information was gained. Because of this second group there will be many pressures to suppress valid information that should be considered public knowledge. Civil suits, delays in fiscal funding, and other tactics are the most common ways to hamper investigations and information releases.

Determining what guidelines will be necessary for the release of information has had extensive study. The following guideline, although not following the procedures of all major intelligence units, is fairly representative and is cited as a logical guide.

Category 1.　Information for the internal use of NYSIIS only—cannot be released to other agencies.

Category 2.　Information releasable to specific agencies—restriction placed on use by donor.

Category 3.　Information releasable to any participating agency.

Category 4.　Information releasable to any criminal justice agency.[14]

---

[14]New York State Identification Intelligence System, *Security System for Organized Crime Intelligence Capability* (NYSIIS, Albany, 1970), p. 6a. These classifications are still valid and in principle concur with The Privacy Act of 1974. This act called on government to police itself, requiring agencies to limit their recordkeeping activities and to prevent disclosure of information except under special circumstances. The law set up procedures under which individual citizens could gain access to their records and challenge those that were inaccurate. Also see the Computer Security Act of 1987.

To further safeguard intelligence data, it can be classified as S—sensitive, or E—extra sensitive.[15] Both classifications are designed to ensure against information getting to the wrong people.

In reality, intelligence information, if it is to be effective, must be regarded in a different way. Much intelligence information, such as verified criminal associations, illegal business transactions, and many other illegal activities that are now classified should be designated as open to the public and subject to analysis by intelligence experts. If verified, this information should then be published by interested news media. Historically, intelligence records have been dead files providing little tactical value.

With ethical considerations far from resolved, it is, however, appropriate to analyze the intelligence records system to determine what information is being gathered and how it is processed.

INTELLIGENCE RECORDS ORGANIZATION

Policy makers at all levels of an organization are finding that a systematic information processing unit requires special administrative consideration.[16] To keep a system compatible with advances in technology, the organizational hierarchy is constantly changing to keep the intelligence processes within normal channels of communication and under the administrative direction of the management structure. Historically, law enforcement administrators have been able to maintain control of information through records distribution, staff meetings, and training sessions. With the infusion of federal money into local departments for highly specialized intelligence and organized crime units, the older methods cannot control the necessary processing of information coming to a department.

In an intelligence records system, three distinct kinds of information will be generated:

1. Services to an agency head that will assist in making broad decisions concerning the impact of organized crime on the total agency operation.
2. Information concerning the criminal clientele directly concerned with operations of specialized units in an agency.
3. Information that concerns an agency's operation and relationship with other criminal justice groups.

Information coming to an agency that reflects managerial processes may concern such matters as these:

[15]Ibid., p. 7. The various systems have their own codes and symbols.
[16]Harris, *Basic Elements of Intelligence*, p. 9.

1. Identifying staff functions through development of reporting policy. For example, all intelligence personnel should be able to report directly to the chief. Thus, information is not "filtered."
2. Separation of function in allocating responsibility for work to be performed. For example, in most cases, intelligence will not be a "personnel" or "internal affairs" function. Intelligence may assist as a service unit, but it should not have the responsibility for everyday enforcement activities. (This may vary with the size of an enforcement unit.)
3. Division of labor within a unit should be explicitly set out in policy and procedures manuals. Where there is an overlap of function, it should be deliberately designed to offer a "check and balance" to the system.
4. External relations, both within and outside an agency, is a key managerial consideration. There are techniques for the forced flow of information that must be pursued. For example, mandatory reporting and distribution, staff brainstorm sessions, and training so extensive that an officer accepts liaison and communication as a responsibility rather than as an occasional luxury.

The author assumes that agency managers are aware of intelligence dangers and strengths. Thus, emphasis here will not be on management processes, but on the processing of information about the criminal clientele, which begins at the international level.

The Intelligence Establishment by Harry H. Ransom contains a comprehensive analysis of the national intelligence network. With the success of the Central Intelligence Agency and allied units in international intelligence, there is pressure to develop a similar system for domestic intelligence. The National Crime Information Center (NCIC) has been the organization that decides who uses the system. The following section is an endeavor to project the type of information that is evolving from present systems.

To adopt any automated system is ultimately demeaning to human dignity and a threat to individual liberty, as described in Arthur Miller's *The Assault on Privacy*. Before a domestic intelligence system is fully developed, there will be many hard decisions and much soul searching. Areas for discussion will be (1) the rationale for intelligence collection, (2) identification of functional concepts for a records system, and (3) common methods of data collection.

The Rationale for Intelligence Collection

The intelligence processes are basically the developing of techniques to collect, evaluate, interpret, and synthesize information into an estimate that can be used by decision makers. In illustrating the various tyes of domestic data-gathering functions, we should keep in mind that the present NCIC data gathering applies only to the solution of a crime. A fact that assists in interpreting other facts or strategic intelligence information that has little or no relationship to a crime or a series of crimes under investigation is not presently entered into NCIC. This lends some assurance, for whatever it may be worth, that NCIC is an operational file rather than one designed for intelligence. Thus, any intelligence generated from the NCIC file is a secondary function. This system may offer some security to individual citizens. In actuality, this fragments the intelligence system to such an extent that much of the data needed for strategic and operational activity lie untapped.

The history of military intelligence, with a greater degree of sophistication, has had the same growing pains as are presently being experienced in domestic intelligence gathering. Questions regarding the controlling political body, the structure for gathering data, and the dissemination of selective facts are still unanswered problems. Both the police and the public fear any intelligence apparatus because there are judgment guidelines to say what type of information and dissemination capability an intelligence system should have.

Many publishing companies issue directories of individuals with common interests or backgrounds, for example, Who's Who, Dunn and Bradstreet, Standard and Poor's Register of Corporations, Directors and Executives, Moody's Bank and Financial Manual, and hundreds of others, many of which are now automated.

Historically, domestic intelligence on criminals, including business monopolies and conspiracies, has been segmented and suppressed for political and military reasons and in general has been of little value.

The development of national data has appeared to take this approach. The Federal Bureau of Investigation, in accepting administrative control of NCIC, has indicated that it will develop intelligence internally from its own agents and operators and from data acquired from operational data, which is a part of NCIC. The SEARCH Project has claimed the area that is identified as "subject in process." Present data-processing units are not focused on collecting information for pure strategic intelligence. Perhaps the most effective national organization for generating intelligence information is the Law Enforcement Intelligence Unit (LEIU). This unit, an ad hoc group of law enforcement agencies, exchanges information on an informal basis from local and state intelligence files. Although LEIU has done much to promote the exchange of information, there is neither adequate financial support nor statutory responsibility for a great degree of expertise in the strategic intelligence field.

In the past decade with the advance of intelligence-gathering technology and the dramatic increase in customs and drug crime, it is foolish to believe that sophisticated computer systems that maintain data on long-range operations of known drug dealers and known associates do not exist. The Irangate investigation confirmed that these systems do exist.

Identifying Functional Aspects of a Record System

With improved recordkeeping systems and the utilization of an integrated computer system, organized crime records will become a separate but an integral part of a centralized records system. The inquiry will be limited to key stations and codes so that confidential information will not be given to unauthorized sources (Figure 13–1). Hundreds of automated systems have been developed for cities and regions. Systems such as TRACER, developed by the Norfolk, Virginia, Police Department, are examples of systems that serve the tactical operations of a multicity region.[17]

Information on organized crime can be entered into a records system from a number of sources (refer to Appendix C):

1. Information on arrestee, location, and type of crime charged comes from booking records.
2. Information on complaints, suspects, and location is taken from the complaint form.
3. License and permit information, on at least a regional basis, is automatically entered from agencies concerned with the licensing function. For example, if the city clerk's office issues business licenses, data on ownership, type of business, etc., would become a part of the information system.[18]

The system should be designed so that certain violations occurring at given locations will be entered into the system and on proper inquiry the system will supply a complete background file on a subject or location under investigation. When a location file is queried by an authorized intelligence officer, all recorded information on a given address will immediately become a part of the investigation. Background inquiry such as this should include a current photo of those connected with the business enterprise. A list of known associates from arrest reports, intelligence reports, and from field interrogation cards assists the officer in investigating organized crime.

Information on all complaints, electronically checked against past complaints on the location, suspects, and arrestees, will come to the investigator as part of the preinvestigation for a business enterprise or location being checked. In addition, vehicles, utility hookups, business licenses, or permit records will be checked when a new organized crime complaint comes to an intelligence unit.

Bringing speed and flexibility to intelligence records will undoubtedly be the greatest accomplishment in organized crime control during the next ten years. Direct access to past police history, methods of operation, and cur-

[17]J. W. Nixon and Ellen Posivach, "TRACER: Computerized Service for the Criminal Justice System," *FBI Law Enforcement Bulletin,* December 1978, pp. 7–11.

[18]James W. Stevens, *State and Regional Information Systems: The Criminal Justice Component* (Institute of Urban Studies, The University of Texas at Arlington, February 1970), pp. 10–20.

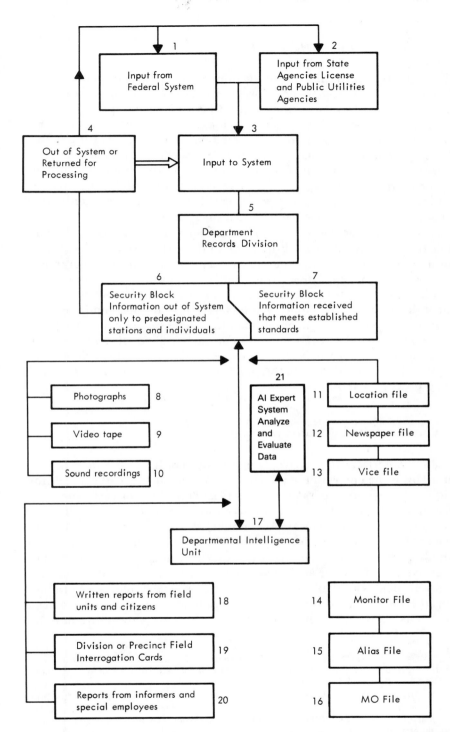

FIGURE 13-1 Configuration of system security for information entering and leaving the system.

rent illegal activities for use in investigations will support better prosecutions and improve the management information system. This information will focus on improved investigations and on better cases for prosecutions.[19]

Organized criminal records will no longer be separate entities but will be part of an integrated criminal justice system. In a data processing system, records of a confidential nature will be more secure than is now possible in a manual records system. The police administrator should begin planning for an integrated computer records system with intelligence records as an integral part of a centralized system. This concept has been part of most sophisticated intelligence information systems.

The extent and depth of inquiry on organized criminal intelligence will be limited only by the sophistication of the system and the accuracy of information entered into it. Remote inquiry stations can be programmed to receive only specific information; thus, the central storage unit can be protected against indiscriminate inquiry and will even note the source of an unauthorized inquiry. Godfrey and Harris indicate that computer technology has progressed to the point that multiple users can concurrently access a common database. In such a system, each individual user can get all the information he or she is allowed to see, and any information entering the system is safeguarded from the public disclosure.[20] The proposed intelligence process is shown in Figure 13–2.

Common Data Collection Methods

Most Americans today have their profile recorded in several computer banks. This is the end result of all types of automated data gathering. Information gathering on all persons is a practice that will not be easily remedied by legislation. As long as private industry and government pour millions of dollars into computer hardware, it is unlikely the indiscriminate collection of data will cease. Data collected by private business and government are dissimilar, yet each bit of information gathered goes to make up a comprehensive file of interrelated facts. All information collected by business and government is available to the other, through legal or illegal means. Both data-gathering systems are equally dangerous in terms of the uses being made of the collected data. It is not the purpose of this book to debate morality

[19]All systems in the NCIC net can be designed to receive all the intelligence information generated by the criminal justice system. National Space Agency sattelite systems are operational and collect intelligence data that are international in scope.

[20]E. Drexel Godfrey and Don R. Harris, *Basic Elements of Intelligence: A Manual of Theory, Structure and Procedures for Use by Law Enforcement Agencies against Organized Crime* (LEAA, U.S. Department of Justice, 1972), p. 275a. Artificial Intelligence Systems are now coming into common use in major police agencies.

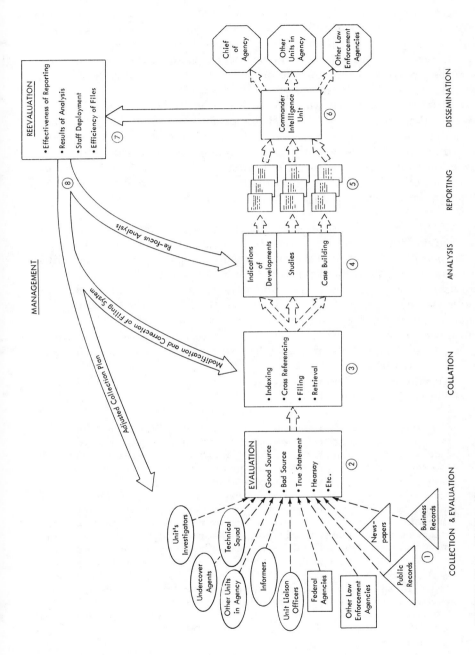

FIGURE 13-2 The intelligence process.

COLLECTION & EVALUATION   COLLATION   ANALYSIS   REPORTING   DISSEMINATION

215

or legality in terms of the information collected. Unless the law specifically prohibits certain acts of information gathering, it is presumed that both private business and government agencies will use techniques that are necessary to maintain a place in the business world or that law enforcement believes are necessary to equalize the technological advantage held by the criminal engaged in organized crime.[21]

A legal methodology with a realistic chance for success must be established if there is to be a sound basis for public agencies to be in the data-gathering business. Techniques used by the criminal must dictate the counter-measures imposed by law enforcement agencies. As we discuss the role of law enforcement in information gathering, it is important to observe a few of the information-gathering techniques used by sophisticated criminal groups that ultimately must be countered by law enforcement.

Criminal use of information technology. Organized criminal conspiracies are not concerned about constitutional guarantees such as "the right of the people to be secure in their persons, houses, papers and effects against unreasonable searches and seizures." They are interested only in desired results and that is what they get for the money they spend. The criminal conspiracies are not in the least worried about the Fair Credit Reporting Act. They will, in spite of legal restrictions, get desired information through apparently legitimate sources. To counter this type of activity, law enforcement agencies must have the same advantage, in terms of technology and legal guidelines within which to work.

To show how the criminal may use information-gathering devices, these brief illustrations are cited:

> Consumer fraud practices are so common as to defy individual identity. For example, price fixing, securities manipulation, and other forms of theft depend on the flow of massive amounts of information. Cooperative wholesale grocery associations, for example, frequently do not rely on supply and demand, but on monopolies in fixing food prices.
>
> Banking institutions are prime candidates because loan sharks are often tied in with legitimate lending institutions. Usurious rates and other credit dodges fluctuate on computer information. Credit information such as financial status and assets are for sale to criminal organizations through some credit reporting associations. This same information is available to extortionists, promoters, and others. No laws presently in use or proposed can stop or slow this practice.
>
> Wire services that furnish gambling information are important. Information such as the opening line and closing line on sports activities use computer services for carrying coded messages. These services are all provided on a contract basis as a part of a legitimate business enterprise such as sports networks and data transmission of seemingly innocent business data.

---

[21]U.S. Department of Treasury publishes *Statistics of Income* and the Internal Revenue Service uses files from the income tax returns to prosecute individuals in organized crime.

Information on swindled securities, antitrust violations, and sophisticated theft operations depend on automated information gathering and transmission. Information obtained by surveillance may be used for bribery, extortion, and shakedowns in a large number of ways. This type of activity is extremely effective when dealing with political figures and those who hold positions of trust. Any situation that demands additional persuasion can secure it through the use of surveillance instruments and data-gathering techniques.

The only way law enforcement can counter these types of operations is to have more advanced equipment and better technical personnel than that possessed by the criminal. The problem of dealing with criminal conspiracies is not going to be solved by laws that are unenforceable and procedures and guidelines that no one will follow. Eventually appropriate investigative techniques must be employed to counter equipment used by syndicate operations.

Countermeasures by law enforcement agencies. Decision making in organized crime control is based on data secured through the intelligence function. To make these vital decisions, government agencies need not receive carte blanche authority to pursue investigations without legal safeguards. They do need, however, a succinct set of rules to pursue an effective investigation. It is important to identify the procedures that are legal and to establish the basis on which administrative decisions and court cases are to be decided. Investigators rarely need to know all the personal habits, traits, and information about an individual for court prosecution. In the decision-making area, however, it is important to assess this type of information. Some is available to criminal leaders through certain kinds of private business transactions. It seems ironic that the legally designated agents of government are prohibited from securing comprehensive information.

The countermeasures by law enforcement have been the subject of many abuses. There can be no question that information on innocent persons has gone into intelligence files under the auspices of national security. A person in public life will have his or her name entered into intelligence files on many different occasions. The prime question should not be whether the name is in fact in the file, but whether or not the information gives a true and accurate picture of what transpired at that given time.

Analysis of Collected Data

Law enforcement is still weak in the analysis and linking of collected data. For the overall analysis of data, one or more persons must be trained as analysts. The analyst must be capable of developing patterns, networks, connections, and new areas of organized crime penetration from the file records and the incoming raw information. Without the analyst, the information flow cannot be used effectively. Without the analyst, much of the incoming raw information will remain just that.[22]

The analysis procedure consists of three steps.[23] (1) summarize, (2) compare, and (3) explain. Using the computer, an important new technique in analysis has emerged. This is called *linking,* and the technique determines the presence or absence of links among individuals.[24] The database usually consists of such information as investigation reports, arrest records, informant reports, financial statements, and newspaper articles.

The linking analysis is completed in six steps: (1) assembling the information, (2) abstracting information relevant to individual relationships and affiliations, (3) preparing an association matrix (an array of the relationships among a set of individuals, noting the strength of the links), (4) developing a preliminary link diagram, (5) incorporating organizations into the diagram, and (6) refining the link diagram. With more prosecutions under the RICO statute, this phase of analysis will become vital in the proof of a case. The issue of entering a person's name into an intelligence file is not as important as the absolute accuracy of such information.

The nature of the intelligence process does not necessitate massive collection of data by law enforcement officers. The data are available in hundreds of published documents and from persons who are interested in revealing information about an enemy. The real need is for clear-cut lines of policy and law to control the collection and dissemination of such information.

All types of information concerning some individuals have been collected indiscriminately by both government and business; there is little question that the individual's right of privacy has been violated by the forces who collect the information. There must be a closer look at how intelligence is collected and who is doing the collecting. How intelligence is processed and the role of the intelligence establishment must also be identified if logical laws to regulate its proliferation are to evolve. Intelligence gathering has lived under a cloak of secrecy, not through necessity, but because of vested interests and a blatant disregard for the right of the public to know what is being done.

SUMMARY

A great number of legal and moral issues must be resolved before comprehensive intelligence gathering can be achieved. Some techniques for control have been achieved by the SEARCH committee for effective data gathering and public protection. With new technology, the job is continuous.

[22]Godfrey and Harris, *Basic Elements of Intelligence,* p. 7.

[23]Ibid., pp. 27–37.

[24]W. R. Harper, "Application of Link Analysis to Police Intelligence," *Human Factors,* 17, 2 (April 1975), 157–64. Refer to all 1988 copies of *AI Expert* magazine.

It becomes apparent as the development of automatic data processing evolves that there is danger to the individual's right of privacy. If not curbed by rigid, realistic guidelines, this will destroy our free society.

The SEARCH committee reports offer guidelines on how an effective computerized intelligence system works. The design and organization of intelligence records are key factors in getting maximum usable information from select bits of intelligence. Every step, process, and structure of an intelligence function should be designed for the maintenance of maximum security, accuracy, and a control that provides for the check and balance system. Information must be develped into a records system that can be properly manipulated and made available to field units where it can provide some beneficial impact. If one step or procedure is weak, the entire system is subject to failure.

Many computer systems operated by private businesses and government bodies fail to provide adequate safeguards. As methods of data collection evolve, a warning should be issued concerning computerized intelligence. Unless control standards are established, maintained, and enforced, intelligence information will be used against the attainment of justice. Computerized systems that give the necessary intelligence data and provide protective safeguards must be developed.

QUESTIONS FOR DISCUSSION

1. Why are ethical considerations as important as statutory regulations in the collection and dissemination of intelligence information?
2. Identify major standards as established by the SEARCH committee. How do they affect the intelligence network?
3. Identify the major components of the Fair Credit Reporting Act and assess its value for protecting the citizen.
4. Identify a set of basic rules for the classification of information. Is the classification scheme too secretive or too lax in security?
5. What are the three basic forms of intelligence generated by a good records and reporting system? Do they conform to the 1986 Electronic Communications Privacy Act (ECPA)?
6. Explain how basic organization structure influences the control of intelligence through a "check and balance" system.
7. Will an automated records system offer greater security than a manual system? How safe is an automated system?
8. Explain the concept of "synthesizing" intelligence. How does it relate to linking? How will Artificial Intelligence Systems enhance this operation?
9. Identify factors that should cause concern about excessive intelligence gathering.
10. Assess the priority for accuracy of information being entered into an intelligence storage system.

14

Methods for Organized Crime Control

LEARNING OUTCOMES

1. Gain an overview of accepted methods for organized crime enforcement.
2. Recognize organization and management techniques that can be applied to crime control.
3. Know common control techniques for organized crime at the community level.
4. Understand techniques for field officers and how they affect organized crime control.
5. Know about commissions responsible for establishing policy leading to organized crime control.

There are a number of ways in which the control of organized crime should be pursued. Each of the ways brought out in this text must look to both the citizen and street patrol officer to ensure its success. As illustrated in Figure 14–1, these ways may be described as: (1) education and the development of awareness throughout the community, (2) civic action groups and crime commissions, and (3) punitive enforcement.

EDUCATION

The most positive approach for controlling organized crime is to inform the police and citizens of the magnitude and implications of organized crime in a community. When officer and citizen know the intricate route of money placed on a $2 bet, they may be reluctant to support or condone such an organization. When officer and citizen are aware of and understand that certain businesses are controlled by mobsters and illegal monopolies, economic sanctions will assist in bringing them to a halt.[1]

[1]Morton Mintz and Jerry S. Cohen, *America, Inc.* Copyright © 1971 by Jerry S. Cohen and Morton Mintz. Reprinted by permission of the publisher, Dial Press Inc., New York.

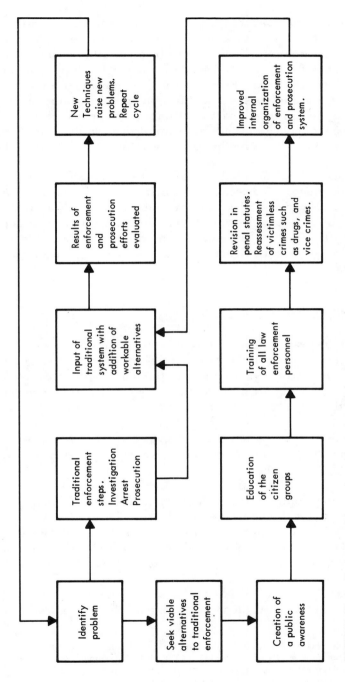

FIGURE 14-1 Programmed sequence for organized crime control.

This type of positive action is based on the premise that legislators have decriminalized the activities society will tolerate. Obviously if activities such as gambling are legalized, they cease to be a law enforcement problem.

Education of the police and general public holds the greatest hope for control of organized crime. Every state and national plan should concentrate on such education. A few law enforcement investigators placed about the state and the nation will have little impact on the problem unless they generate a core of police and citizens so knowledgeable about the techniques of organized crime that "street pressure" will force the confederations out of business.

Most states now include some form of specialized law enforcement training in organized crime techniques, operations, intelligence analysis, and coordination of field activities. Considerable emphasis has been placed on the training of prosecutors, legal advisors, and judges who serve clients involved with strike force operations. It is important to note that judges have been included in the legal orientation necessary to understand and prosecute organized crime.

Model Programs

Model long-range programs have been drawn up for states, to function under the direction of the governors. Through federal, state, and local financing, a variety of organized crime training programs are offered for all local officers. States are also identifying organized crime problems and are moving toward the education of citizens as a means of control for organized crime.

Some model plans could counter organized crime if properly implemented.[2] But the first step is still extensive training for criminal justice personnel.

Training should be structured to reach all personnel involved in organized crime control. For example, seminars open to the police, prosecutors, and judges should be offered throughout the state. These seminars should be followed by presentations to business groups and interested citizens. Following these sessions would be intensive in-service training for specialists engaged in the arrest and prosecution of organized crime offenders.

Because organized crime has such an impact on the economic and social structure of a community, the authors contend that education is the only

---

[2]Robert G. Blakely, Ronald Goldstock, and Charles H. Rogouin, *Rackets Bureau: Investigation and Prosecution of Organized Crime.* (Washington, D.C.: U.S. Government Printing Office, March, 1978). Also see Howard Abadinsky, *Organized Crime,* 2nd ed., (Chicago: Nelson Hall, 1985). A second step in controlling white collar crime was taken in January 1989 when six national task forces to investigate business frauds were created.

technique that will limit organized criminal influence in the community.[3] The federal effort of zeroing in on individuals and finding some statute in which to prosecute can quickly degenerate into persecution. The local approach of identifying a violation and searching for a culprit is equally absurd. The only way a confederation will be weakened is through pressure exerted by all levels of government through approved enforcement techniques. Public education is the only vehicle that can effectively translate many efforts into action.

The commission approach is partially an educational medium and partially an enforcement technique. Thus, considerable emphasis in organized crime suppression should be on the use of crime commission.

CIVIC ACTION GROUPS AND CRIME COMMISSIONS

Organized crime can be controlled, but only with full citizen support to reveal the criminal acts that are most covert. The rackets, which were revealed years ago by the Kefauver Committee, still exist simply because citizens have not taken it upon themselves to force necessary action to bring about prosecutions. There are basically two types of civic action groups. They may be classed as civic action citizens' groups and those established under the framework of government.

These two methods of suppressing organized crime are different; however, both look to the citizen as a main force for crime suppression. Civic action groups are usually ad hoc structures that attack a single problem, whereas the crime commissions are legally constituted bodies of government and should have a more lasting impact on the overall organized crime problem.

Civic Action Groups

The ultimate in prevention of any type of crime is an aroused citizenry. No agency of government can be better than the citizen it represents; thus, civic action groups are potent forces in an overall organized crime suppression effort. Civic groups historically have been the catalyst for reform movements. Public demand for stricter law enforcement and removal of covert vice crimes has had an impact on local organized crime. The prime problem with public participation in ad hoc groups is their short life and

[3]Many articles address this problem, but none arrive at definitive ways in which we should be addressing organized crime. D.C. Smith, Jr., "Organized Crime and American Life," *Society,* 16, 3 (March–April 1979), 32–38. S. L. Hills, "Organized Crime and American Society," *Midwest Quarterly,* 9, 2 (January, 1968), 171–82. William Webster, "Rooting Out Organized Crime: A Coordinated Effort," *Vital Speeches,* 53 (February 15, 1987), 282–86.

the difficult problem of coordination with public agencies. Ad hoc groups of citizens formed not through political necessity, but through community pride, offer sporadic hope for organized crime control.

One example of the type of commission that has been relatively effective is the Chicago Crime Commission. In operation for several decades, the Chicago commission has been a forerunner in the publication of a limited number of syndicate activities. This crime commission must be judged as an effective device for the revealing of certain criminal activities. An example of this commission's work is shown in Figure 14-2.

These comments on the role of the crime commission have been taken from statements made by various members of the National Association of Citizens Crime Commissions.

Increasing public understanding.   Crime commissions can contribute materially to better public understanding and public rejection of organized crime.

Planning citizen involvement.   The citizens' involvement should be programmed and planned rather than allowed to be dissipated on short-term projects of limited value.

Generating community initiative.   The commission should examine the criminal justice functions and make recommendations to enforcement agencies for system improvement.

There are nine recognizable signs that organized crime is moving in on a community:

Social acceptance of hoodlums in decent society.

Community's indifference to ineffective local government.

Notorious mobster personalities in open control of businesses.

Deceptive handling of public funds.

Interest at very high rates to poor risk borrowers (the juice loan).

Close association of mobsters and local authorities.

Arson and bombings.

Terrorized legitimate businesses.

Easily found gambling, narcotics and prostitution.

FIGURE 14-2   The nine danger signs of the social cancer known as organized crime, as identified by the Chicago Crime Commission.

Examining basic political systems.   Commissions should require ethics bills and recommend civil service careers in many areas now in the "spoils" domain.

Involving organized business.   Chambers of commerce and professional associations should encourage the stimulation of programs and seminars to educate and develop blueprints for action within business enterprises.

Expanding the system to include civil sanctions.   Criminal law alone cannot curb organized crime. Civil justice for the purpose of reaching the racketeer who moves into the legitimate business field must be explored.

Encouraging cooperation among criminal justice agencies.   While there has been no endorsement of the "task force concept," those in the commissions indicate a need to coordinate the efforts of the federal agencies, as well as the different units of local government, including the police, courts, and correction agencies. These recommendations are shown in Figure 14–3.

Citizens Crime Commissions' Recommendations for Eliminating Organized Crime

1. The citizens crime commissions must be free from political involvement, thus, financing from private sources is desirable.

2. Have a commission in all major cities to act as an investigative "watch dog" representative of the public interest.

3. Expanded criminal intelligence is rapidly becoming a major function of citizens crime commissions.

4. A dedication to create a climate of communitywide support for innovative programs in juvenile and correctional programs.

5. The business community is encouraged to use the extensive files, research, and consultation services of the citizens commissions.

6. The commissions have interest in legislative changes. Although not a lobbying agency, they are effective in having input into initiation of new laws.

7. Conduct periodic surveys of criminal justice systems to determine if the best form of justice possible is being rendered.

8. Encourage public information campaigns for special anticrime programs and with continued emphasis on organized crime.

FIGURE 14-3 Citizens crime commissions' recommendations for eliminating organized crime. (These goals and statements have been extracted from various speeches made by crime commission members and from position papers.)

Citizen Groups Established Under the Framework of Government

There are increasing pressures to fix the responsibility for organized crime control in multijurisdictional organizations, although some experts recommend keeping the hearing or exposure process separate from the enforcement function. Which method becomes more effective will probably depend on the effectiveness of such groups as the Pennsylvania Crime Commission. It was created in 1968 with the power to subpoena witnesses, to have access to public records, and to make changes and recommendations for legislative action. The report published as a result of investigations during the first two years of this organization should serve as a national model. The publication, entitled *The Report on Organized Crime,* although generally circulated among police agencies, should be published in volume and circulated among all the citizens of the state and perhaps even nationally.

The true effectiveness of this type of group brings us full circle to the realization that politics enters into the selection of the citizen representative. For example, the grand jury is selected in many states by judges or other ranking elected officials who obtain a rubber stamp approval of their appointees. In many instances, the grand jury is kept busy detailing terrible conditions in the jail or other public buildings, returning indictments against run-of-the-mill criminal violators, and puttering with other tasks until the year expires and new appointments are made. Grand jury reports can be the "comedy books" of government ills.

If grand juries are to perform an adequate function, the members should be selected from the general tax rolls, like regular jury members; tenure should be increased to a minimum of two years, with power and staff support to continue certain investigations; and the printing of a report for public consumption should be required. The political nature and lack of budget for operations make present grand juries relatively ineffective against organized crime.

Crime commissions come in a variety of forms and degrees of effectiveness. A crime commission with or without legal structure is going to be worthless unless its findings are followed up with intensive investigation and prosecution. The crime commission consisting of ad hoc citizen representation is of questionable value unless its members can forget political vindictiveness, petty jealousies, and personal aggrandizement.

The legally structured crime commission as an adjunct to a grand jury is in a position to render valuable aid to law enforcement. Unfortunately, this type of commission depends on a strong grand jury. Most grand juries are replaced every year, and because of a restricted budget for investigators, very few organized crime prosecutions are obtained through information furnished by the jury.

Special committees or commissions that have revealed much about organized crime are the Congressional subcommittees at both the national and state levels. Information produced from these organizations, although circulated widely for political purposes, has done much to create public awareness. Here are examples of such committees:

Wickersham Committee, 1928—An early appraisal of crime conditions in the United States

Kefauver Committee, 1950–51—National hearings on all types of organized crime, emphasis on gambling

McClellan Committee, 1957–60—National hearings on all types of organized crime, emphasis on labor reackets.

President's Commission on Organized Crime 1967, 1976, 1983 and 1986. (These are limited hearings and do not entail national investigations.)

International Conference on Drug Abuse and Illicit Trafficking, 1987.

Punitive Enforcement

The primary emphasis, perhaps, should be on punitive enforcement. This method is emphasized because the methods of crime prevention previously discussed cannot be totally effective. Local law enforcement officers fully understand that punitive enforcement cannot be a final solution to organized crime. But until better solutions are developed, punitive methods will be used. Officers are aware that without intensive punitive enforcement at all levels of government, there will be little hope for controlling organized crime. Local law enforcement is, by and large, willing to accept all available assistance at state and national levels. Let us look more closely at the role of the field officer at the local level.

Role of the field officer.   In modern departments, the field officer is heavily involved in organized crime enforcement. If a patrol officer is lax in observing violations, overlooks gambling and prostitution, and fails to make reports regarding suspicious actions, he or she is contributing to the success of organized criminal groups. The role a field officer has in controlling organized crime may be identified as the following:

The collection of facts and the funneling of these facts to specialized units in a department. A field officer through observation can obtain names, addresses, automobile and license numbers of suspects and establish patterns of movement on confederation members living in a district.

The detection of patterns, modus operandi, and other traits that relate to organized crime activity.

The bringing of information to light that will bring about a thorough investigation.

Reduction of personnel through arrest to cause the organization to be more cautious and to minimize victim contacts. The field officer should be in a position to take action on all violations.

Field contact with willing and unwilling victims to develop leads through associates, and to gather other types of information not available to intelligence officers.

Association with local businesspeople so that if these businesses are pressured by racketeers, owner and operators will have the confidence and trust in the officer to report these threats or pressures. The officer then, in turn, refers the material to intelligence officers.[4]

Identification of those who are local organized criminals as opposed to those who have national confederation connections.

The field officer, if well trained in the methods of organized criminals, becomes a field investigator of street activities, many of which ultimately furnish support evidence on top-level hoodlums. If organized crime is to be controlled, the enforcement pressures must come from both street-level and specialized investigatory personnel.

IDENTIFYING ORGANIZED CRIME: HOW THE PATROL OFFICER FUNCTIONS

Because of new and better information from studies about organized crime, we are able to identify at least three types of crimes that may be considered of an organized nature: (1) the common physical crimes such as burglary or robbery, when one or more persons is involved in the planning, execution, or disposition of the spoils of a crime; (2) those crimes that are socially destructive such as embezzlement, consumer fraud, and other crimes classed in the "white collar" category; and (3) the activities of the traditional "syndicated" or confederated groups who are organized for the sole purpose of pursuing illegal gain. It is the latter category that we normally refer to as organized crime, but the first two classifications should be identified as being of an organized nature in specific instances and considered in the police effort. White collar crime is discussed in Chapter 9; here we will look at how common physical crimes relate to traditional organized crime.

The Common Physical Crimes

The field officer lives daily with these crimes, which are viewed by most departments as being individual violations by an antisocial individual. In many instances, they are organized from the basic inception to the final execution of a given violation.

---

[4]This association also works against the field officer who, through such close contacts, may be tempted to connive with such persons to subvert the laws and overlook violations. When contacts with hoodlums are frequent, the entire enforcement process may succumb to bribery and corruption. In 1988, the Los Angeles Police Department had two members of its intelligence division removed because they improperly handled information.

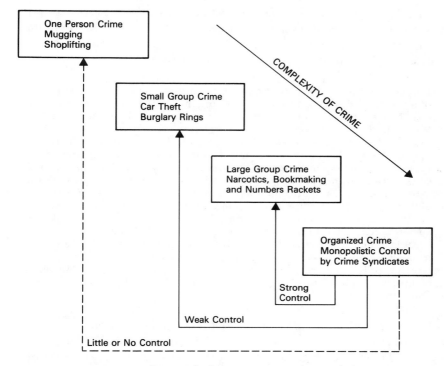

FIGURE 14-4   Degree of control of various crimes by confederations.

The field officer should pursue the investigation of every crime with the idea that more than one individual may be involved. Crime reports, arrests records, and follow-up investigation should meet the same rigid processes of analysis as the investigation of traditional organized criminal violations. The complexity of organized crime, as described by Donald R. Cressey, is shown in Figure 14-4.[5]

As the three classifications of organized crime are analyzed, it becomes apparent that very few crimes are not suspect. It is the intent of these classifications to cause the field officer to see the possible connections that may arise from a stolen car case or a simple house burglary where merchandise is stolen. What is being asked is that the officer, in enforcement and reporting procedures, consider that some form of organization may exist.

[5]Presentation of Professor Donald R. Cressey, University of California, Santa Barbara, at the Third Organized Crime Law Enforcement Training Conference, sponsored by the Law Enforcement Assistance Administration, U.S. Department of Justice, at the University of Oklahoma, Norman, March 4, 1970.

The field officer will be in contact with criminals in this category, and, unless the criminal activities are investigated and documented, there may be no link to organized crime. Each violation has unique characteristics that may cause it to be of an organized criminal nature:

> Burglary, not normally associated with organized crime, has these loose ties of an organized nature. The common burglar needs a "fence" for merchandise. The fence may become the apex of an organization predicated upon theft. When there is a receiver or fence, burglaries may be considered as being organized at the street level. The fence or receiver of stolen property may operate behind loan and pawn shop fronts, or may be in the secondhand business or moving and storage business. He may be a loan shark, in the construction business, or in dozens of trade businesses that can use the stolen merchandise. (It is not uncommon for a building contractor to have a boxcar of lumber, shingles, or pipe stolen from his supply and eventually end up buying them back at a reduced rate.) Burglars will loot warehouses, docks, and airport storage facilities, all of which must have a pipeline to a market. According to news reports, approximately $5 billion in merchandise were stolen from air terminals alone. The rate of burglary clearance was less than 25 percent. There is a vast armada of thieves who appear to work alone, but who in reality are working for the large organizations. Burglary is a major supporting crime for confederations.

Organization may be present in activities of gamblers, loan sharks, and receivers of stolen property. In investigating a crime scene, a field officer may detect the type of criminal activity by the traits of the job. For example:

> The type of merchandise taken—boxcar loads of merchandise, large hauls of furs or jewelry, stock, bonds or other merchandise—may indicate a need for a fence.[6] Large quantities of office machines may be transported interstate and sold in areas that have not been a part of the mandatory crime reporting system, have very ineffective local law enforcement, and are not a part of the National Crime Information System.

The method of operation may, with the introduction of sophisticated data processing systems, become an effective identifier for gang activities. For example:

> One highly organized group, probably not affiliated with any national organization, successfully used a pipe wrench on the front door of the victim's home to gain entry. It was later discovered that these thieves had successfully operated in 12 states, with more than 30 suspects involved.

With the computer systems now being developed, the investigators would have immediately identified the trademarks of the participants. This

---

[6]See Roy Rowan, "How the Mafia Loots JFK Airport," *Fortune*, 115, June 22, 1987, pp. 54–59.

points out to the field officer that every burglary should be investigated with the possibility of identifying organized activity.

Shoplifting is a unique and common form of theft. It should also be approached with the thought of organized involvement. Again, the receiver of stolen property is the key culprit. The field officer who reports the violation is a critical link in identifying those professionally involved in shoplifting and those who are occasional thieves.

The gangs concerned with robbery, although not organized to the extent they had been in the 1930s, still have field units who hit select targets. Postal vehicles, armored cars, and large jewelry consignments have been the prime targets of well-executed action.

Traditional Confederation Crime

The primary thrust of this section is to relate common crimes to the traditional syndicated crimes. Although the traditional organized crime per se may not be the major problem, one of the avowed purposes of this text is to outline how the officer and the citizen must approach the enforcement of such crimes to minimize the impact of organized crime on society.

The field officer's approach to the control of organized crime is the strategy called *violation-response.* This strategy means that when there is a violation of the law, there is an attempt to identify, prosecute, and convict the persons committing the offense. This, as Anderson explains, is the traditional way for local officers to respond to organized crime. The other strategy is the *attrition* approach used by the federal government. This is directed toward finding a statute for which sufficient information exists to prosecute and obtain a conviction.[7]

There is no question that the most effective approach is the latter strategy. Both strategies are used frequently by local officers, including field officers, to the extent that prosecution and not persecution is the ultimate end. The field officer should use both strategies for apprehending organized crime violators. A conclusion drawn by many local officers is that organized crime will not be eliminated by the arrest of a few top-level members, or many top-level members, but will be successful only when the entire body of the organization is torn apart by massive coordinated efforts that will chop off the head of the organization and "rip the guts" from the entire organization. One without the other is doomed to failure.

[7]Annelise Anderson, *Organized Crime: The Need for Research* (Organized Crime, Programs Division LEAA, U.S. Department of Justice, 1971), p. 2. Also see Bob Levin, "A Massive Inquiry into the Mafia," *McLeans,* 99, February 24, 1986, p. 42.

SUMMARY

This chapter briefly discusses three different methods for approaching the control of organized crime. Chances are that the average community will be using the third choice cited in this chapter, that is, punitive control by criminal justice agencies. There is no attempt to play down the importance of punitive control. In principle, this type of enforcement looks good; in practice, punitive enforcement alone has no chance in controlling organized criminal activities.

The method with top priority has been identified as education for both the police and the public. Education of all police officers and the public must be the predominant thrust if there is to be an impact on presently structured organized crime. But this method alone will have little impact on organized crime; education must be coordinated with the efforts of punitive enforcement.

The training and education of a few specialized officers cannot of itself make a workable system. The average citizen in cities throughout our country must be deluged with factual information about the corner bookie, the prostitute, the junkies, and the lotteries that support confederations. Crimes without victims are oriented toward the emasculation and robbery of an entire social structure, not toward just a single victim.

The citizens' war on crime offers some hope. Organized citizens are making their presence known through crime commissions and other activities. The National Association of Citizen Crime Commissions has 21 national affiliate units. These units serve as intelligence sources and action initiation groups. They are not vigilantes. In an attempt to deal in true facts, civic action groups have the potential for being effective because they may probe into any area of criminal misbehavior. The governmental commissions are usually established to investigate specific crime areas. Both types would be more effective if there were longer active tenure. This would create a sustained interest in setting and obtaining long-range goals.

To the extent that education and citizen committees fail, punitive enforcement is the final step in controlling organized crime. But one method of enforcement alone is not sufficient; all must apply. All three methods working together will produce results in the control of criminal confederations.

QUESTIONS FOR DISCUSSION

1. Give logical arguments to substantiate why there must be citizen involvement in the control of organized crime.
2. Cite a number of techniques for bringing the citizen into play against criminal confederations.

3. What are some of the disadvantages in having citizens playing active roles against organized crime?

4. Identify and cite the state requirements for grand juries. How can these units of government be made more effective?

5. Cite some recent statements from local citizen crime commissions. How can they be made more effective?

6. Review the efforts of the national crime commissions. Why have the findings from these commissions not had a greater impact on organized crime?

7. Identify what you believe to be the model role of the field law enforcement officer.

8. Review how traditional crimes, such as burglary and shoplifting, tie into operations of crime confederations.

9. Explain why the federal approach to organized crime control strategy (attrition) cannot solve the local organized crime control problem without also using the violator-response method.

10. Identify other techniques that can be used against organized crime. How do we rid society of organized crime?

Part V

Education and Training

This part surveys problems yet to be answered or solved.

More and more agencies have educated and trained their officers to recognize the dynamics of organized crime. But commitment to training and education in this field is lacking.

In retrospect, the trends are not encouraging. Intelligence files have been compromised. Public support has not materialized because of adverse police public relations, and enforcement efforts have moved from local action to spotty politically oriented action to meet the publicity needs of a politician seeking a higher office. The political manipulation of organized crime enforcement has moved from the local level to state and federal levels because of the flow of money into the enforcement apparatus.

In the June 20, 1988, issue of *Insight* magazine, the dilemma surrounding drug enforcement and the use of the military was addressed based on the action of Congress in approving such military action. Analysts from vested interest groups reasoned why the military could not be used, using arguments that ranged from the lack of training to the wrong kind of training. We should be educating to reduce the demand for drugs, but the next best move is to have adequate support from the military to assist civilian enforcement efforts.

Many of the analysts cited the Posse Comitatus Act of 1878, which stipulated the military could not be used for law enforcement purposes. That Act was passed in a different time, and the needs of the country were different because of the speed of transportation and the mass movement of people. The change in 1981 by Congress to allow the military to serve as surveillance for civil law enforcement helped, but it did not furnish the support that the Congress says is now necessary. It will be interesting to see if honest enforcement policies prevail over vested interest groups. In 1989, use of the military was approved and they are being used in interdiction operations.

15

Education and Training for Organized Crime Control

LEARNING OUTCOMES

1. Have an overall impression of the need for and the importance of education and training in organized crime enforcement.
2. Gain insight into the type of training and education needed.
3. Develop curriculum for both agency and citizen use.
4. Recognize the importance of education and training of the right type at the appropriate level.

One of the weakest links in the struggle against organized crime is education and training at the local level. Public administrators, who are aware that organized crime exists in their community, are not spending sufficient time in educating and training citizens, law enforcement officers, and other members of the criminal justice system. Consequently, local persons with an interest in curbing organized crime are left to their own resources in securing information about those engaged in organized crime. If there is to be a favorable impact on organized crime in a community, the transmittal of technology about these crimes must come to both the members of the criminal justice system and the citizen in an accelerated manner.

There are three modes for transmitting information to those concerned with organized crime control. They are (1) education in academic institutions, (2) specialized training for police officers, and (3) greater public information. To implement one mode of learning without the other two will not produce a desired level of information about the criminal confederations. Neither the citizen nor enforcement officer will have sufficient expertise to expose and apprehend the violators.

EDUCATION IN ACADEMIC INSTITUTIONS

The proper place to transmit technology about a social problem of great magnitude is in the academic classroom. Unfortunately, teachers of the social sciences and government classes are not knowledgeable about the functions of organized criminals. In past years, largely because of money available under the Omnibus Crime Bill, educators have suddenly discovered that teachers should have an orientation on the drug problem. Hours have been spent teaching teachers about pharmacology and other general information concerning drugs. Rarely has a teacher been offered the opportunity or transmitted knowledge about the relationship of drug traffic to the total organized crime picture and the deleterious impact of drugs on the society. This fragmentation of instruction leaves the average citizen and police officer without factual knowledge about organized criminal influence on the total crime picture. Traditionally, education and training concerning organized crime have been restricted to a select number of officers who have been assigned vice and intelligence responsibilities. The general administrative attitude, particularly among departments, seems to be that only a limited number of officers should deal with organized crime. Many police department personnel have no more knowledge about this type of crime than a member of the general public.

Academic instructors are rarely qualified to teach these concepts. These courses should be taught at the high school and junior college level to obtain a broader base of exposure for all citizens. A course in technical education dealing with drugs and other organized crime should be available to students at this level of education. How such a course is structured will depend on the instructor. However, the course should be built on broad social concepts and on how organized crime influences the social and economic structure of a community.

There has been little effort to provide organized crime information in educational programs. Consequently, the government has found it necessary to support high-level training courses as part of organized crime action programs. But it does little good to develop field operations in a department if specialized personnel are the only officers committed to intelligence gathering and prosecution of organized criminals. Police organizations generally tend to exclude organized crime as a high priority. This omission is due in part to a lack of knowledge and in part to political considerations.

An educational institution could offer one of the best sources of conceptual information for local officers and citizens. Academic institutions are usually defensive about their failure to have such instruction. The institution usually states that it has no qualified staff to teach such courses. Nothing could be further from reality. Disciplines such as accounting, economics, business management, computer sciences, and mathematics are staffed with persons who can contribute within the framework of their particular expertise. The subject of organized crime has been studied extensively in small segments in each of these disciplines. It is the responsibility of the educational program to bring these studies into focus.

The "say no to drugs" programs are a beginning in public education about one facet of organized crime. The law enforcement officers, with limited resources, should be educating teachers who, in turn, will have a continuing, integrated program in the regular curriculum that will have a lasting impact on students.

A broad listing of subjects for organized crime study might include the topical categories shown in the following outline.[1]

Projected College Outline for the Study of Organized Crime

An academically oriented course in organized crime may include, but should not be restricted to, these areas:

I. What is organized crime?
   A. The traditional definition and the new concepts for identifying organized crime.
   B. Should organized crime and drug enforcement be fragmented?
   C. How do traditional concepts of organized crime avoid the tie to street crimes?
II. An overview of organized crime in Western societies.
   A. Some history as it relates to current problems. Defining organized crime as it now exists in contemporary society.
   B. The impact on political subdivisions of nations. The need for control.
   C. The present status of international relationships in curbing organized crime. How it influences fiscal policies.
III. The national problem with organized crime.
   A. The national effort for control of criminal activities.
   B. The political and fiscal ramifications in curbing organized crime.
   C. The national social and political climate. How it influences effective enforcement.
IV. The politics of government and organized crime.
   A. The systems—where does organized crime flourish?
   B. Political restraints, such as conflict of interest laws, political donations, and so on.
   C. Trends in corruption in the political system at all levels of government.
V. What is the citizen's role and obligation in organized crime?
   A. Identify the impact of organized crime in low-income neighborhoods.
   B. How does organized crime enforcement reflect on all law enforcement?
   C. What social factors mandate a citizen's participation in organized crime control?

[1]The Chancellor's Office, California Community Colleges. *Administration of Justice; Educational Programs for Community Colleges of California.* Sacramento Calif., 1988, pp. 73–78.

VI. How are units of government organized to challenge criminal inroads?
   A. The regional concept for the organization of enforcement units.
   B. The gathering of legitimate and legal information.
   C. How do governing bodies organize to obtain political and citizen participation?
VII. The legal system—fighting organized crime.
   A. New laws, the national trends.
   B. State laws, state court, and enforcement weaknesses.
   C. How the prosecutorial function should be strengthened.
VIII. The impact of organized crime on local enforcement agencies.
   A. Prevailing concepts in how organized crime should be challenged.
   B. The issues of corruption, how to maintain a system of checks and balances.
   C. What does society want and how can an effective effort be made against select crimes?
IX. Conceptual issues for police administration.
   A. How can organized crime be identified so that law enforcement will receive citizen support?
   B. The role of the police in initiating new laws and administrative procedures for a city.
   C. How does a department relate to the citizenry in organized crime control?
X. Victimless crimes.
   A. What is the rationale for enforcing such crimes? Is this a realistic approach for contemporary society?
   B. Are moral crimes, such as prostitution, pornography, and homosexuality, crimes that police should be prosecuting?
   C. How should laws be changed to make such crimes consistent in scope nationally?
XI. White collar crimes.
   A. Scope of unreported crimes and the effect on business.
   B. How can a tighter control be exerted over these crimes?
   C. How valid are news media exposés? How dangerous?
XII. Focus on concepts for total social involvement in organized crime control.
   A. Pros and cons of the citizen crime commissions.
   B. Involving citizens in programs for crime prevention.
   C. A study of ideologies in how organized crime can be reduced.

SPECIALIZED TRAINING FOR THE LAW ENFORCEMENT OFFICER

Policy makers at the national level are beginning to recognize the need for a federal effort in organized crime control, as shown in the increased use of the RICO statute in enforcement. In addition, intense and highly select training offers the only solution for bringing police, probation officers, courts, and corrections personnel information about what the influence of organized crime on the social structure. It does little good to train the police if judges are not made aware of the problems. Therefore, there should be an orientation course designed for all units of the criminal justice system. The days of generalizations and vague references to what has happened in the past are no longer a valid source for training and instructional material.

Members of the criminal justice system should be informed about cases that are occurring now. Concise briefs on cases that have been investigated and/or adjudicated should be widely circulated. Associates, political manipulations, and so on, should be a part of current information published by national and state criminal justice units. It is an indictment of our system that the news media become a primary source of reference for intelligence specialists and researchers who might contribute to a solution of the problem. Until widespread release of intelligence information becomes the practice rather than the exception, hoodlums will find shelter in administrative weaknesses.

There has been national momentum to train key enforcement personnel. The Law Enforcement Assistance Administration is supporting national, state, and local training efforts. Because of this support, more and more training programs are standardizing the curriculum along the following lines.

Organized Crime Training Outline

   I. A broad overview of organized crime.
      A. Overview of organized crime internationally and nationally.
      B. The structure of criminal syndicates.
         1. The function of the criminal confederations.
         2. Location of organized crime activities.
         3. Identified members of the criminal confederations.
      C. Organized crime family patterns (international and national).
      D. History and development of organized crime at state and local levels.
  II. Statutes relating to organized crime.
      A. The Omnibus Crime Bill of 1970 and 1986, pertinent statutes.
      B. Other federal laws relating to organized crime.
         1. Federal revenue code violations.
         2. U.S. Code violations.
            a. Stock market manipulations
            b. Labor
            c. Smuggling
            d. Bankruptcy
            e. Interstate conspiracy violations
            f. Wire services
            g. Interstate commerce
            h. Loan sharking
      C. State, county, and city laws.
      D. Civil laws used to control organized crime.
      E. Law enforcement agencies—areas of jurisdiction in the system (federal, state, local).
 III. The intelligence system.
      A. Case preparation—interview and interrogation.
      B. Patterns of organized crime established by intelligence.
      C. The structure and ethics of intelligence systems. Manual versus automated applications.

D. Information collection: strategic and tactical intelligence.
1. The federal agencies and state systems.
2. Undercover agents.
3. Informants.
4. The uniformed officer and special units.
5. Records and filing systems.
   a. Analysis
   b. Evaluation
   c. Dissemination
6. Undercover operations.
7. Development and use of informants.
IV. Using technology for investigations.
A. Communications.
1. Law enforcement intelligence units.
2. Computerized intelligence devices.
B. Electronics.
1. Wiretapping.
2. Electronic surveillance.
3. Intercept and "jumper" devices.
C. Photography.
1. Still and motion pictures.
2. Infra red—holograph.
3. Closed-circuit television, remote monitors.
D. Other devices.
1. The polygraph—special uses.
2. Heat sensors—remote stakeouts.
3. Special antiriot control equipment for militant activities.
V. Organization and supervision in organized crime units.
A. Organizational techniques.
1. Effective reporting.
2. Checks and balances.
3. Special reporting techniques.
B. Supervisory responsibilities.
1. Planning strategy.
2. Assessing and interpreting intelligence.
3. Personnel problems.
VI. Gambling.
A. Gambling—national history and techniques used.
1. Lotteries.
   a. Bolita.
   b. Numbers and policy.
   c. Football, basketball, and baseball cards.
2. Floating dice and card games.
3. Bookmaking—on- and off-track systems.
B. Local gambling.
C. Prostitution.
D. Legalized gambling.
1. Skimming of profits.
2. History of legalized gambling in United States and England.
3. Impact of legalized gambling on community.
E. Organized crime involvement in abortion.

VII. Drugs and organized crime.
    A. History of illegal drug use.
    B. Physiological and psychological aspects.
    C. International, state, and local laws.
    D. Drug identification.
    E. Techniques of search.
VIII. Infiltration of organized crime into business and labor.
    A. Legitimate business infiltration.
        1. General technique of identification.
        2. Loan companies, banking institutions, and leasing operations.
        3. Loan sharking.
        4. Extortion.
        5. Hijacking.
        6. Operations and public utilities service.
    B. Labor racketeering.
    C. Special frauds, such as the liquor industry, real estate, credit cards.
    D. Stock market.
    E. Income tax investigations.

Topical areas in this outline have been taken from established training programs from throughout the United States.

CONCEPTUALIZING TRAINING AND EDUCATION PROGRAMS

An example of how a curriculum evolves is shown in Figure 15–1. This example of computer crime and countermeasures shows training levels, types of schemes, sources of evidence, and the appropriate levels of information and the type of institution in which the materials should be presented. This same model could be applied to any subject.

Figure 15–2 carries the plan one step further and gives a sample outline of a 40-hour course. This material is presented at the applied skills and conceptual skills level at Long Beach City College, Long Beach, California. The same principles of curriculum structure would apply to any subject area.

SUMMARY

It is apparent that in organized crime units throughout the country there is a need for better education and training. There are indications that large law enforcement units are operating around the clock without sufficient knowledge to have any effect on organized crime. This need is apparent not only among the specialized intelligence and organized crime units, but also among influential citizens' groups, prosecutor units, and court judges. Recognizing these deficiencies, federal and state agencies are attempting to focus on specialized training.

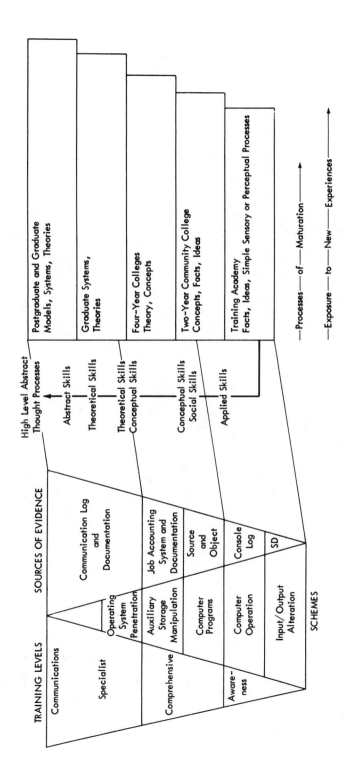

FIGURE 15-1 Computer crime schemes related to appropriate levels of training and education.

Source: The schemes are from Bill Colvin, "Computer Crime Investigators: A New Training Field," *FBI Law Enforcement Journal,* July 1979, pp. 9–12.

	SATURDAY APRIL 19	SATURDAY APRIL 26	SATURDAY MAY 3	SATURDAY MAY 10	SATURDAY MAY 17	SATURDAY MAY 24	SATURDAY MAY 31	SATURDAY JUNE 7
8-9 A.M.	Registration, introduction, defining computer crime — P	Systems organization — L	Fraud and manipulation, theory and practice — L	Administrative control, output control — P	Internal audit — P	Investigative processes, flow charting — B	Special investigative tools — L	— L
9-10	Overview — P	Systems organization — L	Administrative control, internal/external policies, business conduct — L	Administrative controls, error, correction controls — P	Internal audit — P	Investigative processes, flow charting — B	" — L	— L
10-11	State of the art — L	Vulnerabilities of the EDP systems — L	Administrative control, personnel practices and procedures — L	Computer security (hardware) — L	Legal aspects — B	Investigative methods — L	" — L	Case study — P
11-12	Data processing systems Terminology — L	How criminals use the system — P	Administrative and internal controls — P	Computer security (software) — L	Legal aspects — B	Investigative methods — L	" — P	Review and critique — P
12-1	Computer terminology — L	" — P	Administrative control processing — P	Communication and data base systems safeguards — L	Legal aspects/privacy — B	Investigative methods and case studies — L	" — P	Final examination — P

FIGURE 15-2 A 40-hour course in computer fraud and countermeasures.

The topical outlines suggested in this chapter are offered only for orientation. Each agency has its own unique problems. For example, in many areas of the country auto theft by organized groups will take precedence over prostitution or bookmaking. Elsewhere, thefts from airports or from seaport installations may be the prime problems. What we are attempting to emphasize is the importance of getting information out to those who may assist in eliminating organized crime.

QUESTIONS FOR DISCUSSION

1. Discuss the reason why education and training are one of the weakest links in the struggle against organized crime.
2. Name three modes of transmitting information relating to organized crime control to concerned persons.
3. Why is the high school and college a desirable location for transmitting information regarding the social problems relating to organized crime?
4. In the past, to what group of people has organized crime education and training been restricted? Why?
5. Discuss the national interest and actions taken to train key enforcement personnel. Explain.
6. In developing a training curriculum, what are three contributing factors to the type of training required?

16

In Retrospect

LEARNING OUTCOMES

1. Have an awareness of the efforts that have been applied to control organized crime during the past decade.
2. Review the important ideas and concepts contained in this text.
3. Develop some suggestions about an effective enforcement philosophy for the future.

For the past five decades there has been a great debate on defining organized crime by educational novices, and pleas from law enforcement agencies that organized crime is coming to town. While this debate has been going on, crime has become organized and is now firmly entrenched in every prosperous city in this country. During the debate, criminal confederations have quietly built an empire of stocks, property, and political clout. Three decades ago it appeared the debate had ended and that through massive funding and planning there would finally be a national movement to eliminate organized crime. A new dimension in planning emerged with the creation of a National Council on Organized Crime. The council was to formulate a national strategy against organized crime and to coordinate federal control efforts. The objective of this council was to determine the thrust of organized crime control efforts by all agencies of the criminal justice system in the United States.

What happened in the 1980s that emasculated the plans for punitive and nonpunitive enforcement efforts against organized cartels? Where are the plans for economic and administrative sanctions against businesses that support or are controlled by the confederations? The plans, much like those of the 1950s and through the 1980s, seem to fade away when enforcement efforts go beyond the talking stages. It seems that enforcement efforts against criminals are of great political advantage and of tremendous public interest. It remains that way until sanctions begin to affect friends of friends who know someone of influence. At that point, enforcement becomes unpopular and stops.

Since World War II, some of the healthiest organizations in the United States have been the individuals and cartels that form organized crime confederations. These organizations have prospered and expanded for many reasons. Our political system, while offering generous liberties, must at some time face the reality that liberty is laced with responsibility. A republic depends on citizens who assume responsibility for their acts. This responsibility is individual and institutional. If the responsibility is not met by both, there is little hope that liberty, as we have experienced it, will continue. The protection of liberty must begin with the politician, the representative of the justice system, and the individual citizen. When one part of this triad fails to maintain integrity, the entire system is subject to failure.

The more one studies the facets of organized crime, the greater the conviction that very little can be done about it unless there is an awakening of citizens who, in turn, must hold all elements of government accountable for the eradication of organized crime. From legislation, through police, courts, and corrections, accountability can come about only if the laws are realistic, consistently enforced, and fairly adjudicated. To show how to achieve this accountability, we have tried to illustrate how organized crime evolves from street crimes of a vice nature and the more traditional crimes of burglary, robbery, and theft.

We have attempted to be realistic in believing that some organized crime problems would cease if certain violations now classed as crimes were legalized or placed under government control. This feeling, however, has not been supported by the experience of off-track gambling in many states nor of casino gambling in Nevada or New Jersey. In these cases, organized crime either owns or operates the casinos outright. Who is kidding whom about organized crime in these two states? In other states that are under some government constraint on gambling, organized crime operates side by side with the legal systems that have been established. The state offers little competition for organized crime.

The political and legal relationship to organized crime are areas that are not well documented with empirical research. The instances cited are examples of common knowledge to those who have worked in criminal intelligence or instances that have been published in news sources. We hope that by stressing the areas of politics and the legal system as being the keystones to the control of organized crime, citizens, through citizen pressure groups and through the ballot box, can pressure the greedy and the dishonest into the open. The ABSCAM, Irangate, and related investigations are a warning to citizens that unless they insist on clean government, it will never become a reality.

The remaining part of this chapter comments on each chapter and focuses on some of the changes that have occurred or failed to occur, new information, and, in some cases, personal opinions.

PUBLIC AWARENESS AND PROGRESS AGAINST
ORGANIZED CRIME

Organized crime and the community seem to have a workable accommodation, with citizens taking a live and let live attitude. The greatest problem in organized crime enforcement is the failure of the community to acknowledge that organized crime actually exists. Politicians claim that organized crime does not exist in their community, police chiefs pleading for larger budgets say that organized crime is beginning to move into the community, and defense attorneys throw in a complete disclaimer about the existence of organized crime. So, the buck is passed from one agency to another, because there is little or no accountability. The grand jury might be an effective force against organized crime, but it is empaneled for a year and it is kept busy evaluating jail conditions and returning indictments. There is a need for a statewide grand jury that might serve two or three years or on a continuing basis, with new members rotating into the jury at alternate years. There needs to be some plan for the work of the jury.

Research and community awareness techniques have hardly been used effectively. Research in the past decade has been a redefinition of that of the 1960s without practical field applications. The limited research of the 1970s and the 1980s has brought little in the way of positive results. This may not be the fault of the researcher, because I believe it has been demonstrated that research on organized crime cannot be effectively conducted without cooperation of the field enforcement agencies. This was confirmed in the report entitled *Major Issues in Organized Crime Control*, 1987.[1]

One needs only to read and listen to the news media to know that organized crime exists in some far off city, usually in another state. Local news media do not name names and organizations who are involved locally in organized crime. If they did, economic sanctions in the form of withdrawn advertising or huge lawsuits might result. When reporters do not have confirmed proof of a relationship or event, they tend to ignore the story.

The community is not without protection; each year there is some progress made against organized crime. The 1980s have brought massive numbers of indictments against noted Mafia leaders. All of the major cities in the country have lost Mafia members, large drug peddlers, and assorted organized criminals in stings and other operations. RICO indictments are being pursued with good results. For example, in 1987 ten RICO indictments against leaders of the organized crime families in Los Angeles predicted that the families had been crushed. However, not one bookmaking establishment, not one loanshark, nor house of prostitution was closed because of these

---

[1]Herbert Edelhertz, *Major Issues in Organized Crime Control*. Symposium Proceedings, Sept. 25–26, 1986 (Washington, D.C.: National Institute of Justice, 1987).

arrests. Enforcement agencies may be propagandizing the public when they imply that these arrests are crushing the organizations.

It appears that many bodies are being removed from circulation; but the assets of the individual, gained from the fruits of organized crime, are not being seized as mandated by Congress in the RICO statute. Understandably, this broad statute is going to encounter future difficulties and receive some adverse court rulings. Until this happens, federal efforts should be pursued with much vigor.

The role of the prosecutor has been touched on lightly. While the prosecutor's offices is a key position in the prosecution of organized crime, most officers will reflect the temperament of the community. The prosecutor, whether at the federal or local level, is in a position to gauge the efforts being put forth by the criminal justice system in combating organized crime. As an officer of a court, the attorneys can determine the temperament of the judge, assess the efficiency of the police investigator, and know whether there are adequate laws for successful prosecutions. From their positions, they are able to say whether specific cases will be prosecuted, and eventually they are a determining factor in the final sentence and disposition of a case.

The opportunity for corruption is ever present, and the same criteria guide the prosecutor as guide the police officer and the defense attorney. From experience of case investigators, it would appear that the prosecutor is the least vulnerable in the trying of a case; however, deciding whether to prosecute and whether to allow a plea bargain opens many kinds of options for corruption.

PROSTITUTION AND GAMBLING

The discussion of vice crimes has been given priority because these crimes are most susceptible to control with citizen cooperation. While gambling may have fallen to second place as a leading moneymaker for organized crime, it is still a moneymaker for the old, established organized crime families. Gambling does not have the stigma of drug distribution, so those engaged in gambling are an echelon higher in the social structure of organized crime. The experiment in legalized casino gambling in New Jersey has gone as expected. The Atlantic City gambling casinos figured heavily in the ABSCAM investigations when the Justice Department probed bribery of congressmen and state and local government leaders. The attorney general of New Jersey indicated that casinos cannot exist without being an attraction to organized crime.

While the 43 states that now have some form of lottery view it as a way to finance government, contribute to charity, and aid the elderly, it has not raised revenues as expected. The "something for nothing" attitude will eventually undermine the enforcement of illegal gambling. It is only a matter of time until organized crime runs the state system, or runs a parallel system along side the legal system. Gambling money in any form is too easy to be passed up by the confederations.

Prostitution and allied crimes are addressed as a social rather than a law enforcement problem. Punitive enforcement cannot eliminate or even control prostitution, although it has been fairly successful in the area of organized prostitution. There is a strange dichotomy regarding prostitution. The moral majority are actively working against the crime of prostitution, while feminists and younger people do not look at prostitution as a violation that should be addressed by law enforcement. Prostitution is allied to organized crime, although not all prostitutes are a part of organized crime. Groups of prostitutes still follow the harvests, prostitutes are still in "houses," and new and innovative ideas like dating services and massage parlors can be traced to organized affiliation. AIDS will probably have the most lasting impact on the control of prostitution.

DRUGS

The issues of drug distribution have been the same for the past three decades. Basic methods of distribution are the same; only the quantity and the site of the drug origin changes. The U.S. borders are sieves, and users in this country seem to have a voracious appetite for drugs, because they consume all available merchandise. The drug problem grows in relation to the permissiveness of the community; the organization flourishes in the struggles over political and administrative strategies. There are few prospects for a permanent solution to the problem.

The present state of drug usage in this country has grown from individual permissiveness to lack of support for law enforcement and the decriminalization of key narcotic laws. Hundreds of ideological groups spent the 1960s and the 1970s turning people on. As the "turn ons" became national crazes, contraband such as cocaine and marijuana became hot market items. As consumption among upper class groups grew, those charged with enforcing the statutes became benevolent toward drug users and peddlers. The public failed to support law enforcement by permitting unrealistic search and seizure laws; laws that delayed enforcement action so drastically that many police agents just gave up trying to enforce liberalized marijuana laws; restrictive laws governing interrogation; and laws restricting the use of informants. All have combined to discourage arrest except in the most obvious cases. The public attitude toward drugs is reflected in apathy on the part of law enforcement officers who work endless hours on a case, then have it manipulated through the court system by delays and the procedural ploys of highly paid lawyers. This does not mean that the police should be operating without guidelines, but the law should be consistently and universally applied.

When a narcotic such as marijuana is decriminalized and the penalty for the possession of small amounts is lowered to a misdemeanor, it changes the law of arrest under which an agent must operate. It also changes the attitude toward the enforcement of the law. The decriminalization of marijuana laws in many of the states has made the police "arresting pimps" for the legal fraternity. Many officers, as in the days of Prohibition, are releasing small violators rather than arresting them and having them be fleeced by the legal fraternity.

Bureaucratic infighting among the major drug enforcement units has allowed the large drug confederations to operate without pressure. To have an enforcement unit operate effectively means that information must be gained from some source and that information then diligently pursued in an investigation. Often this information is gained outside the drug sphere.

In a speech published in *Vital Speeches* in 1988, FBI Director Sessions outlined the Federal Bureau of Investigation national priority programs in these statements. He said, "The National Chamber of Commerce estimates that white collar crime costs us $45 billion dollars each year . . . bank fraud alone exceeds $1 billion in 1986. . . . In 1987 an additional task force was formed in Dallas to investigate suspected fraud in over 20 North Texas S & L's." (This followed the conviction of 90 suspects in the TEXACON cases where over $100 million had been extorted from lending agencies by inflated property values.) In 1989, additional task forces were assigned nationwide.

He further amplified the role of the Bureau in cooperation with other agencies in intelligence and operations in foreign counterintelligence programs. He said, "Through the FBI's development of the counterintelligence awareness program—called DECA—companies that hold classified contracts with the government are contacted and FBI agents teach their employees to be aware of the recruiting and information-gathering techniques that hostile officers commonly employ."

The third area was to discuss the FBI's newest priority program—drugs. He indicated that . . . "the continuing flow of illegal drugs into our country signals that drugs are still in demand, are still being used by Americans in all walks of life, and are still destroying the lives and future of unprecedented numbers of our teenagers, and young adults, including young professionals."

Political decisions have affected enforcement along the southern coast of the United States. These decisions have focused major enforcement attention along the Florida border. In the meantime, Alabama and Louisiana had a massive influx of drugs. The experience is similar to what has been happening in Arizona and southern California for the past three decades.

The strategy of putting DEA agents in foreign countries, with a program to eliminate narcotics at its source, will serve its purpose well if governments cooperate and political encounters can be minimized.

The solution to the drug problem is not going to be easy; too many people are benefitting from the profits of narcotics. A large force of professional personnel live on narcotic and allied violations. Crime is a big business, and big business generates a flow of money that supports many professional people. This is not meant to imply that drugs are allowed to flow with permission, but rather that all-out efforts are just not exerted to eradicate the problems. The average narcotics peddler is easy to apprehend and simple to isolate and prosecute. Drug peddlers are not known for their intelligence, and the "mules" who do the actual transportation are sacrificed to the system by the money bosses. Thus, the chance to get at the head of the organization is very small.

It does little good to attempt to reinvent the wheel in drug enforcement. As long as the market exists it is doubtful there will be effective control. Alcohol and narcotics share a similar fate. Legalize them, and the profits are localized in a few hands. Decriminalize use, and the legal profession shares in the profits. As long as huge profits flow into political and legal sources, little impact will be made in curbing the flow of drugs into and within this country.

The domestic transporters of narcotics could suffer if the RICO statue were applied in massive enforcement efforts. The real value of RICO is its use as a lever against middle- and lower-level drug dealers who, to avoid forfeiture of property and other assets, will cooperate with federal agents. By injecting fear and mistrust into sales and distribution systems, the enforcement officer is working from a power position. As long as the courts support RICO, there can be many effective enforcement actions.

PORNOGRAPHY

Pornography is another activity that in time will closely parallel the drug trade. The laws are indecisive about pornography, and, as a result, enforcement has been inconsistent or nonexistent. When prosecutors move in on smut peddlers, they are met with public resistance. In a Gallup Poll Report No. 251, August 1986, only 45 percent of the national population sampled believed there should be national standards on pornography. Only 45 percent of the same sample thought there should be stricter enforcement of obscenity law. Without public support, it makes little difference what the criminal juctice system is doing. In the Prybas case in Virginia, where RICO statutes were used in the prosecution, there is an allegation that the penalty is more shocking than the crime. It is esimated that about one half of all videotapes sold in 1988 were "adult titles." If the volume increases, eventually the market for porno may rival that of illegal narcotics and become the number one moneymaker for the confederations.

BUSINESS FRAUD

This text has touched only briefly on the magnitude of frauds and swindles relating to business and to the confederations. There are whole books devoted to explaining these intricate frauds and swindles. The web of private business interests, the influences of confederation-dominated unions, and other conceptual relationships have not been cited in detail because there are many rumors about these relationships but there is not much hard research evidence on how confederations work with legitimate businesses.

Local law enforcement does not become involved in all business frauds. Most big fraud cases are handled by state attorneys general or by a U.S. attorney and their investigators. Thus, the importance to local law enforcement is minimized.

The *President's Commission on Organized Crime Report* of October 1985 clearly identifies the problems of labor union crimes. The Commission found that the history of labor-management racketeering is one of opportunistic exploitation. The Commission recommended that the Department of Labor and the U.S. Attorney strike forces carry out planned campaigns against organized crime in each industry. The Commission indicated that there is now a recognition of a broader influence by organized crime in the market place.

In this report the Commission listed 74 pages of labor union indictments. Many of these indictments are being satisfied with promises by organized crime figures to disassociate themselves from labor union activities.

Organized crime may not control the unions, but it has a very comfortable working relationship with the major unions in the country. What is so vividly pointed up without accusation of fault is that these relationships are virtually impossible to translate into convictions.

MILITANT GROUPS

The policing of militant groups has become a major activity for local police agencies. Gang intelligence groups and SWAT teams to deal with militants have become commonplace in local agencies.

These gangs are not only local and regional, but national and international in scope. Many of the listed gangs have good international connections in narcotics and other criminal enterprises. Thus, local police become not only enforcers of local and state laws, but also necessary intelligence links for group actions against the national government.

There is little question that this country is in for a period of violent actions by these groups. If these groups are met with the tough laws available, terrorism will be restricted to isolated instances. If the groups are met with permissiveness and weak resolve, we can expect increased terrorist activity during the future.

ORGANIZATION AND MANAGEMENT
OF ENFORCEMENT

A section of the book has been devoted to organization and management concepts to point out that dozens of different structures may be established and function equally well. In identifying some supervisory and management techniques, this book also points out the major weaknesses of organized crime control groups in operation today.

Some criticism has been leveled at certain crime control efforts by federal and state agencies primarily because organized crime is not eliminated by the arrest of one or two thousand known members of the confederations. The establishment of organized crime is too heavily insulated to cease because of efforts exerted at the top. The effort must be multidirectional and with full public revelation so that "fixes" do not take place prior to or after trial.

In discussing technology, such as intelligence gathering, there has been an attempt to stress safeguards. There has been some conceptualizing on intelligence processes, and how the information is applied to crime control. From a national perspective, the last decade has not produced much valid empirical research; the studies cited are restatements of old problems.

Since the Watergate scandal, law enforcement agencies have been reluctant to collect the type of domestic intelligence data that are worthwhile. Government spying, after the indictment of two FBI administrators associated with "black bag" operations, has been closely limited and controlled. The guidelines developed in 1976 carry cautionary measures that are being put to work at the present time. The intelligence networks are again geared up for increased activity against organized crime and subversive activities from abroad.

SUMMARY

One major reason why organized crime flourishes so widely is the social chaos surrounding the laws that govern such activities as sexual misbehavior and gambling. The conflicting history of such activities as pornography and obscenity has been offered in some depth so that the citizen and the enforcement officer can understand the complexity of requiring arbitrary social comformity through law. As social attitudes have changed, the laws have not been flexible in meeting these changes. This dichotomy is shown in the fact that 42 states permit some form of gambling. Yet the new laws governing organized crime are designed to make taking bets a major federal felony. There is little congruity in how the problem should be reconciled among the various units of government.

Because there are so many diverse philosophies on what crimes should be enforced, this text cannot be expected to furnish but a few solutions and/or suggestions for organized crime control. But a look at the historical background on a few of the more common crimes may help the reader to view a crime, even if it were minor, as another instrument in making organized crime strong.

Appendix A

Categories of Criminal Activity Engaged in by Organized Criminals

Crimes that fit into this category might be, but are not limited to, the following categories:

Crimes normally conducted by organized groups:

Racketeering by monopoly or extortion
Planned bankruptcy
Black market or prohibited products

Crimes by persons operating on an individual, ad hoc basis (or crimes conducted with a common scheme and thus classed as organized crime):[1]

Purchase on credit with no intention to pay, or purchase by mail in the name of another
Individual income tax violations
Credit card frauds
Bankruptcy frauds
Title II home improvement loan frauds
Frauds with respect to social security, unemployment insurance, or welfare
Unorganized or occasional frauds on insurance companies (theft, casualty, health)
Violations of Federal Reserve regulations by pledging stock for further purchases, flouting margin requirements
Organized or unorganized "lonely hearts" appeals by mail

Crimes in the course of their occupations by those operating inside business, government, or other establishment, in violation of their duty of loyalty and fidelity to employer or client:

[1]Herbert Edelhertz, *The Investigation of White Collar Crime: A Manual for Law Enforcement Agencies* (Washington, D.C.: U.S. Government Printing Office, April 1977).

Commercial bribery and kickbacks by and to buyers, insurance adjusters, contracting officers, quality inspectors, government inspectors, auditors, and so on

Bank violations by bank officers, employees, and directors

Embezzlement by business or union officers and employees

Securities fraud by insiders trading by the use of special knowledge, or causing firms to take positions in the market to benefit themselves

Employee petty larceny and expense account frauds

Frauds by computer, causing unauthorized payouts

"Sweetheart contracts" entered into by union officers

Embezzlement by attorneys, trustees, and fiduciaries

Fraud against the government
  A. Padding of payrolls
  B. Conflicts of interest
  C. False travel, expense, or per diem claims

Crimes incidental to and in furtherance of business operations, but not the central purpose of the business:

Tax violations

Antitrust violations

Commercial bribery of another's employee, officer or fiduciary (including union officers)

Food and drug violations

False weights and measures by retailers

Violations of Truth-in-Lending Act by misrepresentation of credit terms and prices

Submission or publication of false financial statements to obtain credit

Use of fictitious or overvalued collateral

Check-kiting to obtain operating capital on short-term financing

Securities Act violations to obtain operating capital, false proxy statements, manipulation of market to support corporate credit or access to capital markets, and so on

Collusion between physicians and pharmacists to cause the writing of unnecessary prescriptions

Dispensing by pharmacists in violation of law, excluding narcotics traffic

Immigration fraud in support of employment agency operations to provide domestics

Housing code violations by landlords

Deceptive advertising

Fraud against the government:
  A. False claims
  B. False statements:
    1. To induce contracts
    2. AID frauds
    3. Housing frauds
    4. SBA frauds, such as SBIC bootstrapping, self-dealing, cross-dealing, or obtaining direct loans by use of false financial statements

C. Moving contracts in urban renewal

Labor violations (Davis-Bacon Act)

Commercial espionage

White-collar crime as a business, or as the central activity:

Medical or health frauds

Advance fee swindles

Phony contests

Bankruptcy fraud, including schemes devised as salvage operation after insolvency of otherwise legitimate businesses

Securities fraud and commodities fraud

Chain referral schemes

Home improvement schemes

Debt consolidation schemes

Mortgage milking

Merchandise swindles:
  A. Gun and coin swindles
  B. General merchandise
  C. Buying or pyramid clubs

Land frauds

Directory advertising schemes

Charity and religious frauds

Personal improvement schemes:
  A. Diploma mills
  B. Correspondence schools
  C. Modeling schools

Fraudulent application for, use, and /or sale of credit cards, airline tickets, and so on

Insurance frauds:
  A. Phony accident rings
  B. Looting of companies by purchase of overvalued assets, phony management contracts, self-dealing with agents, intercompany transfers, etc.
  C. Frauds by agents writing false policies to obtain advance commissions.
  D. Issuance of annuities or paid-up life insurance, with no consideration, so that they can be used as collateral for loans
  E. Sales by misrepresentation to military personnel or those otherwise uninsurable.

Vanity and song publishing schemes

Ponzi schemes

False security frauds

Purchase of banks, or control thereof, with deliberate intention to loot them

Fraudulent establishment and operation of banks or savings and loan associations

Fraud against the government:
  A. Organized income tax refund swindles, sometimes operated by income tax "counselors"

B. AID frauds
C. FHA frauds
   1. Obtaining guarantees of mortgages on multiple-family housing far in excess of value of property with foreseeable inevitable foreclosure
   2. Home improvement frauds

Executive placement and employment agency frauds

Coupon redemption frauds

Money order swindles.

Appendix B

Organized Crime Control Act of 1970 (Amended in 1978, 1984, and 1987)

The Racketeer Influenced and Corrupt Organizations (RICO) statute is 298 pages long and the purpose of this section is to give the reader an idea of the scope of the law. The RICO statute provides for four separate offenses; three are substantive crimes (18 U.S.C. 1961 [a], [b], and [c]), and the fourth offense involves conspiracy to commit any of the substantive RICO violations (18 U.S.C. 1962 [d]).[1] The latter statute is the one most frequently used and the one that has drawn so much criticism in 1988.

Most states now have RICO statutes of their own patterned after the federal statute, and some prosecutions have been made under those. The federal law has the teeth, and two or three federal prosecutors have tried to implement it against powerful financial frauds and union cases, much to the chagrin of powerful political leaders. The federal statute, in summary, includes the following general titles. Refer to the U.S. Code for full details.

Title I. Grand juries.   Special grand juries under the jurisdiction of district courts to sit for periods of 36 months.

Title II. General immunity.   Provides "use" immunity rather than "transaction" immunity for an organized crime witness.

Title III. Recalcitrant witness.   Authorizes a maximum 18-month civil commitment with respect to witnesses who refuse to testify.

Title IV. False declarations.   Abandons the two-witness and direct evidence rule and authorizes a prosecution for perjury and false declarations based on irreconcilably inconsistent declarations under oath.

Title V. Protected facilities for housing government witnesses.   Authorizes the attorney general to protect and maintain federal or state witnesses and their families.

Title VI. Depositions.   Authorizes the government to preserve testimony by use of a deposition in a criminal proceeding.

Title VII. Litigation concerning sources of evidence.   Omits limits on the disclosure of evidence illegally obtained by the government.

---

[1]Rudolph W. Giuliani, "Legal Remedies for Attacking Organized Crime," *Major Issues in Organized Crime.* (Washington, D.C.: National Institute of Justice, 1987), pp. 103–130.

Title VIII. Syndicated gambling (five parts).   Prohibits the obstruction of state or local law enforcement by making it unlawful for two or more persons to conspire to obstruct the enforcement of law with the intent to facilitate gambling.

Unlawful to engage in conspiracy to gamble in violation of state law by five or more persons, having a gross revenue of more than $2000 per day.

Unlawful to engage in the operation of an illegal gambling business. If inferentially established, property used in violation of the provision may be seized.

A Presidential Crime Commission is established to review gambling and enforcement policies and to recommend alternatives.

Makes possible enforcement of Parts 1 and 2 by court-ordered electronic surveillance. This surveillance is not preempted by state law.

Title IX. Racketeer influence and corrupt organizations.   Makes unlawful the receipt or use of income from racketeering activities.

Prohibits the acquisition of any enterprise engaged in interstate commerce through a "pattern" of "racketeering activity."

Proscribes the operation of any enterprise engaged in interstate commerce through a "pattern" of "racketeering activity."

Title X. Dangerous special offender sentencing. Section 1001.   Authorizes extended sentences of up to 25 years for dangerous offenders.

Title XI. Regulation of Explosives. Section 1102.   Establishes federal controls over interstate and foreign commerce in explosives.

Title XII. National Commission on individual rights.   This commission is designed to conduct comprehensive study and review of federal laws and practices relating to special grand juries and other rights as authorized by law or acquired by executive action.

Title XIII. General provisions.   If parts of the act are held invalid, provisions of other parts are not affected.

The RICO statute did not create a new substantive offense, because any acts punishable under RICO are also punishable under existing state and federal statutes. RICO encompasses a wide variety of state and federal offenses that can be used as predicate acts of racketeering. The statute can be used very broadly in a wide variety of circumstances. Thus, the statute is used only in select cases.

The use of RICO by successful federal prosecutions has brought a storm of protest from the business community and from the civil libertarians. There is a fine line between persecution and prosecution, and big money prosecutions find scapegoats when their clients are convicted and receive long prison terms. Prosecutor Rudolph Guiliani, although highly successful as a prosecutor, approved tactics that are negated in the *RICO Manual for Federal Investigators.*

An editorial in the *Wall Street Journal* implied that RICO policies were violated in the latest cases of securities frauds. The accusations were[2]

---

[2]L. Gordon Crovitz, "RICO's Broken Commandments," *The Wall Street Journal,* January 26, 1989. Editorial.

1. Inclusion of a RICO count in an indictment solely or even primarily to create a bargaining tool for later plea negotiation on lesser counts would not be appropriate and would violate the *Principles of Federal Prosecution.*
2. ... warns against threatening RICO to coerce testimony or cooperation.
3. The manual discourages concocting a RICO case built on tax and secondary allegations such as mail fraud.
4. Supervisors will not approve a proposed RICO indictment that contains as predicates mail fraud charges concerning federal tax evasion or related violation ... unless first cleared with the Tax Division at Main Justice.
5. "Fraud in the sale of securities," but not every securities case is supposed to be a RICO case.

Obviously, the writers of the law and the writers of the procedures did not have the same type of prosecution in mind. In every RICO case, the government uses, although perhaps covertly, the statute to gain plea bargaining and cooperation from witnesses. The strength of the law is implied in those tactics.

In the highly visible cases around the country, there has been much sentiment stirred up that will probably get the statute modified this year. For example, the New York Organized Crime Control Act enacted in 1987 was felt to have a more fair philosophy in its structure about showing the entire scope of an organization and the prohibition of prosecution when defendants are not meaningfully linked to each other, then separate trial must be provided.[3]

[3]Daniel L. Feldman, "Principled Compromise: The New York State Organized Crime Control Act," *Criminal Justice Ethics.* John Jay College, 6, 1 (Winter–Spring 1987), 57.

Appendix C

Regulations That Control NCIC Computer Operations

DATA FILES

The National Crime Information Center (NCIC) contains data on stolen vehicles, missing license plates, lost or stolen guns, lost or stolen articles that are individually serially numbered and valued at $500 or more, wanted persons, and stolen or missing securities (including stocks, bonds, money orders, currency). Criteria for data input are stipulated by the NCIC operating manual. For instance, the following general provisions govern entries made by control terminals.[1]

Vehicle File

It is suggested that unrecovered stolen vehicles be entered in file within 24 hours after the theft. . . . An immediate entry should be considered in instances where the place of theft is in proximity of a state line.

Missing vehicles will not be entered in file unless a formal police theft report is made or a complaint filed and appropriate warrant issued charging embezzlement, etc.

Vehicles wanted in conjunction with felonies or serious misdemeanors may be entered into file immediately.

License Plate File

Unrecovered stolen license plates will be entered on the same basis as stolen vehicles provided all plates issued are missing.

---

[1]The criteria for entry have been abridged from the *Operating Manual* of the National Crime Information Center (Washington, D.C.: U.S. Department of Justice, 1968), pp. 6–8. Information gathering, intelligence processing, and operations of the investigation unit has not actualized because of lack of research, territorial jealousy and restrictive court decisions. See Frederick T. Martens, "The Intelligence Function," *Major Issues in Organized Crime Control* (Washington, D.C.: National Institute of Justice).

Gun File

Serially numbered weapons (stolen or lost).

Weapons recovered in connection with an unsolved crime for which no lost or stolen report is on file may be entered in the file as a "recovered" weapon.

Article File

Individual serially numbered property items valued at $500 or more. Office equipment (adding machines, typewriters, dictating machines, etc.) and color television sets may be entered regardless of value.

Multiple serially numbered property items totalling $5,000 or more in one theft.

Any serially numbered property items may be entered at the discretion of the reporting agency if (1) the circumstances of the theft indicate that there is a probability of interstate movement, or (2) where the seriousness of the crime indicates that such an entry should be made for investigative purposes.

Wanted Person File

Individuals for whom federal warrants are outstanding.

Individuals who have committed or have been identified with an offense which is classified as a felony or misdemeanor under the existing penal statutes of the jurisdiction originating the entry and felony or misdemeanor warrant has been issued for the individual with respect to the offense which was the basis of the entry. Probation and parole violators meeting the foregoing criteria should be entered.

A "Temporary Felony Want" may be entered when a law enforcement agency has need to take prompt action. . . .

Securities File

Stocks, bonds, money orders, currency, etc., will be stored in this file.

These criteria for data input serve as the basis for all agency decisions regarding information that will be processed for entry into the national system. Whereas in some cases restrictive, the provisions provide a fairly flexible working basis for the identification of the major items of data with which law enforcement agencies are concerned.

In regard to these criteria, two primary characteristics should be noted. First, the criteria provide that items of data be uniquely identifiable. Articles that cannot be identified or distinguished as unique cannot be entered, because no point of reference for an inquiring agency is provided. A vehicle must have a license number or identification number; a person must have a name; a gun must have a serial number; currency must have a denomination and serial number. In other words, each data entry must include an identifier that will allow discrimination between like objects.

Second, the system will take information on criminals or wanted persons, but will not take information on crimes. When a criminal offense is committed, no entries can be made unless article, person, vehicle, etc., associated with the crime can be identified positively. This prevents the inclusion of data that would be useless in the solution of crimes and gives evidence to the fact that the NCIC is an operationally based system designed to serve administrative and operational needs, rather than a research or data gathering system that would aid in management control.

RETENTION PERIOD OF NCIC RECORDS

In addition to the control terminal updating or purging provisions to be discussed at a later point, the NCIC has regular purging provisions to keep files current. General regulations have been formulated for discarding data that would be useless after a longer period of time. The decreasing probability of a need for locating particular items of data makes it possible to purge the files periodically, based on a standardized retention period. The following general rules apply to items of data for which no locating information has been received by the NCIC:

Vehicle File

Unrecovered stolen vehicles will remain in file for the year of entry plus 4.

Unrecovered vehicles wanted in conjunction with a felony will remain in file for 90 days after entry. In the event a further record is desired, the vehicle must be reentered.

Unrecovered stolen VIN plates, engines and transmissions will remain in file for the year plus 4.

License Plate File

Unrecovered stolen license plates not associated with a vehicle will remain in file for one year after the end of the year during which the valid period of the plate expires.

Gun File

Unrecovered weapons will be retained in file for an indefinite period until action is taken by the originating agency to clear the record.

Weapons entered in file as "recovered" weapons will remain in file for the balance of the year entered plus 2.

Article File

Stolen articles uncovered will be retained for the balance of the year entered plus one year.

Wanted Person File

Persons not located will remain in this file indefinitely until action is taken by the originating agency to clear the record (except "temporary felony wants").

The data items when purged according to these rules are stored on magnetic tape for future reference. They are not totally purged from the files on the NCIC, but are simply shifted from the active files to inactive files. The same process applies to data files on located property or persons, which are governed by the following rules:

Vehicle, License Plate, and Article Files

Records concerning stolen vehicles, vehicles wanted in conjunction with felonies, vehicle parts ... [license plates, and articles] will remain in file for a period of 10 days subsequent to the date of recovery, as shown in the message clearing the record, and then automatically removed.[2]

Gun File

Records concerning stolen or lost weapons will remain in file for a period of 10 days subsequent to the date of recovery....

Records of "recovered" weapons will be removed from file immediately upon receipt of a stolen report concerning that weapon.

---

[2]*Operating Manual*, pp. 8–9. These are general guidelines and do not necessarily fit the revisions of systems, the upgrades in technology, and the court decisions that govern each state. For example, see Melinda Cabral, "Dissemination and Security of Information," *California Police Recorder*, January 1988, pp. 37–43.

Wanted Person File

Records concerning wanted persons shall remain in file for a period of 30 days subsequent to the date of apprehension, as shown in the message clearing the record, and then automatically removed.[3]

Periodic validity checks of NCIC data files are requested of control terminals. Appropriate data are furnished to control terminals which, in turn, check data entries against original agency records. Quarterly checks are made of data in the vehicle and license plate file; and annual check is made of data in the gun file. No provisions are presently established for frequency and scope of validity checks of the wanted person file, and no validity checks are required of data in the article file because of purge criteria covering this file.

MESSAGES AND DATA REVISION

The NCIC computer will accept six types of messages and make appropriate types of changes in the active files. These include:

Record entry—places a new record in file.

Record modify—adds data to or changes a portion of data previously placed in the NCIC file by a record entry. May be made only by agency originally entering the record.

Record cancel—cancels a record for reasons other than recovery of property or apprehension of a wanted person, i.e., record later determined to be invalid, withdrawal of prosecutive action, etc. May be made only by agency originally entering record. Cancel messages are not to be used for any purpose other than that stated above.

Inquiry—requests a search of the NCIC file against information available to the inquiring agency.

Locate message—shows a temporary change in record status. The message is sent by an agency which has located an item of stolen property or wanted person previously entered in the system.

Record clear—records recovery of stolen/missing property or apprehension of a wanted person, the subject of a previously placed record in the NCIC. May be made only by agency originally entering record.[4]

The NCIC, in turn, will transmit three types of messages to control terminals. These include: (1) acknowledgements of messages other than inquiries, (2) replies to inquiries, and (3) administrative messages. Administrative messages concern operating aspects of the system sent to system

---

[3]*Operating Manual*, pp. 9–10. The procedures described here constitute a database for advanced knowledge systems most likely to be implemented in major departments in the 1990's.

[4]Ibid., pp. 30–35.

participants. Control terminals, however, cannot send administrative messages to NCIC through terminals.

Messages sent to NCIC by control terminals are to be prepared off-line, except for inquiry messages that are prepared on-line.[5] Off-line preparation allows adequate time for verification of data entries by originating agencies to ensure accuracy. On-line preparation of inquiry messages provides instant response to operating needs for information checks. Because inquiry messages are the only type that require immediate response from the NCIC, this pattern of messages provides an effective operational basis for accurate input while allowing immediate response to operational needs.

SCOPE OF DATA IN NCIC FILES

The scope of data in computer files either limits or increases the chances for a variety of types of searches. In the NCIC data format most of the data relevant for search purposes are provided. The vehicle file requires the following items of data on stolen vehicles, vehicle parts (as appropriate), and vehicles involved in felonies (to the extent that data are available):

> License plate number
> License plate state
> License plate year of expiration
> License plate type
> Vehicle identification number
> Year
> Make
> Model
> Style
> Color
> Date of theft
> Originating agency case number

In addition to this basic data on the item involved, the record as contained in the NCIC files includes a message key that instructs the NCIC and its participants as to the intent of the message, an originating agency code, and

---

[5]Off-line is defined as "a system . . . in which the peripheral equipment is not under the control of the central processing unit." On-line refers to "a system . . . in which information reflecting current activity is introduced into the data processing system as soon as it occurs. Thus, directly in-line with the main flow of transaction processing." See *Automatic Data Processing Glossary, Datamation* magazine, 1968.

an NCIC record number. The record provides space for later inclusion of the date the item is located or the record is canceled, the locating agency, and a locating agency case number. A "miscellaneous" field is provided for relevant information or for extension of data not totally contained by established fields. (For instance, when a license plate number exceeds eight digits, the full number must be inserted in the "miscellaneous" field.)

Inquiries concerning stolen vehicles, felony vehicles, stolen parts, and stolen and/or missing license plates are processed as follows:

1. Inquiries should be made by complete license plate number and state of issue and/or complete vehicle identification number, or vehicle part number in instances involving engines and transmissions.
2. When inquiry is by license plate number only and positive response is received, it is necessary to match the remaining identifying data in the NCIC record with the plate being inquired about before taking further action. In this instance, search is by plate number only; thus, multiple "hits" may ensue.
3. Uncommon circumstances may indicate a need for a special off-line search, e.g., for all vehicles of a particular year and make; for a particular model or color; etc. Such requests must be kept to a minimum and only requested where communicated to the NCIC off-line.[6]

Data items on stolen or missing license plates are identical to that on stolen vehicles listed above, with the exception of the six data items descriptive of the vehicle.

Record entries on stolen or missing weapons include the following data items:

> Serial number
> Make
> Caliber
> Type
> Date of theft or missing report

The data entry also provides for a message key, an originating agency number, an originating agency case number, an NCIC number, and a miscellaneous field for date weapon is located or record is canceled, the locating agency, and the locating agency case number. A "recovered" weapon is identified by a code included in the message instructions to the NCIC.

In addition to the normal identifying data field for locating information, the article file entries include the following fields; type, serial number, brand name, and model.

---

[6]*Operating Manual*, p. 45.

Data records on wanted persons are more extensive than those required for other items. Fields of data include:

Name	Operator's license year of
Sex	expiration
Race	Offense
Nationality	Date of warrant
Date of birth	Originating agency case number
Height	License plate number
Weight	License plate state
Color hair	License plate year of expiration
FBI number	License plate type
Fingerprint classification	Vehicle identification number
Miscellaneous number	Year
Social Security number	Make
Operator's license number	Model
Operator's license state	Style
	Color

Provision is made for locating information, an NCIC number, and originating agency identification. In addition, the message key may be coded with "A" if the subject is known to be armed, with "S" if the subject is known to possess suicidal tendencies, and with "Y" if both describers apply.

Duplicate entries on persons will be accepted by the NCIC, if the originating agencies are different. "The agency making the second entry will receive as a hit the record already in file at the time the second entry is acknowledged. Should the entry contain data concerning a vehicle or license plate that has already been entered in the vehicle or license plate file, the agency making the entry will be furnished the record in file at the time the wanted person entry is acknowledged."[7]

Inquiries of the wanted person file are governed by the following provisions:

1. Inquiries may be made by name and at least one of the following numerical identifiers: complete date of birth, FBI number, miscellaneous number, social security number, operator's license number, and originating agency case number.
2. Inquiries may be made by using message code "QW" with license plate number, license plate state, and/or vehicle identification number. In this instance it is not necessary to use a name.
3. Special circumstances may indicate a need for a search by name only. These can be made off-line but ... must be ... requested only where extreme circumstances warrant.[8]

[7]*Operating Manual*, p. 62. A "hit" as used in this quote refers to a positive response from the system that a person, vehicle, or object is wanted by some agency. The requesting agency is then provided the information that a record exists and relevant information on the person, vehicle, or object.

[8]*Operating Manual*, pp. 63–64.

NCIC EXTENSION AND DEVELOPMENT

The NCIC system has grown and matured since its inception in 1967. Each state and adjoining foreign countries now access this system. This type of system supports strategic and tactical intelligence capabilities to each NCIC terminal. For example, if strategic intelligence were requested on a certain vehicle ownership, this could be traced through the system. The ability to keep car and owner together is often important intelligence information. In a tactical intelligence application, this system has been instrumental in curbing the flow of stolen cars into Mexico, which, in turn, resulted in the curbing of narcotics flowing back into the United States.

The advisory group of the NCIC was reportedly considering extension of active files to include "missing" persons in its wanted persons file to facilitate location of such persons through normal activities. The advisory group was also considering storage of criminal identification records. "Such records of arrests and dispositions could be entered or retrieved instantaneously in the NCIC real-time system" and would aid in the NCIC's criminal justice statistical program.

OTHER NATIONAL SYSTEMS

Two other national communication systems are the Law Enforcement Teletype System (LETS) and the National Driver Register Service (NDRS). Law Enforcement Teletype System is simply a teletype connecting system between law enforcement agencies throughout the United States and is primarily devoted to the exchange of general information among police departments. It can supplement NCIC by providing the means for verification of entries, for notifying originating agencies of arrests and dispositions, and for sending administrative messages from control terminals to NCIC.

The National Driver Register Service (NDRS) consists of a computer-based file of "dangerous drivers." Its reason for being is explained by the following statements:

> The purpose of the National Driver register is to provide a central driver-records identification facility containing the names of drivers whose licenses have been denied, suspended or revoked for any reason other than a denial or withdrawal of a license for less than 6 months due to a series of nonmoving violations. It was established by the United States Congress to assist each State in locating all the records available on these drivers, regardless of where in the United States they may have established these records.[9]

---

[9]U.S. Department of Transportation, *The National Driver Register: A State Driver Records Exchange Service* (Washington, D.C.: U.S. Government Printing Office, September 1967), p. i.

The basic file is established from reports sent to the NDRS by each state and serves each state by providing information on requests concerning drivers—within twenty-four hours of receipt of a request for a license search.

The file is theoretically useful to a large number of state and local officials. These include:

> Driver license administrators—for checking on individuals who request to be licensed by the state.
>
> Police—developing complete accident reports (by providing background information on individuals involved in accidents).
>
> Prosecutors—may need driver information to determine whether to file first- or second-offense charges.
>
> Judges—need driver information to determine appropriate sentences after conviction.
>
> School administrators—need driver records in the section of driver education teachers.
>
> Other public authorities—need driver records on job applicants and on employees.
>
> Insurance firms and transportation companies—need complete records for identifying poor risks among applicants for automobile liability insurance and for employment as truck and bus drivers.

Only state and federal officials can obtain information directly from the NDRS, but information can be made available to other officials who need it.

There are so many good sources of information entire volumes are devoted to listing these documents.[10]

---

[10]Beryl Frank, Ed., *Encyclopedia of U.S. Government Benefits* (New York: Dodd, Mead and Company, 1985). Also see Government Data Publications, 1100 17th Street, N.W., Washington, D.C. 20036.

Appendix D

Standard Classification Numbers for Crimes Related to Organized Criminal Activity

SOVEREIGNTY	**0100**	RANSOM—ADULT—GUN	1004
		RANSOM—ADULT	1005
TREASON	0101	RANSOM—ADULT—	
TREASON MISPRISION	0102	STGARM	1006
ESPIONAGE	0103	HOSTAGE FOR ESCAPE	1007
SABOTAGE	0104	ABDUCTION—FAMILY	1008
SEDITION	0105	ABDUCTION—NONFAMILY	1009
SELECT SCV	0106		
		SEXUAL ASSAULT	**1100**
MILITARY	**0200**	RAPE—GUN	1101
DESERTION	0201	RAPE	1102
		RAPE—STGARM	1103
IMMIGRATION	**0300**	SODOMY—BOY—GUN	1104
ILLEGAL ENTRY	0301	SODOMY—MAN—GUN	1105
FALSE CITIZEN	0302	SODOMY—GIRL—GUN	1106
SMUGGLE ALIENS	0303	SODOMY—WOMAN—GUN	1107
		SODOMY—BOY	1108
		SODOMY—MAN	1109
HOMICIDE	**0900**	SODOMY—GIRL	1110
KILL—FAMILY—GUN	0901	SODOMY—WOMAN	1111
KILL—FAMILY	0902	SODOMY—BOY—STGARM	1112
KILL—NONFAM—GUN	0903	SODOMY—MAN—STGARM	1113
KILL—NONFAM	0904	SODOMY—GIRL—STGARM	1114
KILL—PUB OFF—GUN	0905	SODOMY—WOMAN—	
KILL—PUB OFF	0906	STGARM	1115
KILL—POL OFF—GUN	0907	STAT RAPE	1116
KILL—POL OFF	0908		
NEG MANSL—VEHICLE	0909	**ROBBERY**	**1200**
NEG MANSL—NOT VEH	0910	ROB BUSINESS—GUN	1201
		ROB BUSINESS	1202
KIDNAPPING	**1000**	ROB BUSINESS—STGARM	1203
RANSOM—MINOR—GUN	1001	ROB STREET—GUN	1204
RANSOM—MINOR	1002	ROB STREET	1205
RANSOM—MINOR—		ROB STREET—STGARM	1206
STGARM	1003	ROB RESIDENCE—GUN	1207

ROB RESIDENCE	1208		BURG NO FORCED—RES	2204
ROB RESIDENCE—STRGARM	1209		BURG NO FORCED—	
FORC PURSE SNATCH	1210		NONRESS	2205
			BURG TOOLS	2206

ASSAULT	**1300**			
ASLT AGG—FAMILY—GUN	1301		**LARCENY**	**2300**
ASLT AGG—FAMILY	1302		POCKET PICK	2301
ASLT AGG—FAMILY—			PURSE SNATCH	2302
STGARM	1303		SHOPLIFT	2303
ASLT AGG—NONFAMILY—			LARC PARTS FM VEH	2304
GUN	1304		LARC FM AUTO	2305
ASLT AGG—NONFAMILY	1305		LARC FM VEH TRANS	2306
ASLT AGG—NONFAMILY—			LARC FM COIN MACH	2307
STGARM	1306		LARC FM BLDG	2308
ASLT AGG—PUB OFF—GUN	1307		LARC FM YARDS	2309
ASLT AGG—PUB OFF	1308		LARC FM MAILS	2310
ASLT AGG—PUB OFF—				
STGARM	1309			
ASLT AGG—POL OFF—GUN	1310		**STOLEN VEHICLE**	**2400**
ASLT AGG—POL OFF	1311		VEH THEFT SALE	2401
ASLT AGG—POL OFF—			VEH THEFT STRIP	2402
STGARM	1312		VEH THEFT FOR CRIME	2403
ASLT SIMPLE	1313		VEH THEFT	2404
			VEH THEFT BY BAILEE	2405
			VEH RCVING	2406
ABORTION	**1400**		VEH STRIP	2407
ABORT OTHER	1401		VEH POSS	2408
ABORT SELF	1402		TRANSPORT	2409
SOLICIT SUBMIT ABORT	1403		AIRPLANE THEFT	2410
SOLICIT PERFORM ABORT	1404			
ABORTIFACIENT SELL	1405		**FORGERY**	**2500**
			FORG CHECKS	2501
ARSON	**2000**		FORGERY	2502
ARSON BUS—LIFE	2001		COUNTERFEIT	2503
ARSON RES—LIFE	2002		COUNTERFEIT—	
ARSON BUS—INS	2003		TRANSPORT	2504
ARSON RES—INS	2004		COUNTERFEIT TOOLS	2505
ARSON BUSINESS	2005		PASS COUNTERFEIT	2506
ARSON RESIDENCE	2006		PASS FORGED CHECKS	2507
			POSSESS COUNTERFEIT	2508
EXTORTION	**2100**			
EXTORT THREAT PERSON	2101		**FRAUD**	**2600**
EXTORT THREAT			CON GAME	2601
PROPERTY	2102		SWINDLE	2602
EXTORT THREAT			MAIL FRAUD	2603
REPUTATION	2103		IMPERSONATION	2604
			FRAUD CREDIT CARDS	2605
			NSF CHECKS	2606
BURGLARY	**2200**		FALSE STATEMENT	2606
BURG SAFE—VAULT	2201			
BURG FORCED—RES	2202			
BURG FORCED—NONRES	2203		**EMBEZZLE**	**2700**

STOLEN PROP	2800
STOL PROP THEFT SALE	2801
STOL PROP THEFT TRANSPORT	2802
STOL PROP THEFT	2803
STOL PROP TRANSPORT	2804
STOL PROP RECEIV	2805
STOL PROP POSSESS	2806
STOL PROP CONCEALED	2807

PROPERTY DAMAGE	2900
DAM PROP BUS	2901
DAM PROP PRIV	2902
DAM PROP PUB	2903

DANGEROUS DRUGS	3500
HALLUC—MANU	3501
HALLUC—DIST	3502
HALLUC—SELL	3503
HALLUC—POSSESS	3504
HALLUC	3505
HEROIN—SELL	3510
HEROIN—SMUG	3511
HEROIN—POSSESS	3512
HEROIN	3513
OPIUM—SELL	3520
OPIUM—SMUG	3521
OPIUM—POSSESS	3522
OPIUM	3523
COCAINE—SELL	3530
COCAINE—SMUG	3531
COCAINE—POSSESS	3532
COCAINE	3533
SYNTH NARC—SELL	3540
SYNTH NARC—SMUG	3541
SYNTH NARC—POSSESS	3542
SYNTH NARC	3543
NARC EQUIP	3550
MARIJUANA—SELL	3560
MARIJUANA—SMUG	3561
MARIJUANA—POSSESS	3562
MARIJUANA—PROD	3563
MARIJUANA	3564
AMPHET—MANU	3570
AMPHET SELL	3571
AMPHET—POSSESS	3572
AMPHET	3573
BARBIT—MANU	3580
BARBIT—SELL	3581
BARBIT—POSSESS	3582
BARBIT	3583

SEX OFFENSE	3600
SEX CHILD	3601
HOMOSEX GIRL	3602
HOMOSEX BOY	3603
INCEST MINOR	3604
INDEC EXP MINOR	3605
BESTIALITY	3606
INCEST ADULT	3607
INDEC EXP ADULT	3608
SEDUCE ADULT	3609
HOMOSEX WOMAN	3610
HOMOSEX MAN	3611
PEEPING TOM	3612

OBSCENE MATERIAL	3700
MANU OBSCENE	3701
SELL OBSCENE	3702
MAIL OBSCENE	3703
POSSESS OBSCENE	3704
DIST OBSCENE	3705
TRANSPORT OBSCENE	3706
OBSCENE COMM	3707

FAMILY OFF	3800
NEGLECT FAM	3801
CRUEL CHILD	3802
CRUEL WIFE	3803
BIGAMY	3804
CONTRIB DELINQ MINOR	3805
NEGLECT CHILD	3806
NONPAY ALIMONY	3807
NONSUPPORT PARENT	3808

GAMBLING	3900
BOOKMAKE	3901
CARDS—OP	3902
CARDS—PLAY	3903
DICE—OP	3904
DICE—PLAY	3905
GAMBLING DEVICE—POSSESS	3906
GAMBLING DEVICE—TRANSPORT	3907
GAMBLING DEVICE—NOT REGIS	3908
GAMBLING DEVICE	3909
GAMBLING GOODS—POSSESS	3910
GAMBLING GOODS—TRANSPORT	3911
LOTTERY—OP	3912

LOTTERY—RUN	3913	OBSTRUCT JUST	5006
LOTTERY—PLAY	3914	OBSTRUCT COURT	5007
SPORTS TAMPER	3915	MISCONDUCT—JUDIC	
WAGERING INFO—		OFF	5008
TRANSMIT	3916	CONTEMPT CONGR	5009
EST GAMBLING PLACE	3917	CONTEMPT LEGIS	5010

COMMERCIAL SEX	**4000**	**BRIBERY**	**5100**
KEEP BROTHEL	4001	BRIBE GIVE	5101
PROCURE PROSTITUTE	4002	BRIBE OFFER	5102
HOMOSEX PROST	4003	BRIBE RECEIVE	5103
PROSTITUTION	4004	BRIBE SOLICIT	5104
		CONFLICT INT	5105
		GRATUITY GIVE	5106
LIQUOR	**4100**	GRATUITY OFFER	5107
MANU LIQUOR	4101	GRATUITY RECEIVE	5108
SELL LIQUOR	4102	GRATUITY SOLICIT	5109
TRANSPORT LIQUOR	4103	KICKBACK GIVE	5110
POSSESS LIQUOR	4104	KICKBACK OFFER	5111
MISREPRESENT AGE	4105	KICKBACK RECEIVE	5112
LIQUOR	4106	KICKBACK SOLICIT	5113

DRUNK	**4200**	**WEAPON OFFENSE**	**5200**
		ALTER ID ON WPN	5201
OBSTRUCT POLICE	**4800**	CARRY CONCLD WPN	5202
		CARRY PROH WPN	5203
RESIST OFF	4801	EXPLOS—TEACH USE	5204
AID PRIS ESC	4802	EXPLOS—TRANSPORT	5205
HARBOR FUGTV	4803	EXPLOS—USE	5206
OBSTRUCT CRIM INVEST	4804	INCEND DEV—POSSESS	5207
MAKE FALSE REP	4805	INCEND DEV—USE	5208
EVIDENCE—DESTROY	4806	INCEND—TEACH USE	5209
WITNESS—DISSUADE	4807	WPN LIC	5210
WITNESS—DECEIVE	4808	POSSESS EXPL	5211
REFUSING AID OFF	4809	POSSESS WPN	5212
COMPOUND CRIME	4810	FIRE WPN	5213
UNAUTH COMM W		SELL WPN	5214
PRISONER	4811		
ARREST—ILLEGAL	4812	**PUBLIC PEACE**	**5300**

FLIGHT—ESCAPE	**4900**	ANARCHISM	5301
		RIOT—INCITE	5302
ESCAPE	4901	RIOT—ENGAGE	5303
FLIGHT AVOID	4902	RIOT—INTERFERE FIRE	5304
		RIOT—INTERFERE OFF	5305
		RIOT	5306
OBSTRUCT JUDIC		ASSEMBLY—UNLAW	5307
(CONGR., LEGIS.)	**5000**	FALSE ALARM	5308
BAIL—SECURED BOND	5001	HARASS COMM	5309
BAIL—PERSONAL RECOG	5002	DESECRATE FLAG	5310
PERJURY	5003	DISORDERLY COND	5311
PERJURY	5004	DISTURB PEACE	5312
CONTEMPT COURT	5005		

CURFEW	5313	DIVULGE MSG CONTENTS	5703
LOITER	5314	EAVESDROP	5704
		EAVESDROP EQUIP	5705
TRAFFIC OFF	**5400**	OPEN SEALED COMM	5706
		TRESPASS	5707
HIT RUN	5401	WIRETAP—FAILURE REP	5708
TRANSP DANG MATL	5402		
DRIV INFLU DRUGS	5403		
DRIV INFLU LIQ	5404	**SMUGGLE**	**5800**
MOVING TFC	5405	CONTRABAND	5801
NONMOVING TFC	5406	PRISON CONTRABAND	5802
		AVOID PAYING DUTY	5803
HEALTH—SAFETY	**5500**		
DRUGS ADLTD	5501	**ELECTION LAWS**	**5900**
DRUGS—MISBRAND	5502		
DRUGS	5503	**ANTITRUST**	**6000**
FOOD ADLTD	5510		
FOOD—MISBRAND	5511	**TAX—REVENUE**	**6100**
FOOD	5512	INCOME TAX	6101
COSMETICS ADLTD	5520	SALES TAX	6102
COSMETICS—MISBRAND	5521	LIQUOR TAX	6103
COSMETICS	5522		
		CONSERVATION	**6200**
CIVIL RIGHTS	**5600**	ANIMALS CONSERV	6201
		BIRDS CONSERV	6202
INVADE PRIVACY	**5700**	FISH CONSERV	6203
		LICENSE CONSERV	6204
DIVULGE EAVESDROP INFO	5701		
DIVULGE EAVESDROP ORDER	5702	**VAGRANCY**	**6300**

Appendix E

Inquiry Examples

The typical automated communications system, including the Law Enforcement Teletype System (LETS), is now guided by the following formats. These are presented as samples only because users of the system receive operating manuals.

CRIMINAL HISTORY INQUIRY, INTERSTATE IDENTIFICATION INDEX (III)[1]

```
        QH              CRIMINAL   HISTORY   INQUIRY
          OPR ID:
          REQUESTED BY: NAME-------------UNIT------  /REASON------
          --NAME INQUIRY ---CRIME SUMMARY RECORD ----- PERSONAL DATA
          ---NUMERIC INQUIRY   ----NCIC INQUIRY RECORD
          ORG: CA019  ------NAME  ------------------------ SEX ---
          RAC --- HGT--- AGE --- DOB ------(USE AGE OR DOB-NOT BOTH)
          HAI --- EYE ---
          SOC --------- FBI ---------- OLN -------- MNU -----------
          SID --------- CII ---------- INN ---------------
            IF CRIME SUMMARY TRANSCRIPT IS REQUESTED BY MAIL:
            REQUESTING AGENCY CODE:  ------------
*******************   THIS FORMAT IS FOR LAW ENFORCEMENT
** W A R N I N G **   INVESTIGATORS ONLY.
*******************
                      IT IS NOT TO BE USED FOR EMPLOYMENT,
                      LICENSING OR CERTIFICATION PURPOSES.
SIGNON-00    SIGNON ACCEPTED          NO MSGS WAITING
SCREEN FORMATTED
                      --------

RQR INTERSTATE IDENTIFICATION INDEX (III) CRIMINAL HISTORY INQUIRY
OPR ID
FBI-------------   OR     SID --------------
DEPARTMENT          PD ----------------------
BUILDING ----------------------------------------(OPTIONAL)
ADDRESS ---------------------------------------
CITY & STATE -----------------------------------ZIP ---------
** NOTE ** A PERIOD IS NOT ALLOWED IN ANY OF THE ABOVE FIELDS
SCREEN FORMATTED                        NO MSGS WAITING
```

[1]These are general formats used by states for national and international communication. Format may vary from agency to agency. Information order is standardized.

```
ADMIN:                 ADMINISTRATIVE MESSAGE                        PAGE
ENTER DESTINATION(s)------------------------------------------
      FROM ------------------------------ PHONE -----------------
TEXT  -----------------------------------------------------------
      -----------------------------------------------------------
      -----------------------------------------------------------
      -----------------------------------------------------------

      IF NO MORE PAGES REQUIRED, ENTER AN "N" :  Y
SCREEN FORMATTED                              NO MSGS WAITING



NLETS*               NLETS MESSAGE    MESSAGE TYPE AM    ENTER REF NO---
ORIGINATING ORI/AGENCY NAME:    CA019------/-------------INITIALS---
DESTINATION(S) ORI/AGENCY NAMES (S):    1-------- / ---------------
      2 ----------- / ------------------- 3----------/----------------
      4 ----------- / ------------------- 5 --------/----------------
TEXT  -----------------------------------------------------------
      -----------------------------------------------------------
      -----------------------------------------------------------
      -----------------------------------------------------------
SCREEN FORMATTED                              NO MSGS WAITING



ADMIN                  ADMINISTRATIVE MESSAGE
ENTER DESTINATION(S) -----------  --------------  -----------  -------
TEXT  -----------------------------------------------------------
      -----------------------------------------------------------
      -----------------------------------------------------------
      -----------------------------------------------------------
      -----------------------------------------------------------
SCREEN FORMATTED                              NO MSGS WAITING
```

```
ADMIN                 ADMINISTRATIVE MESSAGE
ENTER DESTINATION(S)  C/LTS ----------- ----------- ---------- ----------
TEXT   ---------------------------------------------------------------------
       ---------------------------------------------------------------------
       ---------------------------------------------------------------------
       ---------------------------------------------------------------------
INPUT MSG  003                                    NO MSGS WAITING

AII
15:53  03/30/ YEAR
15:53  03/30/ YEAR
TXT
HAZMAT ON-LINE
RESPONSE TO INQUIRY ON HAZMAT UN NUMBER:       1268
CHEMICAL NAME (S)
NAPTHA DISTILLATE
PETROLEUM DISTILLATE,  N. O. S.
ROAD OIL
THE FOLLOWING INFORMATION IS PROVIDED BY THE NATIONAL SHERIFFS
ASSOCIATION FROM DATA SUPPLIED BY THE U. S. DEPARTMENT OF TRANS-
PORTATION, OFFICE OF HAZARDOUS MATERIALS TRANSPORTATION.
ERG GUIDE NUMBER:  27
F I R E   O R   E X P L O S I O N
FLAMMABLE/COMBUSTIBLE MATERIAL, MAY BE IGNITED BY HEAT, SPARKS OR
FLAMES.  VAPORS MAY TRAVEL TO A SOURCE OF IGNITION AND FLASH BACK.
CONTAINER MAY EXPLODE IN HEAT OR FIRE.
VAPOR EXPLOSION HAZARD INDOORS, OUTDOORS OR IN SEWERS.
RUNOFF TO SEWER MAY CREATE FIRE OR EXPLOSION HAZARD.
H E A L T H   H A Z A R D S
MAY BE POISONOUS IF INHALED OR ABSORBED THROUGH SKIN.
VAPORS MAY CAUSE DIZZINESS OR SUFFOCATION.
CONTACT MAY IRRITATE OR BURN SKIN AND EYES.
FIRE MAY PRODUCE IRRITATION OR POISONOUS GASES.
RUNOFF FROM FIRE CONTROL OR DILUTION WATER MAY CAUSE POLLUTION.
E M E R G E N C Y   A C T I O N
KEEP UNNECESSARY PEOPLE AWAY, ISOLATE HAZARD AREA AND DENY ENTRY.
STAY UPWIND, KEEP OUT OF LOW AREAS
WEAR SELF-CONTAINED (POSITIVE PRESSURE IF AVAILABLE) BREATHING
APPARATUS AND FULL PROTECTIVE CLOTHING.
ISOLATE FOR 1/2 MILE IN ALL DIRECTIONS IF TANK CAR OR TRUCK IS
INVOLVED IN FIRE.
FOR EMERGENCY ASSISTANCE CALL CHEMTREC (800) 424-9300
IF WATER POLLUTION OCCURS, NOTIFY APPROPRIATE AUTHORITIES
F I R E
SMALL FIRES: DRY CHEMICAL, CO2, WATER SPRAY OR FOAM.
LARGE FIRES: WATER SPRAY, FOG OR FOAM.
MOVE CONTAINER FROM FIRE AREA IF YOU CAN DO IT WITHOUT RISK.
(OTHER INSTRUCTIONS MAY FOLLOW)
```

Example: Hazardous Materials Reporting Format.

Bibliography

This partial bibliography includes publications from 1960 to the present. Articles and short research reports may be secured from the National Criminal Justice Reference Service, Box 6000, Rockville, Maryland 20850.

Abadinsky, Howard. *Organized Crime.* Boston: Allyn and Bacon, 1981.

Albini, Joseph L. *The American Mafia: Genesis of a Legend.* New York: Appleton-Century-Crofts, 1971.

Allen, Edward J. *Merchants of Menace—The Mafia, A Study of Organized Crime.* Springfield, Ill.: Charles C Thomas, 1962.

Anderson, Annelise G. *The Business of Organized Crime: A Cosa Nostra Family.* Palo Alto, Calif.: Hoover Institute Press, 1979.

Bailey, William G., ed. *The Encyclopedia of Police Science.* New York: Garland Publishing, 1989.

Becker, Jay. *The Investigation of Computer Crime.* Seattle: Battelle Law and Justice Study Center, 1978.

Bequai, August. *Computer Crime.* Lexington, Mass.: D.C. Heath, 1978.

Bequai, August. *Organized Crime: The Fifth Estate.* Lexington, Mass.: D.C. Heath, 1979.

Bequai, August. *The Cashless Society: EFTS at the Crossroads.* New York: Wiley, 1981.

Bers, Melvin K. *The Penetration of Legitimate Business by Organized Crime: An Analysis.* Washington, D.C.: U.S. Department of Justice, LEAA, 1970.

Blakely, G. R. "On the Waterfront—RICO (Racketeer Influenced and Corrupt Organizations) and Labor Racketeering," *American Criminal Law Review,* 17, 3 (Winter 1980.)

Blakely, G. R., and C. H. Rogovin. *Techniques in the Investigation and Prosecution of Organized Crime: The Rackets Bureau Concept. General Standards for the Operation of Organized Crime Control Units.* Washington, D.C.: U.S. Department of Justice, LEAA, 1977.

Blakely, G. Robert, Ronald Goldstock, and Charles H. Rogovin. *Rackets Bureau: Investigation and Prosecution of Organized Crime.* Washington, D.C.: U.S. Government Printing Office, March 1978.

Block, Alan A., and Frank Scarpitti. *Poisoning for Profit: The Mafia and Toxic Waste in America.* New York: William Marrow & Co., 1985.

Buse, Renee. *The Deadly Silence,* Garden City, N.Y.: Doubleday, 1965.

Bynum, Timothy S., ed. *Organized Crime in America: Concepts and Controversy.* New York: Criminal Justice Press, 1986.

California Department of Justice. *Proceedings of Symposium 87—White Collar: Institutional Crime—Its Measure and Analysis.* Sacramento, 1987.

Carroll, John M. *Secrets of Electronic Espionage.* New York: Dutton, 1966.

Chaiken, Marcia R., and Bruce D. Johnson. *Characteristics of Different Types of Drug Involved Offenders.* Rockville, Md.: U.S. Justice Department, 1988.

Chamber of Commerce of the United States. *Deskbook on Organized Crime.* Washington, D.C.: An Urban Affairs Publication, 1969.

Chamber of Commerce of the United States. *Marshaling Citizen Power against Crime.* Washington, D.C., 1970.

Chamber of Commerce of the United States. *Mafia.* Greenwich, Conn.: Fawcett, 1972.

Cole, George S. *Criminal Justice: Law and Politics,* 5th ed. Belmont, Calif.: Cole Publishing Co., 1988.

Coleman, James W. *The Criminal Elite: The Sociology of White Collar Crime.* New York: St. Martins Press, 1985.

Cook, James, and Jane Carmichael (part 3). "The Invisible Enterprise," *Forbes,* September 29–November 24, 1980. Four-part series.

Drzazga, John. *Wheels of Fortune.* Springfield, Ill.: Charles C Thomas, 1963.

Dulles, Allen W. *The Craft of Intelligence.* New York: Harper & Row, 1968.

Dulles, Allen W. *The Secret Surrender.* New York: Harper & Row, 1966.

Edelhertz, Herbert. *The Nature, Impact and Prosecution of White-Collar Crime.* Washington, D.C.: National Institute of Law Enforcement and Criminal Justice, May 1970, ICR 70–1.

Edelhertz, Herbert. *The Investigation of White Collar Crime: A Manual for Law Enforcement Agencies.* Washington, D.C.: U.S. Government Printing Office, April 1977.

Ernst, Morris L., and Alan U. Schwartz. *Censorship, The Search for the Obscene.* New York: Macmillan, 1964.

Gardiner, John A. *The Politics of Corruption: Organized Crime in an American City.* New York: Russell Sage, 1970.

Geis, Gilbert, and Robert F. Meier. *White Collar Crime: Offenses in Business, Politics and the Professions.* New York: Free Press, 1977.

Geis, Gilbert, and Ezra Statland, eds. *White Collar Crime: Theory and Research.* New York: Sage, 1980.

Godfrey, E. Drexel, Jr., and Don R. Harris. *Basic Elements of Intelligence.* Washington, D.C.: U.S. Department of Justice, LEAA, 1972.

Goulden, Joseph C. *Truth Is the First Casualty.* Chicago: Rand McNally, 1969.

Gugliotta, Guy, and Jeff Leen. *Kings of Cocaine,* New York: Simon & Schuster, 1989.

Halper, Albert, ed. *The Chicago Crime Book.* New York: World, 1967.

Harris, Don R. *Basic Elements of Intelligence: A Manual for Law Enforcement Officers.* Washington, D.C.: U.S. Government Printing Office, September 1976.

Hill, Albert F. *The North Avenue Irregulars: A Suburb Battles the Mafia.* New York: Cowles, 1968.

Hilsman, Roger. *To Move a Nation.* Garden City, N.Y.: Doubleday, 1967.

Homer, F. D. "Conflicting Images of Organized Crime." In *Critical Issues in Criminal Justice,* R. G. Iacovetta and Dae H. Chang. Durham, N.C.: Carolina Academic Press, 1979.

Homer, F. D. *Guns and Garlic: Myths and Realities in Organized Crime.* Purdue: Purdue University Press, 1974.

Ianni, Francis A., and E. R. Ianni. *A Family Business: Kinship and Control in Organized Crime.* New York: Russell Sage, 1972.

Jennings, Dean. *We Only Kill Each Other: The Life and Bad Times of Bugsy Seigal.* Englewood Cliffs, N.J.: Prentice-Hall, 1967.

Kahn, David. *The Code Breakers: History of Secret Communication.* New York: Macmillan, 1967.

Kefauver, Estes. *Crime in America.* Garden City, N.Y.: Doubleday, 1951.

Kelly, R. J. "A Study in the Production of Knowledge by Law Enforcement Specialists." Ph.D. dissertation, New York University, 1978.

Kennedy, Robert F. *The Enemy Within.* New York: Harper & Row, 1960.

Kennedy, Robert F. *The Pursuit of Justice.* New York: Harper & Row, 1964.

King, Rufus. *Gambling and Organized Crime.* Washington, D.C.: Public Affairs Press, 1969.

Kinsey, Alfred C., Wardell B. Pomeroy, and Clyde E. Martin. *Sexual Behavior in the Human Male.* New York: Saunders, 1948.

Krauss, Leonard, and Aileen MacGahan. *Computer Fraud and Countermeasures.* Englewood Cliffs, N.J.: Prentice-Hall, 1979.

Landesco, John. *Organized Crime in Chicago.* 2nd ed. Chicago: University of Chicago Press, 1968.

Law Enforcement Assistance Administration, Organized Crime Program Division. *The Role of State Organized Crime Prevention Councils.* Washington, D.C., 1970.

Lewis, Jerry D., ed. *Crusade against Crime.* New York: Bernard Geis, 1962.

Lewis, Norman. *The Honored Society.* New York: Putnam, 1964.

Lyman, Theodore R., Thomas W. Fletcher, and John A. Gardiner. *Prevention, Detection, and Correction of Corruption in Local Government.* Washington, D.C.: U.S. Government Printing Office, November 1978.

Maas, Peter. *The Valachi Papers.* New York: Putnam, 1968.

Madison, Charles A. *American Labor Leaders.* New York: Ungar, 1962.

Martin, David C., and John Walcott. *Best Laid Plans: The Inside Story of America's War against Terrorism.* New York: Harper & Row, 1988.

Martin, Raymond V. *Revolt in the Mafia.* New York: Duell, Sloan, and Pearce, 1963.

Matthews, John D. *My Name is Violence.* New York: Belmont Books, 1962.

Maxwell, Edward. "Why the Rise in Teenage Veneral Disease?" *Today's Health,* 1965.

McClellan, John L. *Crime without Punishment.* New York: Duell, Sloan, and Pearce, 1962.

McGovern, James. *Crossbow and Overcast.* London: Hutchinson, 1965.

McLaughlin, Donald. *Room 38: A Study in Naval Intelligence.* New York: Atheneum, 1968.

Messick, Hank. *The Silent Syndicate.* New York: Macmillan, 1967.

Messick, Hank. *Syndicate in the Sun.* New York: Macmillan, 1968.

Messick, Hank. *Lansky.* New York: Macmillan, 1971.

Miller, Arthur R. *The Assault on Privacy: Computers, Data Banks, and Dossiers.* Ann Arbor: University of Michigan Press, 1971.

Mollenhoff, Clark R. *Tentacles of Power: The Story of Jimmy Hoffa.* Cleveland: World, 1963.

Mori, Cesare. *The Last Struggle of the Mafia.* New York: Putnam, 1963.

Moscow, Alvin. *Merchants of Heroin.* New York: Dial Press, 1968.

Municipal Police Administration. Chicago: International City Managers' Association, 1961.

National Advisory Committee on Criminal Justice Standards and Goals. *Organized Crime, Report of the Task Force on Organized Crime.* Washington, D.C.: U.S. Government Printing Office, December 1976.

National District Attorneys Association, Economic Crime Project. *Insurance Fraud Manual.* Chicago, 1981.

National Institute of Justice. *Major Issues in Organized Crime Control. Symposium Proceedings.* Washington, D.C.: U.S. Government Printing Office, September 1987.

New Mexico Governor's Organized Crime Prevention. *Annual Report, 1979.* Albuquerque, 1979.

New York State Commission of Investigation. *Racketeer Infiltration into Legitimate Business.* March 1970.

Norton, Augustus R., and Martin H. Greenberg. *International Terrorism: An Annotated Bibliography and Research Guide.* Boulder, Colo.: Westview Press, 1980.

Oglesby, E. W., Samual J. Faber, and Stuart J. Faber. *Angel Dust: What Everyone Should Know About PCP.* Los Angeles: Charing Cross Publishing, 1982.

Oyster Bay (New York) Conference on Combating Organized Crime, 1965. *Combating Organized Crime.* Albany, 1966.

Pace, Denny F. *Handbook on Vice Control.* Englewood Cliffs, N.J.: Prentice-Hall, 1971.

Pace, Denny F., and Jimmie C. Styles. *Handbook on Narcotics.* Englewood Cliffs, N.J.: Prentice-Hall, 1972.

Pantaleone, Michele. *The Mafia and Politics.* New York: Coward-McCann, 1966.

Penkovskiy, Oleg. *The Penkovskiy Papers.* Garden City, N.Y.: Doubleday, 1965.

Pennsylvania Crime Commission. *Report on Organized Crime.* Harrisburg, Pa.: Office of the Attorney General, Department of Justice, 1970.

President's Commission on Organized Crime, Report to the President and the Attorney General. *America's Drug Habit: Drug Abuse, Drug Trafficking and Organized Crime.* Washington, D.C.: U.S. Government Printing Office, March 1986.

President's Commission on Organized Crime, Report to the President and the Attorney General. *The Edge: Organized Crime, Business, and Labor Unions.* Washington, D.C.: U.S. Government Printing Office, March 1986. VIII.

President's Council on Integrity and Efficiency. *Characteristics of Successful Procurement and Financial Investigations.* Washington, D.C.: U.S. Department of Justice, 1988.

Project SEARCH (System for Electronic Analysis and Retrieval of Criminal History), Committee on Security and Privacy. *Security and Privacy Considerations in Criminal History Information Systems.* Sacramento, Calif.: Project SEARCH staff, California Crime Technological Research Foundation, July 1970. Technical Report No. 2.

Puzo, Mario. *The Godfather.* New York: Putnam, 1969.

Quebec Commission de Police. *Organized Crime and the Business World* (Crime Organise et le Monde des Affaires), Quebec, Canada 1977.

Ransom, Harry Howe. "Intelligence, Political and Military." *International Encyclopedia of the Social Sciences,* VII, pp. 415–21. New York: Macmillan, 1968.

Ransom, Harry Howe. *The Intelligence Establishment.* Cambridge, Mass.: Harvard University Press, 1970.

Reber, Jan, and Paul Shaw. *Executive Protection Manual.* San Francisco: Assets Protection, 1980.

Redston, George, and Kendall F. Crossen. *The Conspiracy of Death.* Indianapolis: Bobbs-Merrill, 1965.

Reid, Ed, and Ovid Demaris. *The Green Felt Jungle.* New York: Trident Press, 1963.

Reuter, Peter. *Disorganized Crime: Illegal Markets and the Mafia.* Cambridge, Mass.: The MIT Press, 1983.

Reuter, Peter. *Racketeering in Legitimate Industries: A Study in the Economics of Intimidation.* Santa Monica, Calif.: The Rand Corp., 1987.

Rhodes, Robert P. *Organized Crime: Crime Control vs Civil Liberties.* New York: Random House, 1984.

Rucker, William B., ed. *Drugs, Society and Behavior.* Guildford, Conn.: The Dushkin Publishing Groups, Inc., yearly.

Salerno, Ralph. *The Crime Confederation: Cosa Nostra and Allied Operations in Organized Crime.* Garden City, N.Y.: Doubleday, 1969.

Schabeck, Tim A. *Computer Crime Investigation Manual.* San Francisco: Assets Protection, 1981.

Schiavo, Giovanni. *The Truth about the Mafia.* New York: Vigo Press, 1962.

Schur, Edwin M. *Narcotic Addiction in Britain and America.* Bloomington: Indiana University Press, 1962.

Sciascia, Leonardo. *Mafia Vendetta.* New York: Knopf, 1964.

Seidly, John Michael. " 'Upon the Hip'—A Study of the Criminal Loan Shark Industry." Ph.D. dissertation, Harvard University, 1969.

Sheldon, Jonathan A., and George Z. Weibel. *Survey of Consumer Fraud Law.* Washington, D.C.: U.S. Government Printing Office, June 1978.

Sondern, Frederic, *Brotherhood of Evil, the Mafia.* New York: Farrar, Straus and Giroux, 1959.

Spergel, Irving. *Racketville, Slumtown.* Chicago: The University of Chicago Press, 1964.

Sterling, Claire. *The Terror Network.* New York: Holt, Rinehart and Winston, 1981.

Sterling, Claire. *Octopus: The Long Reach of the International Sicilian Mafia.* New York: W. W. Norton and Company, 1990.

Stratton, John G. "The Terrorist Act of Hostage Taking: Considerations for Law Enforcement." *Journal of Police Science and Administration,* June 1978, pp. 123–34.

Sullivan, J., and Joseph Victor, ed. *Criminal Justice 1987–88.* Guilford, Conn.: The Dushkin Publishing Group, 1987.

Swanson, C. R., and L. Terri. "Computer Crime Dimensions, Types, Causes, Investigation." *Journal of Police Science and Administration,* September 1980, pp. 304–11.

Tien, Hames M., Thomas F. Rich, and Michael F. Cohn. *Computer Crime: Electronic Fund Transfer Systems Fraud.* U.S. Department of Justice. Cambridge, Mass.: Public Systems Evaluation Inc., 1986.

Treback, Arnold S. *Drugs, Crime and Politics.* New York: Praeger, 1978.

Trubow, George. *Privacy and Security of Criminal History Information: An Analysis of Privacy Issues.* Washington, D.C.: U.S. Government Printing Office, 1978.

Tully, Andrew. *Treasury Agent.* New York: Simon & Schuster, 1958.

Turkus, Burton, and Sid Feder. *Murder Inc.* New York: Farrar, Straus and Giroux, 1951.

Tyler, Gus. *Organized Crime in America.* Ann Arbor: University of Michigan Press, 1962.

United Aircraft—Corporate Systems Center. *Definition of Proposed NYSIIS Organized Crime Intelligence Capabilities.* Farmington, Conn., 1966.

U.S. Department of Justice. *Cargo Theft and Organized Crime: A Handbook for Management and Law Enforcement.* Washington, D.C.: U.S. Government Printing Office, December 1972.

U.S. Department of Justice. *Report to the Nation on Crime and Justice.* Washington, D.C.: Bureau of Justice Statistics, 1988.

U.S. Department of Justice. *Executive Summary: FY 1988 Report on Drug Control.* Washington, D.C.: Bureau of Justice Statistics, 1989.

U.S. Department of Justice, LEAA. *Intergovernmental Cooperation in Organized Crime Control: Examples of States' Activities.* Washington, D.C.: U.S. Government Printing Office, 1979.

U.S. Department of Justice. *Racketeer Influenced and Corrupt Organizations (RICO): A Manual for Federal Prosecutors.* Washington, D.C.: U.S. Government Printing Office, 1985.

U.S. Department of Justice, LEAA. *The Investigation of White Collar Crime: A Manual for Law Enforcement Agencies.* Washington, D.C.: U.S. Government Printing Office, April 1977.

U.S. General Accounting Office. *War on Organized Crime Faltering, Federal Strike Forces Not Getting the Job Done—Department of Justice.* Report to the Congress by the U.S. Comptroller General, 1977.

U.S. Senate. *Organized Criminal Activities, South Florida and U.S. Penitentiary, Atlanta, Ga., Hearings before the Senate Permanent Subcommittee on Investigations.* Part 3, 95th Congress, 2nd Session, October 24–25, 1978.

Walker, Bruce J., and Ian F. Blake. *Computer Security and Protection Structure.* Stroudsburg, Pa.: Dowden, Hutchinson and Ross, 1980.

Walsh, T. J., and R. J. Healy. *Protection of Assets Manual.* San Francisco: Assets Protection, 1981.

Wheeler, Stanton. *On Record: Files and Dossiers in American Life.* New York: Russell Sage, 1969.

Wilson, James Q. *Crime and American Culture.* Lanham, Mass.: University Press of America, 1983.

Wise, David, and Thomas B. Ross. *The Invisible Government.* New York: Random House, 1964.

Wyden, Peter. *The Hired Killers.* New York: Morrow, 1963.

Wykes, Alan. *The Complete Illustrated Guide to Gambling.* Garden City, N.Y.: Doubleday, 1964.

Index

ABSCAM probe, 34, 53, 157, 247, 249

Academic institutions, organized crime studied in, 237–239

Accountability in law enforcement agencies, 181, 183, 188–190

Accounting of expenses in enforcement agencies, 191–193

Acquired Immune Deficiency Syndrome (AIDS), 87–89
incidence of, 87, 88–89
and prostitution, 87–89, 250

Adams, Nathan, 159

Administration of enforcement agencies, 190, 193–198

Afghanistan, drug traffic from, 96

Agencies in control of organized crime, operation of, 179–234

Air freight industry, corruption in, 134, 138

Air transportation, government regulation of, 158

Alabama, drug traffic in, 251

American Bar Association, 39, 40

Amphetamines, 94, 99
code numbers on possession and sale of, 275

Anderson, Annelise, 232

Antitrust violations, 157, 257, 277

A & P coercion case, 138

Arizona
drug traffic in, 109, 251
Mafia families in, 15

Arkansas, gambling in, 50

Arson, code numbers on, 274

Article file in National Crime Information Center, 264, 266

Associations and organizations in racketeering, 141

Attrition approach to law enforcement, 182, 232

Automobiles
and national register of dangerous drivers, 271–272
repairs of
confederation activity in, 155
fraudulent practices in, 155
stolen, records on
code numbers in, 274
in National Crime Information Center, 263, 265, 266, 268, 269, 274

Banking industry
computer crimes in, 162
fraudulent practices in, 158, 251

Bankruptcy fraud, 134, 135, 137, 151, 256, 258

Bars and restaurants, involvement of organized crime in, 135, 149, 150
in gambling operations, 57–58

Bennett, William J., appointed as drug czar, 1

Bers, Melvin, 136, 137–138

Betting, 54–63. See also Gambling

Bingo games, state laws on, 53

Blackmail on sexual behavior, 80

Black market operations, 144–146, 256

Boiler room fraud, 151–152

Bombings by militant groups, 169, 171

Bonds and stocks, manipulation and theft of. See Stocks and bonds, manipulation and theft of

Bookmaking, 7, 49, 54–62
  in bars, 57–58
  in community, 13, 16, 23, 35
  computer systems in, 162
  confederation control of, 47, 58
  by employees, 57
  enforcement of laws on, 41
  evidence of, 59, 60, 61
  in fixed spot, 58
  memory system in, 57
  on sporting events, 62
  state laws on, 38, 41
  telephone equipment in, 58–59
Boston, Mafia families in, 15
Boyle, W. A. "Tony," 156
Brennan, William J., Supreme Court
    Justice, 115
Bribery, 260
  code numbers on, 276
  in gambling on sporting events, 72
Brown, William, 86–87
Burglary. *See* Thefts
Business enterprises
  in civic action groups for crime
      control, 224
  computer crimes in, 159–165
  fraudulent practices of, 151–158. *See
      also* Fraudulent practices
  government regulation of, 157–158
  legitimate, of confederations, 14, 17,
      18, 21, 22, 129–130
  monopolies in, 134, 137, 138–139,
      217
    in black market operations, 144,
        145
    in racketeering, 140–141
  penetrated by organized crime, 134,
      135, 136–139
  racketeering tactics in, 149–151
  price fixing in, 134, 137, 141, 217
  stock manipulation and theft in,
      151, 152–154
  white collar crimes in, 129, 131–148,
      159–165

California
  AIDS cases in, 88
  campaign contributions in, and
      political corruption, 30, 31, 32
  computer crimes in, 159, 161, 162
  crime families in, 15, 187, 248
  drug traffic in, 109, 183, 185, 251
  gambling in, 40–41, 63, 68

gang violence in, 167
illegal or unethical conduct of
    judges in, 39
influence of organized crime on
    government contracts in, 150
information exchange system in,
    185–187
investments of organized crime in,
    159
militant groups in, 174
obscenity and pornography in, 117
organization of police departments
    in, 196
prostitution in, 80
regional enforcement agencies in,
    187
stock manipulation and theft in, 153
training programs on crime control
    in, 242
venereal disease in, 84–85, 86
wire-tapping in, 176
Campaign contributions, 28, 30–31,
    32, 156–157
  amount spent, 32, 33
Canada, Mafia families in, 15
Capone, Al, 18
Card games
  gambling on, 63–64
  historical aspects of, 52
Chicago
  civic action groups for crime control
      in, 225
  Mafia families in, 15
Children, sex offenses of adults involv-
    ing, 122, 273, 275
Citizen involvement in organized
    crime control, 5, 224–228, 233
Civic action groups in crime control,
    224–228, 233
Civil Aeronautics Board, law enforce-
    ment activities of, 158
Classification numbers for crimes,
    standardized system of, 203,
    273–277
Cocaine, 96, 101–102, 250
  code numbers on, 275
  seizures of, 103
Code numbers on crimes, standardized
    system of, 203, 273–277
Colleges, organized crime studied in,
    237, 238–239
Collusive agreement in racketeering,
    140

Colombo shooting, 34
Colorado, Mafia families in, 15
Columbia, drug traffic from, 94, 96
Colvin, Bill, 165
Communications, government regulation of, 158
Communist Party in United States, 170, 171–172
Community, 3–11
    assessment of law enforcement needs in, 190
    attitude toward crime in, 6, 9–10, 17, 50, 133
    awareness of organized crime in. *See* Public awareness of organized crime
    civic actions groups for crime control in, 224–228, 233
    crime commissions in, 13, 225, 226, 227–228
    cultural values in, 3, 5–6
    disorganizing forces in, 3, 6–7
    education programs for crime control in, 221–224, 233, 236, 237–239
    entropy in, 6–7
    exposés on organized crime in, 12–13
    formal and informal groups for crime control in, 4, 10
    impact of organized crime in, 1–2
    inputs and outputs in theory on, 7–8
    signs of organized crime in, 12–25, 225
    standards on pornography and obscenity in, 115, 116, 120, 125
Computer systems
    crimes related to, 159–165
        in conspiracies, 217–218
        in dating services associated with prostitution, 79–80
        future trends in, 163–165
        investigation of, 161, 162, 163, 165
        involvement of organized crime in, 162–163
        laws on, 161–162
        training on, 244, 245
        vulnerability to, 163, 164
    of enforcement agencies, 203, 204, 212, 213–215, 263–272
        in investigation procedures, 213–215, 231

    in National Crime Information Center, 203, 263–272
    SEARCH guidelines on, 203–205, 206, 212, 219, 220
    security of information in, 204, 205–209
    standardized coding of data for, 203
Confederations, criminal
    annual income of, 14
    in burglary or robbery, 229–232
    campaign contributions from, 30, 31, 32
    common elements and activities of, 21
    in computer crimes, 162–163
    control of various crimes, 230
        identification of, 229–232
    in drug traffic, 91–92, 97, 98, 109, 252
    evolution of, 17–24
    exposés on, 12–13
    family ties in, 19
    fraudulent business practices of, 256
    gambling activities of, 47, 49, 53, 54, 55–59, 62, 135, 247, 249
        numbers games in, 68, 69
    indictments against leaders of, 248
    lawyers representing, 38–39
    legitimate business enterprises of, 14, 17, 18, 21, 22, 129–130
    nonconfrontation policies of, 17–19
    in obscenity and pornography, 112, 116–117, 123, 125, 252
    organization of, 14, 16, 19, 20
    organization and management problems in control of, 180–201
    penetration of business enterprises, 134, 135, 136–139
        by racketeering, 149–151
    problems in local control of, 16, 22, 133, 197
    in prostitution, 17, 22, 47, 79, 81
    protection of leaders in, 16, 22, 133, 197
    signs of activities in community, 12–25, 225
    in stock manipulation and theft, 151, 152–153
    types of criminal activities of, 23, 256–259
        compared to traditional crime, 25

Confederations, criminal (*continued*)
standardized coding system on,
273–277
in urban areas, 22–23, 24
disputes among groups in, 34
in open and closed cities, 22
using Fifth Amendment privilege of
silence, 42
in vice crimes, 47–48
in white collar crimes, 131–132,
133–134, 147
loan sharking, 142, 143, 144
racketeering, 139–140, 141
Conspiracies
computer systems used in, 217–218
international, militant groups in,
169–172
national, militant groups in,
172–173
Constitution
Fifth Amendment rights in, 42
First Amendment rights in, 112–114,
115, 118, 120, 125
Construction contracts, influence of
organized crime in, 150
Contracts with government, influence
of organized crime in, 150
Controlled substances, 100, 102–103
Cook, Fred J., 18–19, 20, 50
Cornell Institute on Organized Crime,
39–40
Corruption
of enforcement agencies, 188, 198
political
investigation of, 43
patterns of, 27–30
Cosa Nostra, 17, 19, 151. *See also* Mafia
Counterfeiting
code numbers on, 274
in computer crimes, 160
convictions on, 160
of stocks and bonds, 152, 153
Course outlines in study of organized
crime, 238–239, 240–242
Court cases
on antitrust violations, 157
on gambling, 63
legality of evidence in, 176, 260
on obscenity and pornography,
124–125, 126
Supreme Court decisions on,
114–116, 118–119, 124, 125–126

RICO law as basis of, 261–262
role of prosecutor in, 249
testimony of witnesses in, 182, 260
false declarations in, 260
immunity for, 42, 260
protection for, 180, 260
in white collar crimes, 133, 139, 142
Crack cocaine, 101–102
Credit card frauds, 132, 154, 163, 256
Cressey, Donald R., 136, 230
Crime commissions, 13–14, 41, 43–44
citizen participation in, 13, 225, 226,
227–228
Crime control. *See* Law enforcement
Cultural values in control of organized
crime, 3, 5–6
Curriculum guides in study of organized crime, 238–239, 240–242
Customs Service, in control of drug
traffic, 103, 183

Data collection in investigation procedures, 202–209
and analysis of collected data,
218–219
common methods of, 215–218
Dating services, computerized, prostitution associated with, 79–80
Defense Department, in control of
drug traffic, 103
Defense lawyers, relationship with
criminal clients, 27, 29, 38–40
Detroit, crime families in, 15
Dice games, 64–65, 66, 67
historical aspects of, 52, 64, 65
Diggs, Charles, 162
Dissemination of information in
records, 6, 10, 207–208, 209–210
in exposés, 12–13
guidelines on, 209–210
privacy rights and security concerns
in, 204, 205–209, 213, 214
in research projects, 207–208
Dixie Mafia, 14
Douglas, William Orville, Supreme
Court Justice, 119
Drivers, dangerous, national register
of, 271–272
Drug Diversion Units, 108
Drug Enforcement Administration, 48,
105, 107, 108
Drug traffic, 23, 91–111, 250–252, 257

code numbers on, 275
confederation activity in, 91–92, 97, 98, 109, 252
education programs in control of, 237, 238
enforcement of laws on, 94–97, 99, 103, 105, 106, 250–252
 coordination of efforts in, 107–109
 double standard in, 48
 government units in, 103–105, 183
 international programs in, 106
 military action in, 235
 national strategies in, 105–107
 regional agencies in, 185
from foreign countries, 95–97, 103, 104, 105–106, 250
 in golden triangle area, 23, 48, 97
 sealing borders of United States to, 94–95
historical aspects of, 92–94
investigation of, 106, 108, 251
patterns of, 97, 98
political influences on, 35, 92, 103, 109, 251
proposals on legalization of, 250, 251, 252
and prostitution, 78
public attitude toward, 250
social issues in, 1, 91
types of drugs in, 99–103
United Nations action against, 93–94
violence related to, 102
Dyson, Frank, 122–123

Economic issues
 in accounting of expenses in enforcement agencies, 191–193
 in funding of election campaigns, 28, 30–31, 32, 156–157
 in local control of organized crime, 16
 in white collar crime, 134–136, 137, 138, 142–143, 251
Edelhertz, Herbert, 131, 133
Education and training, 221–224, 233, 235, 236–245
 in academic institutions, 237–239
 on computer crimes, 243, 244
 on drugs, 237, 238
 of law enforcement officers, 182, 221–224, 236, 237, 239–242

on investigation procedures, 197, 204, 206
 model programs in, 223–224
 outlines of courses in, 238–239, 240–242
 of public, as control of organized crime, 221–224, 233, 236, 237–239
Elderly victims of fraudulent practices, 154–155
Elections
 amount spent on, 32, 33
 campaign contributions in, 28, 30–31, 32, 156–157
Embezzlement, 132, 257
 code numbers on, 274
 convictions on, 160
 investigation of, 146
 in labor unions, 156
Enforcement agencies, 179–234. *See also* Law enforcement
 intelligence gathering and dissemination in, 202–209
 organization and management of, 180–201
England
 gambling in, 51, 64–65
 obscenity and pornography in, 117
 prostitution in, 76, 77, 82
Entertainment industry, involvement of organized crime in, 135
Entropy in social controls, 6–7
Ethical issues in investigation procedures, 203–210
Ethnic groups
 involvement in organized crime, 14
 in militant organizations, 174
 promoting growth of organized crime, 22–23
 vice control in neighborhoods of, 34–35
Evidence gathering. *See* Investigation procedures
Expense accounting in enforcement agencies, 191–193
Exposés on organized crime, 12–13
Extortion, code numbers on, 274

Fair Credit Reporting Act, 158, 206
Families involved in organized crime, 14, 15, 24

Federal Bureau of Investigation, role
in law enforcement, 251
in computer crimes, 161
in drug traffic, 103, 105
in obscenity and pornography, 117
Federal Communications Commission,
158
Federal law enforcement agencies, 183,
184
cooperation with state and local
agencies, 107–109
Federal Trade Commission, 157
Fences, sale of stolen merchandise to,
158–159, 231
Feshbach, Seymour, 121
Field officer, role in crime control,
228–232
Fifth Amendment privilege of silence,
42
First Amendment rights, and enforcement of laws on obscenity and
pornography, 112–114, 115, 118,
120, 125
Florida
drug traffic in, 106, 251
Mafia families in, 15
venereal disease in, 84, 85, 86
Foreign countries
AIDS cases in, 88–89
drug traffic from, 23, 95–97, 103,
104, 105–106, 251
from golden triangle area, 23, 48,
97
sealing borders of United States
to, 94–95
gambling in, 33, 51, 64–65
militant groups in, 169–71
obscenity and pornography in, 117
prostitution in, 76, 77, 82
Forfeiture of illegal assets, 185, 187
Forgery
code numbers on, 274
convictions on, 160
Fratianno, Jimmy, 18
Fraudulent practices, 129, 130,
151–158, 253
boiler room scheme, 151–152
code numbers on, 274
in computer crimes, 159–165
convictions on, 160
credit card, 132, 154, 163, 256
elderly victims of, 154–155

medical, 156, 258
in savings and loans institutions,
158, 251
in stock manipulation and theft. *See*
Stocks and bonds, manipulation
and theft of
types of, 256, 257, 258–259
in welfare programs, 155, 256
Funding
of local enforcement agencies, 16
of political campaigns, 28, 30–31,
32, 156–157
Futures market, manipulation of,
153–154

Gallo-Profaci feud, 34
Gambling, 9, 10, 23, 49–73, 249–253
betting syndicate in, 54–56
bookmaking system in, 49, 54–62
and bribery, 72
in card games, 63–64
code numbers on, 275–276
computer systems in, 162, 163
corruption in, 53, 54
court testimony on, 63
devices used in, 63–68
in dice games, 64–65, 66, 67
disclosure of information on, 10
elimination of competition in, 33
enforcement of laws on, 49, 50,
249–250, 255
double standard in, 9, 48, 53
inconsistency in, 41
political influences in, 49, 50
problems in, 249–250, 255
federal laws on, 54, 70–71, 261
and growth of vice crimes, 48
handbook in, 54, 55–56, 57
historical aspects of, 51–54
investigation of, 63, 261
betting markers as evidence in,
59, 60, 61
on card games, 64
on skimming of profits, 71–72
involvement of organized crime in,
47, 49, 53, 54, 55–59, 62, 135,
247, 249
in numbers games, 68, 69
in lotteries, 49, 68–71. *See also*
Lotteries
moral issues in, 9, 50–51
opposition to and support of, 50–51

problems in laws on, 40–41
public acceptance of, 9, 10, 17, 50,
    133
skimming of profits in, 71–72, 140
on slot machines, 66–68
on sporting events, 62–63, 69, 70,
    163
  and bribery, 72
state laws on, 41, 52–53, 56, 63
white collar crimes associated with,
    132, 133, 143, 146
wire service information in, 56, 217
Gang violence, 167
  related to drug traffic, 102
Garment industry, involvement of
    organized crime in, 135, 141
Gerver, Israel, 168
Glueck, Sheldon and Eleanor, 121
Godfrey, E. Crexel, 215
Golden triangle area, drug traffic
    from, 23, 48, 97
Gonorrhea
  incidence of, 84, 85
  and prostitution, 83
Government
  corruption of officials in, 27–30, 43
  crime commissions in, 43–44
  influence of organized crime on
      contracts with, 150
  law enforcement agencies of, 184,
      185
  regulatory agencies of, 157–158
Grand juries, 227, 248, 260
Guiliani, Rudolph, 142, 261
Guns
  code numbers on criminal offenses
      related to, 276
  stolen or lost, records of National
      Crime Information Center on,
      264, 266, 269

Hallucinogenic substances, 94, 102
  code numbers on, 275
Handbook (bookie), 54, 55–56, 57
Handicapping on sporting events, 62
Hanna, Kenneth, 123
Harlan, John Marshall, Supreme Court
    Justice, 119
Harris, Don R., 215
Harrison Act (1914), 92
Hazardous materials, 280
Heroin, 92–93, 101, 105, 109

code numbers on, 275
seizures of, 103
Hicklin decision on obscenity, 118
Hijacking by militant groups, 169, 171
Historical aspects
  of drug traffic, 92–94
  of gambling, 51–54
  of pornography and obscenity,
      117–119
of prostitution, 75–77, 85, 86
Homicide, code numbers on, 273
Hoover, J. Edgar, 151
Howton, F. William, 168
Humphrey, Hubert H., contributions
    to election campaign of, 156

Illinois
  civic action groups for crime control
      in, 225
  Mafia families in, 15
  white collar crimes in, 140
Immunity for witnesses, 42, 260
Information gathering. *See* Investiga-
    tion procedures
Injunctions, in enforcement of
    obscenity laws, 124
In rem actions in obscenity, 124
Insurance fraud, 155, 256
Intelligence gathering in investigation
    procedures, 202–209. *See also* In-
    vestigation procedures
Internal Revenue Service role in law
    enforcement
  in computer crimes, 163
  in drug traffic, 105
  in white collar crimes, 137
International Police Organization in
    control of drug traffic, 103
Investigation procedures, 183,
    202–209
  access to information from, 207–208
  accounting of expenses in, 191–193
  allocation of personnel for, 191
  analysis of data in, 218–219
  on burglary or robbery, identifica-
      tion of organized crime involve-
      ment in, 229–232
  coding of information in, 203,
      273–277
  collection of data in, 215–218
  on computer crimes, 161, 162, 163,
      165

Investigation procedures (*continued*)
  computer systems used in, 213–215,
    231
  on conspiracies, 217–218
  of crime commissions, 227–228
  on drug traffic, 106, 108, 251
  ethical issues in, 203–210
  exchange of information in
    among enforcement agencies,
      185–187, 188
    within enforcement agency, 197
  of field officer, 228–232
  on gambling, 63, 261. *See also*
    Gambling, investigation of
  of grand juries, 227, 248
  guidelines on, 254
    in SEARCH, 203–205, 206, 212,
      219, 220
  incorrect or unreliable information
    in, 206, 260
  Law Enforcement Teletype System
    in, 271, 278
  on leaders of organized crime, 197
  legality of, 176, 260
  of local enforcement agencies, 16
  on militant groups, 168, 171–172,
    173, 174–175, 176
  of multicounty agencies, 188
  National Crime Information Center
    in, 203, 211, 212, 263–272
    inquiries to, 267, 268, 269
  on obscenity and pornography, 122,
    126
  organization of information in,
    210–219
  privacy rights in, 203, 204, 205–209
  public awareness of, 6
  purchase of information in, 191, 192
  rationale for, 211–212
  records of, 202–209. *See also* Record
    systems
  relationship of organized crime
    member and enforcement of-
    ficer in, 199
  release of information from, 206,
    208, 209–210
    guidelines on, 209–210
    for research programs, 207–208
  security of information in, 204,
    205–209, 213, 214
  supervisory responsibilities in,
    194–195
  training on, 197, 204, 206
  units responsible for, organization
    and administration of, 194, 195,
    197
  on white collar crimes, 145–147
  wire-tapping in, 176

Judicial system, 37–45. *See also* Legal
    system
Justice Department, 157
  in drug control efforts, 103, 106,
    107
  organization of, 183

Kansas City area, Mafia families in, 15
Kaplan case on obscenity, 118
Kefauver Committee hearings, 41, 224,
    228
Kickbacks, 257
Kidnapping
  code numbers on, 273
  by militant groups, 169, 171
King, Rufus, 42
Kinsey report on prostitution, 81–82

Labor unions
  involvement of organized crime in,
    253
  political involvement of, 156
  racketeering activities of, 253
  and white collar crimes, 134,
    141–142, 147, 148
Las Vegas. *See* Nevada
Latin America, drug traffic from,
    95–96
Law(s)
  adequate for enforcement, 40–41
  on campaign contributions, 156–157
  on computer crimes, 161–162
  on drug traffic, 92–94, 109
  enforcement of. *See* Law
    enforcement
  on gambling, 9, 40–41, 54, 56, 63,
    70–71, 261
    state differences in, 41, 52–53
  immunity from, 42, 260
  lack of uniformity in, 9–10, 40–41
  on pornography and obscenity,
    Supreme Court decisions on,
    114–116, 118–119
  on prostitution, 82
  of states and local communities, 42, 182

Law enforcement, 179–234
accountability in, 181, 183, 188–190
adequacy of laws for, 40–41
administrative problems in, 193–198
agency operation in, 179–234
assessment of community needs for,
190
attrition approach to, 181, 232
citizen involvement in, 247, 248, 249
in civic action groups, 224–228,
233
cooperation among agencies in,
107–109, 226
crime commissions in, 13–14, 41,
43–44, 225, 226, 227–228
double standards in, 9, 48, 53
on drug traffic. *See* Drug traffic, enforcement of laws on education
and training in, 182, 197,
221–224, 233, 236, 236–245
expense accounting in, 191–193
exchange of information in
among agencies, 185–187, 188
within agency, 197
federal agencies in, 183, 184
cooperation with state and local
agencies, 107–108
field officer in, 228–232
on gambling. *See* Gambling, enforcement of laws on inconsistency
in, 41–42
investigation procedures in. *See* Investigation procedures at local
level, 42, 228–229. *See also* Local
control of crime moral issues
in, 9, 10, 198–200
multicounty agencies in, 188–189,
189
National Crime Information Center
in, 263–272. *See also* National
Crime Information Center
on obscenity and pornography,
112–114, 118–125, 252
police function in, 122–123, 125,
126
organization and management of,
181–201, 254
patrol officer in, 228
in permissive society, 9–10, 133
personnel allocation in, 190–191
philosophy of, 198–200
policy development in, 188–193

on prostitution, 77, 82, 87, 89–90
record systems in. *See* Record
systems
regional agencies in, 185–188
regulatory agencies of government
in, 157–158
relationship of organized crime
member and enforcement officer in, 198
sequence of, 222
state differences in, 9–10, 182
strike force concept in, 103–105,
108, 183, 185, 186
supervisory responsibilities in,
194–195, 197
trends in, 246–247
violation-response approach to, 181,
232
Law Enforcement Assistance Administration, 240
Law Enforcement Intelligence Unit,
212
Law Enforcement Teletype System,
271, 278
requests for information from,
278–280
Lawyers
involvement in organized crime, 27,
38–39
relationship with criminal clients,
27, 29, 38–40
Legal system, 37–45
controls on organized crime in, 4, 6,
7
corruption of, 27, 28
in government crime commissions,
43, 44
internal discipline in, 39–40
in investigation of organized crime,
40
laws in, 40–42. *See also* Law(s)
relationship of lawyers with criminal
clients in, 27, 29, 38–40
state differences in, 9–10, 182
unethical or illegal conduct of
judges in, 39
License plates, stolen, records of National Crime Information
Center on, 263, 265, 266, 268,
269
Liquor laws
adequate for enforcement, 41

Liquor laws (*continued*)
  code numbers related to, 276
  in dry areas, 22
Listening devices, legal use of, 71–72, 176
Lobbyists, influence of, 29
Loan shark business, 132, 137, 141, 142–144, 148, 217
  flow of money in, 144, 145
Local control of crime, 42, 228–229
  in business frauds, 253
  in drug traffic, 108–109
    coordination with federal efforts, 107–109
  of militant groups, 168, 172, 176
  protection of confederations from, 16, 22, 133, 197
  role of field officer in, 228–229
  in urban areas, 27
Lotteries, 9, 49, 53, 69–71
  federal laws on, 54, 70–71
  and growth of vice crimes, 48
  historical aspects of, 52
  state laws on, 54, 69, 249–250
Louisiana
  drug traffic in, 251
  Mafia families in, 15, 19

Mafia, 17–19, 20. *See also* Confederations, criminal
  in drug traffic, 91–92
  families involved in, 15
  indictments against leaders of, 248
  legitimate business enterprises of, 22
  origin of, 19
  in stock manipulation and theft, 151
Mail
  crimes related to, 10
  fraudulent materials in, 262
  lottery tickets in, 71
  obscene and pornographic materials in, 118
Malamath, Neal, 121
Mann Act (1910), 82
Marijuana, 95, 96, 102, 109, 250, 251
  code numbers on, 275
Massachusetts
  Mafia families in, 15
  obscenity and pornography in, 118
Massage parlors, prostitution activities in, 81
McClellan Committee, 228

Medical fraud, 156, 258
Meese, Edwin, Attorney General, 30
Metropolitan areas, organization of enforcement agencies in, 187, 188
Mexico
  drug traffic from, 23, 94, 95–96, 97, 105–106
  gambling in, 33
Michigan
  information exchange system in, 185
  Mafia families in, 15
Middle East, drug taffic from, 96–97
Militant groups, 130, 167–177, 253–257
  in international conspiracies, 169–172
  investigation of, 168, 171–172, 173, 174–175, 176
  in national conspiracies, 172–173
  problems in local control of, 168, 172, 176
  social issues in, 168
  in splinter organizations, 173–174
  strategies of, 174–176
  terrorist activities of, 169, 171, 176, 253–254
  types of, 168–174
Military
  intelligence gathering by, 203, 211, 212
  role in law enforcement, 235
Miller, Arthur, 211
Miller case on obscenity, 115, 118, 120, 125
Monopolies in business, 134, 137, 138–139, 217
  in black market operations, 144, 145
  in racketeering, 140–141
Moral issues, 9, 10
  in gambling, 9, 50–51
  in obscenity and pornography, 112, 116–117
  in philosophy of law enforcement, 198–201
Morphine, 92, 99
Multicounty law enforcement agencies, 188–189, 189
Multistate law enforcement agencies, 185
Myth of organized crime, and reality, 13–16

Nader, Ralph, on ethical issues in investigations, 203
Narcotics
code numbers on, 275
distribution of, 251, 252. *See also* Drug traffic
National Council on Organized Crime, 246
National Crime Information Center, 203, 211, 212, 263–272
compared to other national systems, 271–272
exchange of information with, 267–268
extension and development of, 271
files in, 263–265
requests for information from, 267, 268, 269
retention of records in, 265–267
revision of records in, 267
scope of data in, 268–270
National Driver Register Services, 270–272
Nevada
gambling in, 50, 53, 54, 63
competition from Mexico, 33
involvement of organized crime in, 247
moral issues in, 50
skimming of profits in, 71, 140
on slot machines, 66
on sporting events, 62
prostitution in, 82
New Jersey
gambling in, 53
involvement of organized crime in, 247, 249
skimming of profits in, 71
Mafia families in, 15
New Mexico, drug traffic in, 109
New Orleans, Mafia families in, 15, 19
New York
AIDS cases in, 88
crime families in, 15, 21, 24
influence of organized crime on government contracts in, 150
information exchange system in, 187
obscenity and pornography in, 118, 124
Organized Crime Control Act in, 262
stock manipulation and theft in, 153

venereal disease in, 84, 85, 86
Nonconfrontation policies of criminal confederations, 17–19
Numbers for classification of crimes, 273–277
Numbers games, 68–71

Obscenity, 112–127. *See also* Pornography and obscenity definition of, 114, 118–119
Ohio
information exchange system in, 185
Mafia families in, 15
Oklahoma, computer crimes in, 162
Omnibus Crime Bills
on drug traffic, 102, 105, 106, 107–108
on gambling, 54, 63
on listening devices, 72
as model for state laws, 182
Opium, 92, 97, 99, 101
code numbers on, 275
Organization of law enforcement agencies, 180–201
Organized Crime Control Act (1970), 41, 260–262
Racketeer Influenced and Corrupt Organizations (RICO) section of, 261–262. *See also* RICO law

Pakistan, drug traffic from, 96
Paris Adult Theatre case on obscenity, 118, 120
Parker, Donn B., 162
Parson's polity concept, 7
Patrol officer, role in crime control, 229
Pennsylvania
crime commission in, 227
Mafia families in, 15
white collar crimes in, 131
Permissive attitudes in society, 9–10
and gambling, 9, 10, 133
and white collar crimes, 133
Personnel allocation in enforcement agencies, 190–191
Peru, drug traffic from, 96
Peterson, Virgil, 50
Photo studios, prostitution activities in, 80–81
Police departments
checks and balances in, 188, 190

Police departments (*continued*)
  education and training in, as control
    on organized crime, 221–224,
    236, 237, 239
  exchange of information among,
    271
  obligations incurred in, 28
  organization and administration of,
    194, 196
  policies of, 190
  record systems of, 207, 213, 215
    access to information in, 207
  role in interpretation and enforce-
    ment of laws, 9
  on obscenity and pornography,
    122–123, 125, 126
  on white collar crimes, 146–147
Policies of law enforcement agencies,
  development of, 188–193
Policy (numbers) game, 68–71
Political action committees, 31–32,
  156–157
Political issues, 26–36
  in campaign contributions, 28,
    30–31, 32, 156–157
  in civic action groups for crime
    control, 226
  in corruption, 27–30, 43
  in crime commissions, 43–44
  in double standard of law enforce-
    ment, 48
  in drug traffic, 35, 92, 103, 109, 251
  in gambling, 49, 50
  in influence of party in power,
    34–35
  in militant groups, 167, 169–172
  in prostitution, 35, 74
  in sting operations, 31
  in vice control in ethnic
    neighborhoods, 34–35
Polity concept, 8, 9
Pope case on obscenity, 115, 119
Pornography and obscenity, 112–127,
  252
  in black market operations, 144
  confederation activity in, 112,
    116–117, 123, 125, 252
  court cases on, 124–125, 126
    Supreme Court decisions on,
      114–116, 118–119, 124, 125–126
  definition of, 114, 118–119
  enforcement of laws on, 112–114,
    119–125, 252

  police function in, 122–123, 125,
    126
  historical aspects of, 117–119
  investigation of, 122, 126
  legal issues in, 112, 114–116
  moral issues in, 112, 116–117
  public attitude toward, 252
  social issues in, 120–122, 254
Postal Service. *See* Mail
President's Commission on Organized
  Crime, 14, 228, 253
Price fixing, 134, 137, 141, 217
Privacy rights
  code numbers on activities in inva-
    sion of, 277
  in investigation procedures, 203,
    204, 205–209
Property items, serially numbered,
  records on theft of, 264, 266
Prosecution in court cases. *See* Court
  cases
Prostitution, 71, 74–90, 250
  and AIDS, 87–89, 250
  code numbers on, 276
  in community, 13, 23
  confederation control of, 17, 22, 47,
    79, 81
  and drug use, 78
  enforcement of laws on, 77, 82, 87,
    89–90
  federal laws on, 82
  historical aspects of, 75–77, 85, 86
  Kinsey report on, 81–82
  local control of, 16
  political issues in, 35, 74
  proposals on legalization of, 75
  social issues in, 77–78, 250
  types of operations in, 78–81
  and venereal disease, 83–89
Public awareness of organized crime,
  4–5, 6, 7, 10, 247, 248–249
  and civic action groups in crime
    control, 224–228, 233
  education programs increasing,
    221–224, 233, 236, 237–239
  exposés increasing, 12–13
  and political corruption, 34
Public relations firms, prostitution activities of, 80

Racketeer Influenced and Corrupt
  Organizations (RICO) law. *See*
  RICO law

Racketeering, 7, 41, 54, 130, 134, 139–142, 148, 256
  associations in, 141
  businesses acquired in, 149–151
  collusive agreements in, 140
  investigation of, 198
  labor unions in, 253
  prosecution of, 139, 142
  RICO law on. *See* RICO law
  simon-pure, 140
  social acceptance of, 17
Ransom, Harry H., 212
Reagan, Nancy, 106–107
Real estate development, involvement of organized crime in, 135
Reckless, Walter C., 140, 141
Record systems, 202–209
  access to information in, 207–208
  analysis of data in, 218–219
  article file in, 264, 266
  coding of information in, 203, 273–277
  collection of data for, 215–218
  computerized system of, 203, 204, 212, 213–215, 220, 263–272
  confidential information in, 209, 210, 215
  data content of, 205
  exchange of information in
    among enforcement agencies, 185–187, 188
    within enforcement agency, 197
  gun file in, 264, 266, 269
  on innocent persons, 218
  Law Enforcement Teletype System, 271, 278
    requests for information from, 278–280
  license plate file in, 263, 265, 266, 268, 269
  of National Crime Information Center, 203, 209, 210, 263–272
  organization of, 210–219
  privacy rights and security concerns in, 204, 205–209, 213, 214, 220
  release of information in, 6, 10, 206, 208, 209–210
    guidelines on, 209–210
    for research programs, 209–210
  SEARCH (Systems for Electronic Analysis and Retrieval of Criminal Histories) guidelines on, 203–205, 206, 212, 219, 220

securities file in, 264
  sources of information in, 213
  types of information in, 210–211
  vehicle file in, 263, 265, 266, 268, 269
  on wanted persons, 264, 266, 267, 270
Regional law enforcement agencies, organization of, 185–188
Regulatory agencies of government, in control of organized crime, 157–158
Religious cults, violent behavior of, 173–174
Research on crime, 248
  access to data in information systems for, 207–208
Restaurants and bars, involvement of organized crime in, 135, 149, 150
  in gambling operations, 57–58
RICO (Racketeer Influenced and Corrupt Organizations) law, 130, 139, 142, 219, 248, 249
  on drug traffic, 102, 105, 106, 107–108, 252
  on pornography, 252
  prosecution based on, 248, 261–262
  provisions of, 261–262
Robbery. *See* Thefts
Roselli, Johnny, 18
Rosenberg, Bernard, 168

Salerno, Ralph, 132
Savings and loan frauds, 158, 251
Schools, organized crime studied in, 237–239
Schwartz, Murray L., 38
SEARCH (Systems for Electronic Analysis and Retrieval of Criminal Histories), 203–205, 206, 212, 219, 220
Secretarial services, prostitution activities of, 81
Securities, manipulation and theft of. *See* Stocks and bonds, manipulation and theft of
Security of information in records, 114, 204, 205–209, 214, 220
Seidl, John, 143
Seizures of illegal assets, 103, 185
Senate, crime subcommittees in, 43

Sex offenses
  associated with obscene and porno-
    graphic materials, 121–122
  code numbers on, 273, 275
Shoplifting, 230
Shylocking in loan shark business, 142,
    143, 144
Skimming of gambling profits, 71–72,
    140
Slot machines, 66–68
  state laws on, 66
Social issues, 1–45
  in controls on organized crime,
    3–11
  in drug traffic, 1, 91
  in gambling, 50
  in growth of organized crime,
    254–255
  and legal system, 4, 6, 7, 37–45
  in militant behavior, 168
  in obscenity and pornography,
    120–121, 254
  and political system, 26–36
  in prostitution, 77–78, 250
  in white collar crime, 132–134
Society. *See* Community
South America, drug traffic from, 23,
    94, 96, 97, 104
Southeast Asia, drug traffic from, 23,
    48, 97
Speech freedom, and enforcement of
    laws on obsenity and por-
    nography, 15, 112–114, 118,
    120, 125
Special interest groups, political in-
    fluence of, 30
Splinter organizations of militants,
    173–174
Sporting events, gambling on, 62–63,
    69, 70
  and bribery, 72
  computerized system in, 163
Steffens, Lincoln, 29
Sting operations in political corrup-
    tion, 31
Stocks and bonds, manipulation and
    theft of, 151, 152–154, 256, 257,
    258
  computer systems in, 161, 162, 217,
    218
  economic impact of, 134
  records on, 264
Stokes, Harold R., 7, 8
Streetwalking by prostitutes, 78

Strike force concept in law enforce-
    ment, 183, 185, 186
  in drug control efforts, 103–105, 108
Strong-arm tactics in acquisition of
    businesses, 150–151
Supreme Court decisions
  on evidence gathering, 176
  on obscenity and pornography,
    114–116, 118–119, 124, 125–126
Supervisory responsibilities in en-
    forcement agencies, 194–196,
    197
Swindles. *See* Fraudulent practices
Symptoms of organized crime, 12–25,
    225
Syndicates, criminal. *See* Confedera-
    tions, criminal
Syphilis
  incidence of, 84
  and prostitution, 83–87
  symptoms of, 87
Systems for Electronic Analysis and
    Retrieval of Criminal Histories
    (SEARCH), 203–205, 206, 212

Tax violations, 256, 257, 262
  code numbers of, 277
Telephone equipment
  in bookmaking, 58–59
  in prostitution operations, 78–79, 81
Teletype system connecting law en-
    forcement agencies, 271
  requests for information from,
    278–280
Terrorist activities of militant groups,
    169, 171, 176, 253–254
Testimony in court cases, 182, 260
  false declarations in, 260
  on gambling, 63
  immunity for, 42, 260
  protection for, 182, 260
Texas
  drug traffic in, 109
  liquor laws in, 41
  obscenity and pornography in,
    122–123
  savings and loans frauds in, 251
Thailand, drug traffic from, 97
Thefts
  in attempt to conceal white collar
    crimes, 146
  code numbers on, 273–274, 275
  in computer crimes, 159, 160, 162

of credit cards, 154
identification of organized crime involvement in, 229–232
National Crime Information Center records on, 263–264, 265, 266, 268–269
and sale of stolen merchandise to fences, 158–159, 231
of stocks and bonds. *See* Stocks and bonds, manipulation and theft of
TRACER system, 213
Training. *See* Education and training
Tyler, Gus, 31–32, 33

United Nations actions against drug traffic, 92, 93–94
Urban areas
confederations in, 22–23, 24
disputes among groups in, 34
factors affecting growth of, 22–23
in open or closed cities, 22
enforcement agencies in, 187, 188
political corruption in, 27, 29
vice control in, 34–35

Valachi hearings, 13
Vehicle file in National Crime Information Center, 263, 265, 266, 268, 269
Venereal disease
incidence of, 84–85, 86–87
and prostitution, 83–89
symptoms of, 87
Vice crimes, 47–127, 249–250. *See also specific crimes*
double standards on, 9, 48
drug traffic, 91–111
in ethnic neighborhoods, 34–35
gambling, 49–73
investigation of, 198
philosophy of law enforcement in, 198
pornography and obscenity, 112–127
prostitution, 74–90
units enforcing laws on, organization and administration of, 194, 195
Violation-response approach to law enforcement, 181, 232
Violent behavior
and drug traffic, 102
code numbers on, 273, 274
of militant groups, 167, 253–254

and obscene materials, 121
of religious cults, 173–174
Virginia
computerized records system in, 213
pornography in, 252

Wallach, Robert, 30
Walsh, Denny, 138
Wanted person file in National Crime Information Center, 264, 266, 267, 270
Watergate scandal, 254
Weiner, Norbert, 6
Welfare fraud, 155, 256
Wells, Kenneth M., 140
Weston, Paul B., 140
White collar crimes, 129, 131–148
in black market operations, 144–146
computer-related, 159–165
confederation activity in, 131–132, 133–134, 147
convictions on, 160
economic impact of, 134–136, 137, 138, 142–143, 251
fraudulent practices in. *See* Fraudulent practices
gambling associated with, 132, 133, 143, 146
government regulation of, 157–158, 160
investigation of, 146–147, 148
labor union activities in, 134, 141–142, 147, 148
in loan shark business, 141, 142–144, 148
racketeering in, 139–142, 148
and business acquisitions, 149–151
social issues in, 132–134
stock manipulation and theft in, 151–154
types of, 139–146, 258–259
Wickersham Committee, 228
Wire service information in gambling, 56, 217
Wire-tapping for evidence collection, 176
Witnesses
false declarations of, 260
immunity of, 42, 260
protection of, 183, 260
refusal to testify, 260

Zimmerman, Gereon, 66